This book belongs to:

Name: _____

Phone: _____

Email: _____

Address: _____

If found, please contact me so I can get this book back!

Vocabulary Book for Advanced ASL Students: A Student Workbook of ASL Vocabulary utilizing Transcriptions, Descriptions, & SignWriting

Short Name: **ASL Vocab Book**

Authored by Jacalyn W. Marosi M.Ed, NIC, CI

Contributions by Valerie Sutton, Cheri Wren, and Adam Frost of SignWriting.org

Publisher: Jacalyn W. Marosi
    Self-Published by Jacalyn W. Marosi through CreateSpace

Coeur d Alene, Idaho

First Edition Published June 2014

Printed in the United States of America

ISBN-13: 978-0692221754
ISBN-10: 0692221751

Vocabulary Book

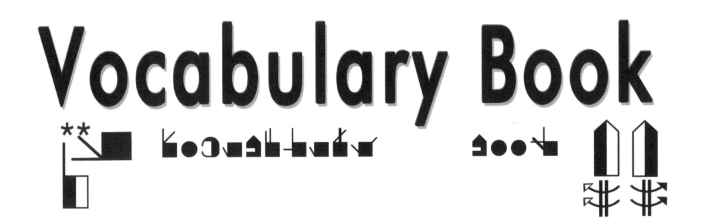

for Advanced

A Student Workbook of ASL Vocabulary
utilizing Transcriptions, Descriptions, & SignWriting

Jacalyn W. Marosi M.Ed, NIC, CI

Table of Contents

Intro & Directions

About This Book   Intro ~ 2

5 Parameters of a Sign (HOLMEs) Chart   Intro ~ 3

Examples of Glossed Vocabulary & Reminder   Intro ~ 4

Transcription Conventions

     Symbols used to write ASL   Intro ~ 5-6

     Symbols used to write ASL Classifiers (depiction)   Intro ~ 7

     Symbols used for Index (IX)   Intro ~ 8

     SignWriting symbols for Palm Orientation   Intro ~ 8

     Symbols for writing Non-Manual Signals (NMS)   Intro ~ 9

SignWriting Handshapes

     Handshapes 1-5   Intro ~ 10

     Handshapes 6-0   Intro ~ 11

     Movement Symbols   Intro ~ 12

     Movement & Tempo Symbols   Intro ~ 13

Alphabet   Intro ~ 14

More Examples of Glossed Vocabulary   Intro ~ 15

Vocabulary Pages – Gloss Boxes   1-150

Handshape Game Directions & Example   152

Handshape Thesaurus with Example   Thesaurus 1-10

Index Pages   Index 1-9

Reference Charts

Language Continuums   Reference -A-

Deaf Community Membership   Reference -B-

ASL Syntax   Reference -C-

Teacher Grade Sheet

Works Cited

ABOUT THIS BOOK:

This workbook is intended for use by advanced ASL students who want to document the new vocabulary they are learning in a classroom setting.

So, STUDENTS?! This is **your** book! Learn it. Use it. Love it.

To help you to document your vocabulary more effectively, there are guidelines from Charlotte Baker-Shenk and Dennis Cokley's ASL Green Books (1980, 1991) which was modified from the late great William Stokoe's method of transcription.

The other featured set of guidelines are from Valerie Sutton's SignWriting. The website (www.signwriting.org) for SignWriting is wonderfully cumulative and worth exploring if you want to learn SignWriting more fluently than the nutshell version explained here.

Thank you, Valerie, for being so supportive of this project!

HOW TO USE THIS BOOK:

1. GET IT
2. DO IT
3. REVIEW IT

GET IT: Before you can use this workbook effectively and efficiently, you must first read and understand the transcription guidelines and/or SignWriting.

DO IT: Once you understand how to document ASL vocabulary, dive in! It will seem tedious at first, but after you become practiced in this skill, it will be easy and very beneficial.

REVIEW IT: After you begin documenting signs to create your own dictionary, the next trick is to review it daily. You will remember your new vocabulary words if you review them daily. **Approximately 10 minutes** a day of review will grow your level of vocab use to levels beyond most other students who do not review daily.

Review it to RETAIN it! ☺

Note: If you would prefer this book to be spiral bound and/or if you want to combine your previous Vocab Book with this new one, take this book to a place like *FedEx* where they can coil bind, laminate, and even combine old with new for less than $10. If feedback is given that the majority students prefer the spiral/coil binding instead of this "perfect binding", the next edition will be bound accordingly.

The 5 Parameters of a Sign

1. Handshape
(the handshape formed with placement of fingers, ie: C or 5)

2. Palm Orientation
(which way the palm is pointing)

3. Location
(where hands are located in relation to your body)

4. Movement
(path/motion/speed of the sign)

5. Non-Manual Signals (NMS)
(GRAMMAR: facial expressions, body posture, head tilt)

Note- NMS is not always considered part of the 5 parameters of a Sign.
"Non-Manual" in this context means "not signed"; the NMS are head and facial movements that indicate grammar, but because its use is imparative to ASL, the NMS are often grouped with the 5 Parameters.

Easy to Remember = H O L M E s

Handshape

Orientation of Palm

Location

Movement

Expressions - NMS

Reis-Rodriguez, D. (2013, June 1). HOLMES. (J. W. Marosi, Lecturee) Gooding, Idaho.

Examples of glossed vocabulary in both Transcription style & SignWriting

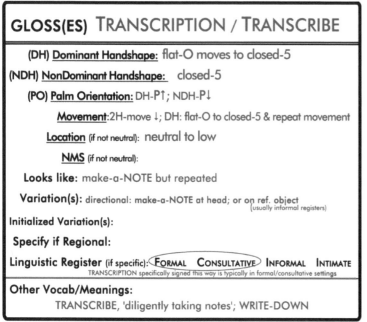

GLOSS(ES) TRANSCRIPTION / TRANSCRIBE

(DH) Dominant Handshape: flat-O moves to closed-5

(NDH) NonDominant Handshape: closed-5

(PO) Palm Orientation: DH-P↑; NDH-P↓

Movement: 2H-move ↓; DH: flat-O to closed-5 & repeat movement

Location (if not neutral): neutral to low

NMS (if not neutral):

Looks like: make-a-NOTE but repeated

Variation(s): directional: make-a-NOTE at head; or on ref. object
(usually informal registers)

Initialized Variation(s):

Specify if Regional:

Linguistic Register (if specific): ⟨FORMAL CONSULTATIVE⟩ INFORMAL INTIMATE
TRANSCRIPTION specifically signed this way is typically in formal/consultative settings

Other Vocab/Meanings:
TRANSCRIBE, 'diligently taking notes'; WRITE-DOWN

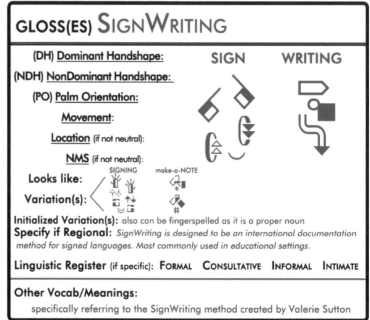

GLOSS(ES) SIGNWRITING

(DH) Dominant Handshape: SIGN   WRITING

(NDH) NonDominant Handshape:

(PO) Palm Orientation:

Movement:

Location (if not neutral):

NMS (if not neutral):

Looks like: SIGNING   make-a-NOTE

Variation(s):

Initialized Variation(s): also can be fingerspelled as it is a proper noun

Specify if Regional: *SignWriting is designed to be an international documentation method for signed languages. Most commonly used in educational settings.*

Linguistic Register (if specific): FORMAL CONSULTATIVE INFORMAL INTIMATE

Other Vocab/Meanings:
specifically referring to the SignWriting method created by Valerie Sutton

10 Minutes of Daily Review...You will remember your
new vocabulary words if you review them daily.

Approximately 10 minutes a day of review will grow your level of vocab use to levels beyond most other students who do not review daily.

Review it to RETAIN it!

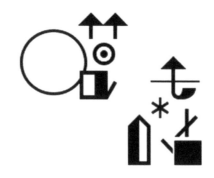

Transcription Conventions: **Symbols Used to Write ASL**

Symbol	Example	Explanation
WORD	**SIGN** **DEAF**	An English word written in capital letters stands for ASL sign (aka "**gloss**"). The meaning of the sign & the English word may not be exactly the same.
/	**REAL/TRUE** **BOLD/TOUGH**	A slash between glosses is used when one sign has **2 different English equivalents**.
#	**#CAR** **#BANK**	the pound sign indicates a lexicalized fingerspelled word; AKA: loan sign
- -	**OH-I-SEE**	When the words for sign glosses are separated with a hyphen, they represent a single sign.
+	**NOT+HERE** **TRUE+WORK**	A plus sign between sign glosses is use used for **compound signs** and **contractions**
fs- or **-**	**fs-BOB** **B-O-B**	"**fs**" is the abbreviation for a 'fingerspelled' word; or use dashes between each letter to indicate fs
" "	**"wave no"**	Quotation marks around lower-case words indicate a **gesture**-like sign.
! !	**!BORED!** **!MUST!**	Exclamation marks are used for signs that are stressed or **emphasized.**
+ +	**DIFFERENT++** **WORK++**	Plus signs after a word indicate **repetitions** of the sign. Also used for habitual or frequent inflection.
-cont	**USE-cont**	The suffix "-cont" indicates **continuous inflection** on verbs.
-char	**MAD-char**	The suffix "-**char**" indicates the modulation on a sign showing a **characteristic**, behavior, or trait

(Charlotte Baker-Shenk, ASL Green Book Series, 1980, 1991)

Transcription Conventions: Symbols Used to Write ASL

<u>Symbol</u>	<u>Example</u>	<u>Explanation</u>
[ ]	[NEAR] [(NDH)B "shelf"/IX-loc…]	Brackets show that **a sign is optional,** not required in a sentence. Also used around separate signs made at the same time; the "wh" or "NDH" symbol indicates non-dominant hand.
(DH) (NDH) RH- LH-	(DH) (NDH) RH- LH-	(DH) stands for "**dominant-hand**" indicating the use of the signer's dominant hand; (NDH) stands for "**non-dominant-hand**". Often signers transcribing for themselves will use RH and LH for "**right hand**" and "**left hand**" because dominant hands are already known
(2h)	(2h)#DO++	(2h) stands for "**2-handed**" and is used when a sign commonly 1-handed is made with both hands.
(2h)alt	(2h)altGUESS	"alt" indicated that both hands move in an alternating manner.
( )	(nod) (shake head) (draws shape) (city)	Words in parentheses indicate an action or movement made without a sign, sometimes with linguistic meaning (i.e. negative or affirmative responses) Also used for variable signs that change in different contexts (i.e. City names)
wg	WHYwg	The suffix "**wg**" shows that the fingers wiggle when making the sign
	BRING*"here"* TAKE-FROM(table) MOTHER*lf*	**Spatial or locative** info about a sign italicized and sometimes in quotes, sometime in parentheses, sometimes abbreviated, immediately after the gloss.
	you-SHOW-TO-*her*	Italicized words before & after inflecting verbs indicated **subject and object of the verb agreement**
POSS		POSS is used for **possessive pronoun.** Specific referents are given in italics and quotes when necessary (i.e., POSS "father" to mean "father's")
	HON / HONOR *(HONORIFIC)*	HON or HONOR or even HONORIFIC is used to indicate that the **formal version** of the sign be used. (i.e., HON-ME)

(Charlotte Baker-Shenk, ASL Green Book Series, 1980, 1991)

Transcription Conventions: Symbols for Classifiers (Depiction)

Symbol	Explanation
DCL: "___"	Descriptive classifier sign used to describe an object or person. What is described is italicized and in quotes (i.e., DCL"*curly hair*"). Sometimes referred to as a size and shape specifiers or SASSes.
LCL:__ "___"	Locative classifier representing an object in a specific place (and sometimes indicting movement). Handshape is given, followed by spatial or locative info italicized and in quotes Example: **LCL:B "leaf drifting to the ground"**
SCL:__ "___"	Semantic classifier sign representing a category of nouns such as vehicle or person. Handshape is given, followed by info about specific movement italicized and in quotes Example: **SCL:1 "person walking stiffly and hurriedly"**
BCL: "___"	Body classifier sign representing in which the body "enacts" the verb of the sentence. Role shifting is usually required. Specific action is describing in italics and quotes: Example: **BCL:"acting macho" and BCL:"put arm around friend"**
BPCL:__ "___"	Body part classifier sign representing a specific part of the body doing the action. Handshape is often indicated and specific action is described in italics and quotes Example: **(2H)BPCL:1"crossing legs" and BPCL:B"taps foot"**
ICL: "___"	Instrument classifier sign in which part of the body (usually the hands) manipulates an object Example: **ICL:"turn crank" and ICL:"play jacks"**
PCL:__ "___"	Plural classifier sign, indicating either specific number of non-specific number Example: **PCL:4:"people walking"; PCL:5"hords of"**
ECL:__ "___"	Element classifier sign representing an element of the earth, such as rain, wind/smoke/gas, fire, and light. Example: **ECL:5wg:"waterfall"; ECL:1"water dripping from a faucet"**

(Charlotte Baker-Shenk, ASL Green Book Series, 1980, 1991)

Transcription Conventions for Index: IX

IX   Short for **index**, IX indicates pointing and is used for 3rd person pronouns (he, she, it, him, her). Specific referents are indicated by italicized words in quotation marks, immediately following the gloss (i.e. IX "father"). IX is also used when explaining primes in sign parameters.

IX-loc   IX-loc means "there" and is used to indicate the **location** of an object or place. Specific info is given in italics and quotes immediately after the gloss (i.e. IX-loc *"under table"*).

IX-dir   IX-dir is used when the pointing gives **directions** or traces a route to a place (i.e. IX-dir *"around the corner to the right"*).

IX-list   These signs are all used in the process of **listing** people or things on the non-dominant hand. Listing usually begins with thumb. IX-mult is used when presenting all items on the list.

IX-*thumb*

IX-*index*

IX-*middle*

IX-*ring*

IX-*pinkie*

IX-*mult*

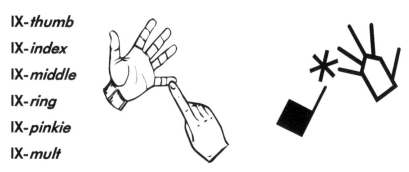

(Charlotte Baker-Shenk, ASL Green Book Series, 1980, 1991)

Palm Orientation (PO)

specified either with P then the appropriate arrow,

$$P\leftarrow \;\; P\rightarrow \;\; P\uparrow \;\; P\downarrow \;\; P\nwarrow \;\; P\nearrow \;\; P\swarrow \;\; P\searrow \;\; \text{or} \;\; LH\rightarrow \;\;\; \leftarrow RH$$

or   **PS**= Palm Self;   **PA**= Palm Away;   **PR**= Palm Right;   **PL**= Palm Left

SignWriting Symbols for Palm Orientation

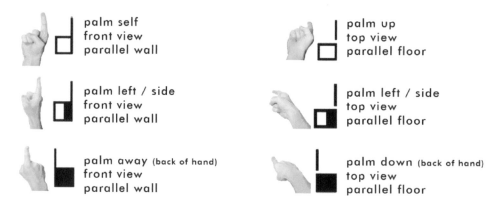

palm self
front view
parallel wall

palm up
top view
parallel floor

palm left / side
front view
parallel wall

palm left / side
top view
parallel floor

palm away (back of hand)
front view
parallel wall

palm down (back of hand)
top view
parallel floor

(Valerie Sutton, Adam Frost, 2013)

Transcription Conventions: Non-Manual Signals (NMS)
(sometimes called "Non-Manual Markers (NMM)")

Symbol	Example Sentence	Explanation	SignWriting Symbol
____t____	____t____ YESTERDAY ME SICK	**topic** (indicates relative clause)	
____q____	____q____ YOU EAT FINISH	**yes/no question**	
____y/n q____	____y/n q____ YOU EAT FINISH	**yes/no question**	
____wh q____	____wh q____ YOUR NAME "what"	**wh-word question**	
____neg____	____neg____ ME EAT NOT-YET	**negation**	
____affirm____	____affirm____ YES KISS-FIST	**affirmation**	
____when____	____when____ ...LUNCH FINISH	similar to conditional sentence, indicating **when** something happens without using the sign	
____cond____	____cond____ #IF RAIN, GAME CANCEL WILL	**conditional clause** "If, then" always 1st part of sentence	
____neg/ q____	____neg/ q____ NOT HURT	**negation & yes/no question** markers at the same time	
____t / q____	____t____ ____/ q____ SEE WOMAN IX-loc	**topic & yes/no question** markers at the same time	
____nod____	____nod____ ME, FINISH SEND-you	**assertion**	
____rhet____	____rhet____ NOT-LIKE, WHY? !BORING!	**rhetorical question**	
<rs: > or <tr: >	<rs:woman "hmm">	**"role shift" or "take role"** indicates the "role" the signer is assuming, maintains role until closing brackets (>)	

SignWriting 1-5 Handshape Symbols
(Adapted with permission from Valerie Sutton, Cheri Wren, & Adam Frost)

1-HAND SYMBOL DESCRIPTION

Symbol	Description
	Index, (IX), 1
	IX on circle, D
	IX on oval, flat D
	IX bent, X
	IX raised knuckle
	IX hinge on fist

2-HAND SYMBOL DESCRIPTION

Symbol	Description
	IX middle (mid), 2
	IX mid bent, bent-V
	IX mid raised knuckles
	IX mid hinge
	IX up mid hinge
	IX mid unit, U
	IX mid cross, R
	mid bent over IX, R

3-HAND SYMBOL DESCRIPTION

Symbol	Description
	IX mid thumb, 3
	IX mid bent, thumb straight
	IX mid thumb bent
	IX mid thumb cup
	IX mid thumb hinge
	IX mid unit thumb side
	IX mid unit hinge thumb side
	IX mid cross thumb side
	IX mid unit thumb forward
	mid thumb circle IX up, small-D
	IX thumb angle out mid up
	IX mid thumb unit hinge, G
	IX mid thumb angle out
	IX mid thumb angle
	mid thumb angle out IX up,
	mid thumb angle IX up

4-HAND SYMBOL DESCRIPTION

Symbol	Description
	4 fingers, 4
	4 fingers bent
	4 fingers unit, B
	4 fingers unit claw
	4 fingers unit bent, S
	4 fingers unit hinge

5-HAND SYMBOL DESCRIPTION

Symbol	Description
	5 fingers spread, 5
	5 fingers spread 4 bent, bent-5
	5 fingers spread bent, open-claw
	5 fingers spread bent heel
	5 fingers spread thumb forward
	5 fingers spread cup, open-C
	5 fingers spread hinge thumb side
	5 fingers spread hinge no thumb
	flat, closed-5
	flat, between palm facing
	flat heel
	flat thumb side
	flat thumb side heel
	flat thumb bent
	flat thumb forward
	flat split center, thumb side
	closed claw
	cup open, open-C
	cup, C

SignWriting 6-0 Handshape Symbols

(Adapted with permission from Valerie Sutton, Cheri Wren, & Adam Frost)

6-Hand

Symbol	Description
	IX mid ring on circle, 6, W
	IX mid ring unit
	IX mid ring unit hinge; open M
	baby up, i
	baby up on fist thumb under
	baby up on angle
	baby & thumb, Y
	baby thumb on hinge
	baby, IX, thumb; ILY
	baby & IX, "rock on"hand
	baby & IX on circle
	baby & IX on angle

7-Hand

Symbol	Description
	IX, mid, baby; 7
	ring hinge
	IX mid & baby on angle
	ring down
	ring up

8-Hand

Symbol	Description
	IX, ring, baby; 8
	IX ring baby on hook out
	mid hinge
	mid-up
	mid up, thumb side
	mid thumb baby

9-Hand

Symbol	Description
	mid ring & baby, 9
	mid ring & baby on circle, F
	mid ring & baby on ciurlicue
	IX & thumb side, L
	IX & thumb diagonal
	IX & thumb side unit
	IX bent & thumb side
	IX hinge & thumb
	IX straight & thumb forward
	IX & thumb hook
	IX & thumb curlicue
	IX & curved thumb inside; T
	IX & thumb circle; 'baby-O'
	IX & thumb cup; 'baby-C'
	IX & thumb cup open
	IX & thumb hinge, G
	IX & thumb angle in
	IX & thumb angle; 'closed-G'

10-Hand

Symbol	Description
	thumb; 'open-A'; 10
	thumb heel
	thumb side diagonal, A
	thumb forward
	thumb between IX & mid, T
	thumb between mid & ring, N
	thumb between ring & baby; M
	thumb under 2 fingers, N
	thumb over 2 fingers, S
	thumb under 3 fingers, M
	thumb under 4 fingers
	thumb over 4, raised knuckles
	fist; S

0-Hand

Symbol	Description
	curlicue open
	curlicue
	circle
	oval, 'flat-O'
	oval thumb side
	oval no thumb
	hinge open
	hinge open, thumb fwrd
	hinge
	hinge small
	hinge open, thumb side
	hinge, thumb side; RAH (right angle hand)
	hinge open, no thumb
	hinge, no thumb
	angle, "and hand"

SignWriting Movement Symbols

(Adapted with permission from Valerie Sutton and Cheri Wren)

Indicate larger or smaller movements by correspondently altering the lengths of the lines and/or shapes.

Contact

Symbol	Description
*	Touch Single
**	Touch Mult
|*|	Touch Between
+	Grasp Single
++	Grasp Mult
|+|	Grasp Between
#	Strike Single
##	Strike Mult
|#|	Strike Between
⊙	Brush Single
⊙⊙	Brush Mult
|⊙|	Brush Between
℮	Rub Single
℮℮	Rub Mult
|℮|	Rub Between
	Surface Symbols
	Surface Between

Straight, Diagonal Plane

Symbol	Description
	Diagonal Away
	Diagonal Towards Mov
	Diagonal Between Away
	Diagonal Between Towards

Straight, Wall Plane

Symbol	Description
	Single Straight Mov
	Single Wrist Flex
	Double Straight Mov
	Double Wrist Flex
	Double Alt Mov
	Double Alt Wrist Flex
	Cross Movement
	Triple Straight Mov
	Triple Wrist Flex
	Triple Alternating Mov
	Triple Alternating Wrist Flex
	Bend
	Corner
	Corner with Rotation
	Check
	Box
	Zigzag
	Peaks
	Single Travel Rotation
	Double Travel Rotation
	Alt Travel Rotation
	Travel Shaking
	Single Travel Arm Spiral
	Double Travel Arm Spiral
	Triple Travel Arm Spiral
	Single Travel Rotation
	Double Travel Rotation
	Alt Travel Rotation

Movement, Floor Plane

Symbol	Description
	Single Straight Mov
	Single Wrist Flex
	Double Straight Mov
	Double Wrist Flex
	Double Alt Mov
	Double Alt Wrist Flex
	Cross Mov
	Triple Straight Mov
	Triple Wrist Flex
	Triple Alt Mov
	Triple Alt Wrist Flex
	Bend
	Corner
	Check
	Box
	Zigzag
	Peaks
	Single Travel Rotation
	Double Travel Rotation
	Alt Travel Rotation
	Single Travel Rotation
	Double Travel Rotation
	Alt Travel Rotation
	Travel Shaking

Curves Parallel, Wall Plane

Symbol	Description
	Curve 1/4
	Curve 1/2 Circle
	Curve 3/4 Circle
	Hump
	Loop
	Double Loop
	2 Curves Wave
	3 Curves Wave
	Curve Then Straight
	Curved Cross
	Rotation Single
	Rotation Double
	Rotation Alt
	Shaking

Finger Movement

Symbol	Description
	Single Squeeze
	Mult Squeeze
	Squeeze Sequential
	Single Flick
	Mult Flick
	Flick Sequential
	Squeeze Flick Alt
	Hinge Mov, ↑↓
	Hinge Mov, ↑ Sequential
	Hinge Mov, ↓ Sequential
	Alt Hinge Mov, ↑↓
	Hinge Mov, ↔ , Scissors ✄
	Finger Contact Mov, Wall Plane
	Finger Contact Mov, Floor Plane

SignWriting Movement & Tempo Symbols

(Adapted with permission from Valerie Sutton and Cheri Wren)

Indicate larger or smaller movements by correspondently altering the lengths of the lines and/or shapes.

Curves Hit, Wall Plane & Chest	
Symbol	Description
	Curve Hits, Front Wall
	Hump Hits, Front Wall
	Loop Hits, Front Wall
	Wave Hits, Front Wall
	Rotation Single Hits, Front Wall
	Rotation Double Hits, Front Wall
	Rotation Alt Hits, Front Wall
	Curve Hits, Chest
	Hump Hits, Chest
	Loop Hits, Chest
	Wave Hits, Chest
	Rotation Single Hits, Chest
	Rotation Double Hits, Chest
	Rotation Alt Hits, Chest
	Wave Diagonal Path

Curves Hit, Ceiling & Floor Plane	
Symbol	Description
	Curve Hits, Ceiling
	2 Humps Hits, Ceiling
	3 Humps Hits, Ceiling
	Single Loop Hits, Ceiling
	Double Loop Hits, Ceiling
	Wave Hits, Ceiling
	Single Rotation Hits, Ceiling
	Double Rotation Hits, Ceiling
	Alt Rotation Hits, Ceiling
	Curve Hits, Floor
	2 Humps Hits, Floor
	3 Humps Hits, Floor
	Single Loop Hits, Floor
	Double Loop Hits, Floor
	Wave Hits, Floor
	Single Rotation Hits, Floor
	Double Rotation Hits, Floor
	Alt Rotation Hits, Floor

Curves Parallel, Floor Plane	
Symbol	Description
	Curve
	Curve Combined
	Hump
	Loop
	Wave, Snake
	Wave
	Single Rotation
	Double Rotation
	Alt Rotation
	Parallel Shaking

Circles, Wall	
Symbol	Description
	Single Arm Circle
	Double Arm Circle
	Single Arm Circle Hits
	Double Arm Circle Hits
	Single Wrist Circle Front
	Double Wrist Circle Front
	Single Wrist Circle Hits
	Double Wrist Circle Hits
	Single Finger Circles
	Double Finger Circles
	Single Finger Circles Hits
	Double Finger Circles Hits

Tempo

Symbol	Name
	Fast
	Slow
	Tense
	Relaxed
	Same Time
	Same Time Alternating
	Every Other Time
	Gradual

American Manual Alphabet & Numbers 0-10

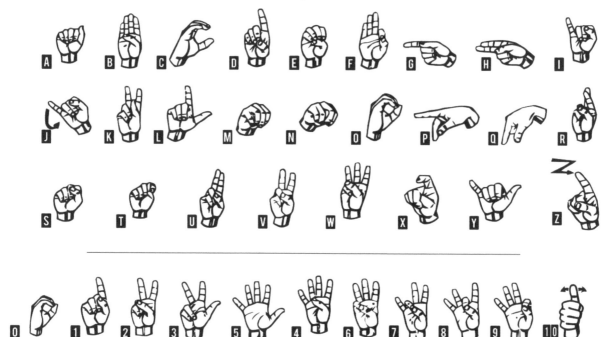

Fonts: signs language tfb,
Gallaudet Regular

Sutton ASL Alphabet & Numbers 0 - 15

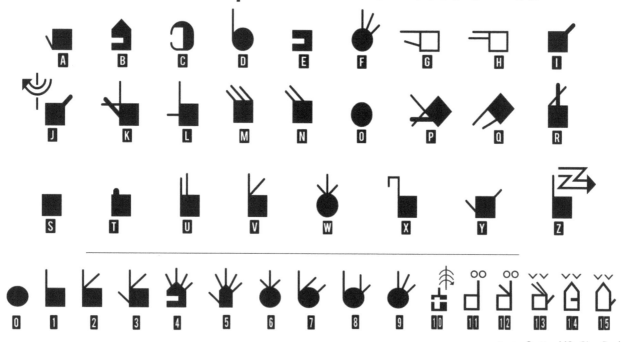

Fonts: SuttonUS, SignPuddle
signs language tfb

MORE Examples of Glossed Vocabulary in both Transcription style and SignWriting.

GLOSS(ES) PERSONAL / PERSONALITY

(DH) Dominant Handshape: P

(NDH) NonDominant Handshape:

(PO) Palm Orientation: self

Movement: circle then touch

Location (if not neutral): heart

NMS (if not neutral):

Looks like: COP but circles and touches

Variation(s):

Initialized Variation(s): C=CHARACTER; L=LOYAL / LOYALTY;

Specify if Regional: Q=QUALITY / QUALIFY (but PO makes the Q look like G)

Linguistic Register (if specific): FORMAL CONSULTATIVE INFORMAL INTIMATE

Other Vocab/Meanings:

GLOSS(ES) PERSONAL / PERSONALITY

(DH) Dominant Handshape:

(NDH) NonDominant Handshape:

(PO) Palm Orientation:

Movement:

Location (if not neutral):

NMS (if not neutral):

Looks like: COP but circles and touches

Variation(s):

Initialized Variation(s): C=CHARACTER; L=LOYAL / LOYALTY;

Specify if Regional: Q=QUALITY / QUALIFY (but PO makes the Q look like G)

Linguistic Register (if specific): FORMAL CONSULTATIVE INFORMAL INTIMATE

Other Vocab/Meanings:

GLOSS(ES) SPECIAL / UNIQUE / EXCEPT

(DH) Dominant Handshape: F

(NDH) NonDominant Handshape: IX

(PO) Palm Orientation: F is P↓; IX is P-self

Movement: F picks up IX upward

Location (if not neutral): low to high

NMS (if not neutral):

Looks like: FIND but add IX

Variation(s): NDH is 5, not IX

Initialized Variation(s):

Specify if Regional:

Linguistic Register (if specific): FORMAL CONSULTATIVE INFORMAL INTIMATE

Other Vocab/Meanings: EXCEPTION
SPECIALIZE; SPECIAL+agent = SPECIALIST

GLOSS(ES) SPECIAL / UNIQUE / EXCEPT

(DH) Dominant Handshape:

(NDH) NonDominant Handshape:

(PO) Palm Orientation:

Movement:

Location (if not neutral):

NMS (if not neutral):

Looks like:

Variation(s):

Initialized Variation(s):

Specify if Regional:

Linguistic Register (if specific): FORMAL CONSULTATIVE INFORMAL INTIMATE

Other Vocab/Meanings: EXCEPTION
SPECIALIZE; SPECIAL+agent = SPECIALIST

GLOSS(ES) SELF

(DH) Dominant Handshape: A at (NDH) IX

(NDH) NonDominant Handshape: IX or directional (including self)

(PO) Palm Orientation: DH-PL; nDH- PA

Movement: taps twice on IX

Location (if not neutral): neutral or directional

NMS (if not neutral):

Looks like: HIT (but soft movement tapping)

Variation(s): no NDH for MYSELF

Initialized Variation(s):

Specify if Regional: region often dictates PO or Loc differences

Linguistic Register (if specific): FORMAL CONSULTATIVE INFORMAL INTIMATE

Other Vocab/Meanings: HIMSELF / HERSELF / ITSELF / YOURSELF
used to *specify* something or someone

GLOSS(ES) SELF

(DH) Dominant Handshape:

(NDH) NonDominant Handshape:

(PO) Palm Orientation:

Movement:

Location (if not neutral):

NMS (if not neutral):

Looks like:

Variation(s): MYSELF

Initialized Variation(s):

Specify if Regional: region often dictates PO or Loc differences

Linguistic Register (if specific): FORMAL CONSULTATIVE INFORMAL INTIMATE

Other Vocab/Meanings: HIMSELF / HERSELF / ITSELF / YOURSELF
used to *specify* something or someone

GLOSS(ES)

(DH) <u>Dominant Handshape</u>:

(NDH) <u>NonDominant Handshape</u>:

(PO) <u>Palm Orientation</u>:

<u>Movement</u>:

<u>Location</u> (if not neutral):

<u>NMS</u> (if not neutral):

Looks like:

Variation(s):

Initialized Variation(s):

Specify if Regional:

Linguistic Register (if specific): FORMAL CONSULTATIVE INFORMAL INTIMATE

Other Vocab/Meanings:

GLOSS(ES)

(DH) <u>Dominant Handshape</u>:

(NDH) <u>NonDominant Handshape</u>:

(PO) <u>Palm Orientation</u>:

<u>Movement</u>:

<u>Location</u> (if not neutral):

<u>NMS</u> (if not neutral):

Looks like:

Variation(s):

Initialized Variation(s):

Specify if Regional:

Linguistic Register (if specific): FORMAL CONSULTATIVE INFORMAL INTIMATE

Other Vocab/Meanings:

GLOSS(ES)

(DH) <u>Dominant Handshape</u>:

(NDH) <u>NonDominant Handshape</u>:

(PO) <u>Palm Orientation</u>:

<u>Movement</u>:

<u>Location</u> (if not neutral):

<u>NMS</u> (if not neutral):

Looks like:

Variation(s):

Initialized Variation(s):

Specify if Regional:

Linguistic Register (if specific): FORMAL CONSULTATIVE INFORMAL INTIMATE

Other Vocab/Meanings:

GLOSS(ES)

(DH) <u>Dominant Handshape</u>:

(NDH) <u>NonDominant Handshape</u>:

(PO) <u>Palm Orientation</u>:

<u>Movement</u>:

<u>Location</u> (if not neutral):

<u>NMS</u> (if not neutral):

Looks like:

Variation(s):

Initialized Variation(s):

Specify if Regional:

Linguistic Register (if specific): FORMAL CONSULTATIVE INFORMAL INTIMATE

Other Vocab/Meanings:

GLOSS(ES)

(DH) <u>Dominant Handshape</u>:

(NDH) <u>NonDominant Handshape</u>:

(PO) <u>Palm Orientation</u>:

<u>Movement</u>:

<u>Location</u> (if not neutral):

<u>NMS</u> (if not neutral):

Looks like:

Variation(s):

Initialized Variation(s):

Specify if Regional:

Linguistic Register (if specific): FORMAL CONSULTATIVE INFORMAL INTIMATE

Other Vocab/Meanings:

GLOSS(ES)

(DH) <u>Dominant Handshape</u>:

(NDH) <u>NonDominant Handshape</u>:

(PO) <u>Palm Orientation</u>:

<u>Movement</u>:

<u>Location</u> (if not neutral):

<u>NMS</u> (if not neutral):

Looks like:

Variation(s):

Initialized Variation(s):

Specify if Regional:

Linguistic Register (if specific): FORMAL CONSULTATIVE INFORMAL INTIMATE

Other Vocab/Meanings:

GLOSS(ES)

(DH) Dominant Handshape:

(NDH) NonDominant Handshape:

(PO) Palm Orientation:

Movement:

Location (if not neutral):

NMS (if not neutral):

Looks like:

Variation(s):

Initialized Variation(s):

Specify if Regional:

Linguistic Register (if specific): FORMAL CONSULTATIVE INFORMAL INTIMATE

Other Vocab/Meanings:

GLOSS(ES)

(DH) Dominant Handshape:

(NDH) NonDominant Handshape:

(PO) Palm Orientation:

Movement:

Location (if not neutral):

NMS (if not neutral):

Looks like:

Variation(s):

Initialized Variation(s):

Specify if Regional:

Linguistic Register (if specific): FORMAL CONSULTATIVE INFORMAL INTIMATE

Other Vocab/Meanings:

GLOSS(ES)

(DH) Dominant Handshape:

(NDH) NonDominant Handshape:

(PO) Palm Orientation:

Movement:

Location (if not neutral):

NMS (if not neutral):

Looks like:

Variation(s):

Initialized Variation(s):

Specify if Regional:

Linguistic Register (if specific): FORMAL CONSULTATIVE INFORMAL INTIMATE

Other Vocab/Meanings:

GLOSS(ES)

(DH) Dominant Handshape:

(NDH) NonDominant Handshape:

(PO) Palm Orientation:

Movement:

Location (if not neutral):

NMS (if not neutral):

Looks like:

Variation(s):

Initialized Variation(s):

Specify if Regional:

Linguistic Register (if specific): FORMAL CONSULTATIVE INFORMAL INTIMATE

Other Vocab/Meanings:

GLOSS(ES)

(DH) Dominant Handshape:

(NDH) NonDominant Handshape:

(PO) Palm Orientation:

Movement:

Location (if not neutral):

NMS (if not neutral):

Looks like:

Variation(s):

Initialized Variation(s):

Specify if Regional:

Linguistic Register (if specific): FORMAL CONSULTATIVE INFORMAL INTIMATE

Other Vocab/Meanings:

GLOSS(ES)

(DH) Dominant Handshape:

(NDH) NonDominant Handshape:

(PO) Palm Orientation:

Movement:

Location (if not neutral):

NMS (if not neutral):

Looks like:

Variation(s):

Initialized Variation(s):

Specify if Regional:

Linguistic Register (if specific): FORMAL CONSULTATIVE INFORMAL INTIMATE

Other Vocab/Meanings:

GLOSS(ES)

(DH) <u>Dominant Handshape</u>:

(NDH) <u>NonDominant Handshape</u>:

(PO) <u>Palm Orientation</u>:

<u>Movement</u>:

<u>Location</u> (if not neutral):

<u>NMS</u> (if not neutral):

Looks like:

Variation(s):

Initialized Variation(s):

Specify if Regional:

Linguistic Register (if specific): FORMAL CONSULTATIVE INFORMAL INTIMATE

Other Vocab/Meanings:

GLOSS(ES)

(DH) <u>Dominant Handshape</u>:

(NDH) <u>NonDominant Handshape</u>:

(PO) <u>Palm Orientation</u>:

<u>Movement</u>:

<u>Location</u> (if not neutral):

<u>NMS</u> (if not neutral):

Looks like:

Variation(s):

Initialized Variation(s):

Specify if Regional:

Linguistic Register (if specific): FORMAL CONSULTATIVE INFORMAL INTIMATE

Other Vocab/Meanings:

GLOSS(ES)

(DH) <u>Dominant Handshape</u>:

(NDH) <u>NonDominant Handshape</u>:

(PO) <u>Palm Orientation</u>:

<u>Movement</u>:

<u>Location</u> (if not neutral):

<u>NMS</u> (if not neutral):

Looks like:

Variation(s):

Initialized Variation(s):

Specify if Regional:

Linguistic Register (if specific): FORMAL CONSULTATIVE INFORMAL INTIMATE

Other Vocab/Meanings:

GLOSS(ES)

(DH) <u>Dominant Handshape</u>:

(NDH) <u>NonDominant Handshape</u>:

(PO) <u>Palm Orientation</u>:

<u>Movement</u>:

<u>Location</u> (if not neutral):

<u>NMS</u> (if not neutral):

Looks like:

Variation(s):

Initialized Variation(s):

Specify if Regional:

Linguistic Register (if specific): FORMAL CONSULTATIVE INFORMAL INTIMATE

Other Vocab/Meanings:

GLOSS(ES)

(DH) <u>Dominant Handshape</u>:

(NDH) <u>NonDominant Handshape</u>:

(PO) <u>Palm Orientation</u>:

<u>Movement</u>:

<u>Location</u> (if not neutral):

<u>NMS</u> (if not neutral):

Looks like:

Variation(s):

Initialized Variation(s):

Specify if Regional:

Linguistic Register (if specific): FORMAL CONSULTATIVE INFORMAL INTIMATE

Other Vocab/Meanings:

GLOSS(ES)

(DH) <u>Dominant Handshape</u>:

(NDH) <u>NonDominant Handshape</u>:

(PO) <u>Palm Orientation</u>:

<u>Movement</u>:

<u>Location</u> (if not neutral):

<u>NMS</u> (if not neutral):

Looks like:

Variation(s):

Initialized Variation(s):

Specify if Regional:

Linguistic Register (if specific): FORMAL CONSULTATIVE INFORMAL INTIMATE

Other Vocab/Meanings:

GLOSS(ES)

(DH) <u>Dominant Handshape</u>:

(NDH) <u>NonDominant Handshape</u>:

(PO) <u>Palm Orientation</u>:

<u>Movement</u>:

<u>Location</u> (if not neutral):

<u>NMS</u> (if not neutral):

Looks like:

Variation(s):

Initialized Variation(s):

Specify if Regional:

Linguistic Register (if specific): FORMAL   CONSULTATIVE   INFORMAL   INTIMATE

Other Vocab/Meanings:

GLOSS(ES)

(DH) <u>Dominant Handshape</u>:

(NDH) <u>NonDominant Handshape</u>:

(PO) <u>Palm Orientation</u>:

<u>Movement</u>:

<u>Location</u> (if not neutral):

<u>NMS</u> (if not neutral):

Looks like:

Variation(s):

Initialized Variation(s):

Specify if Regional:

Linguistic Register (if specific): FORMAL   CONSULTATIVE   INFORMAL   INTIMATE

Other Vocab/Meanings:

GLOSS(ES)

(DH) <u>Dominant Handshape</u>:

(NDH) <u>NonDominant Handshape</u>:

(PO) <u>Palm Orientation</u>:

<u>Movement</u>:

<u>Location</u> (if not neutral):

<u>NMS</u> (if not neutral):

Looks like:

Variation(s):

Initialized Variation(s):

Specify if Regional:

Linguistic Register (if specific): FORMAL   CONSULTATIVE   INFORMAL   INTIMATE

Other Vocab/Meanings:

GLOSS(ES)

(DH) <u>Dominant Handshape</u>:

(NDH) <u>NonDominant Handshape</u>:

(PO) <u>Palm Orientation</u>:

<u>Movement</u>:

<u>Location</u> (if not neutral):

<u>NMS</u> (if not neutral):

Looks like:

Variation(s):

Initialized Variation(s):

Specify if Regional:

Linguistic Register (if specific): FORMAL   CONSULTATIVE   INFORMAL   INTIMATE

Other Vocab/Meanings:

GLOSS(ES)

(DH) <u>Dominant Handshape</u>:

(NDH) <u>NonDominant Handshape</u>:

(PO) <u>Palm Orientation</u>:

<u>Movement</u>:

<u>Location</u> (if not neutral):

<u>NMS</u> (if not neutral):

Looks like:

Variation(s):

Initialized Variation(s):

Specify if Regional:

Linguistic Register (if specific): FORMAL   CONSULTATIVE   INFORMAL   INTIMATE

Other Vocab/Meanings:

GLOSS(ES)

(DH) <u>Dominant Handshape</u>:

(NDH) <u>NonDominant Handshape</u>:

(PO) <u>Palm Orientation</u>:

<u>Movement</u>:

<u>Location</u> (if not neutral):

<u>NMS</u> (if not neutral):

Looks like:

Variation(s):

Initialized Variation(s):

Specify if Regional:

Linguistic Register (if specific): FORMAL   CONSULTATIVE   INFORMAL   INTIMATE

Other Vocab/Meanings:

GLOSS(ES)

(DH) <u>Dominant Handshape</u>:

(NDH) <u>NonDominant Handshape</u>:

(PO) <u>Palm Orientation</u>:

<u>Movement</u>:

<u>Location</u> (if not neutral):

<u>NMS</u> (if not neutral):

Looks like:

Variation(s):

Initialized Variation(s):

Specify if Regional:

Linguistic Register (if specific): FORMAL CONSULTATIVE INFORMAL INTIMATE

Other Vocab/Meanings:

GLOSS(ES)

(DH) <u>Dominant Handshape</u>:

(NDH) <u>NonDominant Handshape</u>:

(PO) <u>Palm Orientation</u>:

<u>Movement</u>:

<u>Location</u> (if not neutral):

<u>NMS</u> (if not neutral):

Looks like:

Variation(s):

Initialized Variation(s):

Specify if Regional:

Linguistic Register (if specific): FORMAL CONSULTATIVE INFORMAL INTIMATE

Other Vocab/Meanings:

GLOSS(ES)

(DH) <u>Dominant Handshape</u>:

(NDH) <u>NonDominant Handshape</u>:

(PO) <u>Palm Orientation</u>:

<u>Movement</u>:

<u>Location</u> (if not neutral):

<u>NMS</u> (if not neutral):

Looks like:

Variation(s):

Initialized Variation(s):

Specify if Regional:

Linguistic Register (if specific): FORMAL CONSULTATIVE INFORMAL INTIMATE

Other Vocab/Meanings:

GLOSS(ES)

(DH) <u>Dominant Handshape</u>:

(NDH) <u>NonDominant Handshape</u>:

(PO) <u>Palm Orientation</u>:

<u>Movement</u>:

<u>Location</u> (if not neutral):

<u>NMS</u> (if not neutral):

Looks like:

Variation(s):

Initialized Variation(s):

Specify if Regional:

Linguistic Register (if specific): FORMAL CONSULTATIVE INFORMAL INTIMATE

Other Vocab/Meanings:

GLOSS(ES)

(DH) <u>Dominant Handshape</u>:

(NDH) <u>NonDominant Handshape</u>:

(PO) <u>Palm Orientation</u>:

<u>Movement</u>:

<u>Location</u> (if not neutral):

<u>NMS</u> (if not neutral):

Looks like:

Variation(s):

Initialized Variation(s):

Specify if Regional:

Linguistic Register (if specific): FORMAL CONSULTATIVE INFORMAL INTIMATE

Other Vocab/Meanings:

GLOSS(ES)

(DH) <u>Dominant Handshape</u>:

(NDH) <u>NonDominant Handshape</u>:

(PO) <u>Palm Orientation</u>:

<u>Movement</u>:

<u>Location</u> (if not neutral):

<u>NMS</u> (if not neutral):

Looks like:

Variation(s):

Initialized Variation(s):

Specify if Regional:

Linguistic Register (if specific): FORMAL CONSULTATIVE INFORMAL INTIMATE

Other Vocab/Meanings:

GLOSS(ES)

(DH) <u>Dominant Handshape</u>:

(NDH) <u>NonDominant Handshape</u>:

(PO) <u>Palm Orientation</u>:

<u>Movement</u>:

<u>Location</u> (if not neutral):

<u>NMS</u> (if not neutral):

Looks like:

Variation(s):

Initialized Variation(s):

Specify if Regional:

Linguistic Register (if specific): FORMAL   CONSULTATIVE   INFORMAL   INTIMATE

Other Vocab/Meanings:

GLOSS(ES)

(DH) <u>Dominant Handshape</u>:

(NDH) <u>NonDominant Handshape</u>:

(PO) <u>Palm Orientation</u>:

<u>Movement</u>:

<u>Location</u> (if not neutral):

<u>NMS</u> (if not neutral):

Looks like:

Variation(s):

Initialized Variation(s):

Specify if Regional:

Linguistic Register (if specific): FORMAL   CONSULTATIVE   INFORMAL   INTIMATE

Other Vocab/Meanings:

GLOSS(ES)

(DH) <u>Dominant Handshape</u>:

(NDH) <u>NonDominant Handshape</u>:

(PO) <u>Palm Orientation</u>:

<u>Movement</u>:

<u>Location</u> (if not neutral):

<u>NMS</u> (if not neutral):

Looks like:

Variation(s):

Initialized Variation(s):

Specify if Regional:

Linguistic Register (if specific): FORMAL   CONSULTATIVE   INFORMAL   INTIMATE

Other Vocab/Meanings:

GLOSS(ES)

(DH) <u>Dominant Handshape</u>:

(NDH) <u>NonDominant Handshape</u>:

(PO) <u>Palm Orientation</u>:

<u>Movement</u>:

<u>Location</u> (if not neutral):

<u>NMS</u> (if not neutral):

Looks like:

Variation(s):

Initialized Variation(s):

Specify if Regional:

Linguistic Register (if specific): FORMAL   CONSULTATIVE   INFORMAL   INTIMATE

Other Vocab/Meanings:

GLOSS(ES)

(DH) <u>Dominant Handshape</u>:

(NDH) <u>NonDominant Handshape</u>:

(PO) <u>Palm Orientation</u>:

<u>Movement</u>:

<u>Location</u> (if not neutral):

<u>NMS</u> (if not neutral):

Looks like:

Variation(s):

Initialized Variation(s):

Specify if Regional:

Linguistic Register (if specific): FORMAL   CONSULTATIVE   INFORMAL   INTIMATE

Other Vocab/Meanings:

GLOSS(ES)

(DH) <u>Dominant Handshape</u>:

(NDH) <u>NonDominant Handshape</u>:

(PO) <u>Palm Orientation</u>:

<u>Movement</u>:

<u>Location</u> (if not neutral):

<u>NMS</u> (if not neutral):

Looks like:

Variation(s):

Initialized Variation(s):

Specify if Regional:

Linguistic Register (if specific): FORMAL   CONSULTATIVE   INFORMAL   INTIMATE

Other Vocab/Meanings:

GLOSS(ES)

(DH) <u>Dominant Handshape</u>:

(NDH) <u>NonDominant Handshape</u>:

(PO) <u>Palm Orientation</u>:

<u>Movement</u>:

<u>Location</u> (if not neutral):

<u>NMS</u> (if not neutral):

Looks like:

Variation(s):

Initialized Variation(s):

Specify if Regional:

Linguistic Register (if specific): FORMAL   CONSULTATIVE   INFORMAL   INTIMATE

Other Vocab/Meanings:

GLOSS(ES)

(DH) <u>Dominant Handshape</u>:

(NDH) <u>NonDominant Handshape</u>:

(PO) <u>Palm Orientation</u>:

<u>Movement</u>:

<u>Location</u> (if not neutral):

<u>NMS</u> (if not neutral):

Looks like:

Variation(s):

Initialized Variation(s):

Specify if Regional:

Linguistic Register (if specific): FORMAL   CONSULTATIVE   INFORMAL   INTIMATE

Other Vocab/Meanings:

GLOSS(ES)

(DH) <u>Dominant Handshape</u>:

(NDH) <u>NonDominant Handshape</u>:

(PO) <u>Palm Orientation</u>:

<u>Movement</u>:

<u>Location</u> (if not neutral):

<u>NMS</u> (if not neutral):

Looks like:

Variation(s):

Initialized Variation(s):

Specify if Regional:

Linguistic Register (if specific): FORMAL   CONSULTATIVE   INFORMAL   INTIMATE

Other Vocab/Meanings:

GLOSS(ES)

(DH) <u>Dominant Handshape</u>:

(NDH) <u>NonDominant Handshape</u>:

(PO) <u>Palm Orientation</u>:

<u>Movement</u>:

<u>Location</u> (if not neutral):

<u>NMS</u> (if not neutral):

Looks like:

Variation(s):

Initialized Variation(s):

Specify if Regional:

Linguistic Register (if specific): FORMAL   CONSULTATIVE   INFORMAL   INTIMATE

Other Vocab/Meanings:

GLOSS(ES)

(DH) <u>Dominant Handshape</u>:

(NDH) <u>NonDominant Handshape</u>:

(PO) <u>Palm Orientation</u>:

<u>Movement</u>:

<u>Location</u> (if not neutral):

<u>NMS</u> (if not neutral):

Looks like:

Variation(s):

Initialized Variation(s):

Specify if Regional:

Linguistic Register (if specific): FORMAL   CONSULTATIVE   INFORMAL   INTIMATE

Other Vocab/Meanings:

GLOSS(ES)

(DH) <u>Dominant Handshape</u>:

(NDH) <u>NonDominant Handshape</u>:

(PO) <u>Palm Orientation</u>:

<u>Movement</u>:

<u>Location</u> (if not neutral):

<u>NMS</u> (if not neutral):

Looks like:

Variation(s):

Initialized Variation(s):

Specify if Regional:

Linguistic Register (if specific): FORMAL   CONSULTATIVE   INFORMAL   INTIMATE

Other Vocab/Meanings:

GLOSS(ES)

    (DH) Dominant Handshape:

(NDH) NonDominant Handshape:

    (PO) Palm Orientation:

        Movement:

        Location (if not neutral):

        NMS (if not neutral):

    Looks like:

    Variation(s):

Initialized Variation(s):

    Specify if Regional:

    Linguistic Register (if specific): FORMAL CONSULTATIVE INFORMAL INTIMATE

Other Vocab/Meanings:

GLOSS(ES)

    (DH) Dominant Handshape:

(NDH) NonDominant Handshape:

    (PO) Palm Orientation:

        Movement:

        Location (if not neutral):

        NMS (if not neutral):

    Looks like:

    Variation(s):

Initialized Variation(s):

    Specify if Regional:

    Linguistic Register (if specific): FORMAL CONSULTATIVE INFORMAL INTIMATE

Other Vocab/Meanings:

GLOSS(ES)

    (DH) Dominant Handshape:

(NDH) NonDominant Handshape:

    (PO) Palm Orientation:

        Movement:

        Location (if not neutral):

        NMS (if not neutral):

    Looks like:

    Variation(s):

Initialized Variation(s):

    Specify if Regional:

    Linguistic Register (if specific): FORMAL CONSULTATIVE INFORMAL INTIMATE

Other Vocab/Meanings:

GLOSS(ES)

    (DH) Dominant Handshape:

(NDH) NonDominant Handshape:

    (PO) Palm Orientation:

        Movement:

        Location (if not neutral):

        NMS (if not neutral):

    Looks like:

    Variation(s):

Initialized Variation(s):

    Specify if Regional:

    Linguistic Register (if specific): FORMAL CONSULTATIVE INFORMAL INTIMATE

Other Vocab/Meanings:

GLOSS(ES)

    (DH) Dominant Handshape:

(NDH) NonDominant Handshape:

    (PO) Palm Orientation:

        Movement:

        Location (if not neutral):

        NMS (if not neutral):

    Looks like:

    Variation(s):

Initialized Variation(s):

    Specify if Regional:

    Linguistic Register (if specific): FORMAL CONSULTATIVE INFORMAL INTIMATE

Other Vocab/Meanings:

GLOSS(ES)

    (DH) Dominant Handshape:

(NDH) NonDominant Handshape:

    (PO) Palm Orientation:

        Movement:

        Location (if not neutral):

        NMS (if not neutral):

    Looks like:

    Variation(s):

Initialized Variation(s):

    Specify if Regional:

    Linguistic Register (if specific): FORMAL CONSULTATIVE INFORMAL INTIMATE

Other Vocab/Meanings:

GLOSS(ES)

(DH) <u>Dominant Handshape</u>:

(NDH) <u>NonDominant Handshape</u>:

(PO) <u>Palm Orientation</u>:

<u>Movement</u>:

<u>Location</u> (if not neutral):

<u>NMS</u> (if not neutral):

Looks like:

Variation(s):

Initialized Variation(s):

Specify if Regional:

Linguistic Register (if specific): FORMAL   CONSULTATIVE   INFORMAL   INTIMATE

Other Vocab/Meanings:

GLOSS(ES)

(DH) <u>Dominant Handshape</u>:

(NDH) <u>NonDominant Handshape</u>:

(PO) <u>Palm Orientation</u>:

<u>Movement</u>:

<u>Location</u> (if not neutral):

<u>NMS</u> (if not neutral):

Looks like:

Variation(s):

Initialized Variation(s):

Specify if Regional:

Linguistic Register (if specific): FORMAL   CONSULTATIVE   INFORMAL   INTIMATE

Other Vocab/Meanings:

GLOSS(ES)

(DH) <u>Dominant Handshape</u>:

(NDH) <u>NonDominant Handshape</u>:

(PO) <u>Palm Orientation</u>:

<u>Movement</u>:

<u>Location</u> (if not neutral):

<u>NMS</u> (if not neutral):

Looks like:

Variation(s):

Initialized Variation(s):

Specify if Regional:

Linguistic Register (if specific): FORMAL   CONSULTATIVE   INFORMAL   INTIMATE

Other Vocab/Meanings:

GLOSS(ES)

(DH) <u>Dominant Handshape</u>:

(NDH) <u>NonDominant Handshape</u>:

(PO) <u>Palm Orientation</u>:

<u>Movement</u>:

<u>Location</u> (if not neutral):

<u>NMS</u> (if not neutral):

Looks like:

Variation(s):

Initialized Variation(s):

Specify if Regional:

Linguistic Register (if specific): FORMAL   CONSULTATIVE   INFORMAL   INTIMATE

Other Vocab/Meanings:

GLOSS(ES)

(DH) <u>Dominant Handshape</u>:

(NDH) <u>NonDominant Handshape</u>:

(PO) <u>Palm Orientation</u>:

<u>Movement</u>:

<u>Location</u> (if not neutral):

<u>NMS</u> (if not neutral):

Looks like:

Variation(s):

Initialized Variation(s):

Specify if Regional:

Linguistic Register (if specific): FORMAL   CONSULTATIVE   INFORMAL   INTIMATE

Other Vocab/Meanings:

GLOSS(ES)

(DH) <u>Dominant Handshape</u>:

(NDH) <u>NonDominant Handshape</u>:

(PO) <u>Palm Orientation</u>:

<u>Movement</u>:

<u>Location</u> (if not neutral):

<u>NMS</u> (if not neutral):

Looks like:

Variation(s):

Initialized Variation(s):

Specify if Regional:

Linguistic Register (if specific): FORMAL   CONSULTATIVE   INFORMAL   INTIMATE

Other Vocab/Meanings:

GLOSS(ES)

(DH) Dominant Handshape:

(NDH) NonDominant Handshape:

(PO) Palm Orientation:

Movement:

Location (if not neutral):

NMS (if not neutral):

Looks like:

Variation(s):

Initialized Variation(s):

Specify if Regional:

Linguistic Register (if specific): FORMAL   CONSULTATIVE   INFORMAL   INTIMATE

Other Vocab/Meanings:

GLOSS(ES)

(DH) Dominant Handshape:

(NDH) NonDominant Handshape:

(PO) Palm Orientation:

Movement:

Location (if not neutral):

NMS (if not neutral):

Looks like:

Variation(s):

Initialized Variation(s):

Specify if Regional:

Linguistic Register (if specific): FORMAL   CONSULTATIVE   INFORMAL   INTIMATE

Other Vocab/Meanings:

GLOSS(ES)

(DH) Dominant Handshape:

(NDH) NonDominant Handshape:

(PO) Palm Orientation:

Movement:

Location (if not neutral):

NMS (if not neutral):

Looks like:

Variation(s):

Initialized Variation(s):

Specify if Regional:

Linguistic Register (if specific): FORMAL   CONSULTATIVE   INFORMAL   INTIMATE

Other Vocab/Meanings:

GLOSS(ES)

(DH) Dominant Handshape:

(NDH) NonDominant Handshape:

(PO) Palm Orientation:

Movement:

Location (if not neutral):

NMS (if not neutral):

Looks like:

Variation(s):

Initialized Variation(s):

Specify if Regional:

Linguistic Register (if specific): FORMAL   CONSULTATIVE   INFORMAL   INTIMATE

Other Vocab/Meanings:

GLOSS(ES)

(DH) Dominant Handshape:

(NDH) NonDominant Handshape:

(PO) Palm Orientation:

Movement:

Location (if not neutral):

NMS (if not neutral):

Looks like:

Variation(s):

Initialized Variation(s):

Specify if Regional:

Linguistic Register (if specific): FORMAL   CONSULTATIVE   INFORMAL   INTIMATE

Other Vocab/Meanings:

GLOSS(ES)

(DH) Dominant Handshape:

(NDH) NonDominant Handshape:

(PO) Palm Orientation:

Movement:

Location (if not neutral):

NMS (if not neutral):

Looks like:

Variation(s):

Initialized Variation(s):

Specify if Regional:

Linguistic Register (if specific): FORMAL   CONSULTATIVE   INFORMAL   INTIMATE

Other Vocab/Meanings:

GLOSS(ES)

(DH) Dominant Handshape:

(NDH) NonDominant Handshape:

(PO) Palm Orientation:

Movement:

Location (if not neutral):

NMS (if not neutral):

Looks like:

Variation(s):

Initialized Variation(s):

Specify if Regional:

Linguistic Register (if specific): FORMAL CONSULTATIVE INFORMAL INTIMATE

Other Vocab/Meanings:

GLOSS(ES)

(DH) Dominant Handshape:

(NDH) NonDominant Handshape:

(PO) Palm Orientation:

Movement:

Location (if not neutral):

NMS (if not neutral):

Looks like:

Variation(s):

Initialized Variation(s):

Specify if Regional:

Linguistic Register (if specific): FORMAL CONSULTATIVE INFORMAL INTIMATE

Other Vocab/Meanings:

GLOSS(ES)

(DH) Dominant Handshape:

(NDH) NonDominant Handshape:

(PO) Palm Orientation:

Movement:

Location (if not neutral):

NMS (if not neutral):

Looks like:

Variation(s):

Initialized Variation(s):

Specify if Regional:

Linguistic Register (if specific): FORMAL CONSULTATIVE INFORMAL INTIMATE

Other Vocab/Meanings:

GLOSS(ES)

(DH) Dominant Handshape:

(NDH) NonDominant Handshape:

(PO) Palm Orientation:

Movement:

Location (if not neutral):

NMS (if not neutral):

Looks like:

Variation(s):

Initialized Variation(s):

Specify if Regional:

Linguistic Register (if specific): FORMAL CONSULTATIVE INFORMAL INTIMATE

Other Vocab/Meanings:

GLOSS(ES)

(DH) Dominant Handshape:

(NDH) NonDominant Handshape:

(PO) Palm Orientation:

Movement:

Location (if not neutral):

NMS (if not neutral):

Looks like:

Variation(s):

Initialized Variation(s):

Specify if Regional:

Linguistic Register (if specific): FORMAL CONSULTATIVE INFORMAL INTIMATE

Other Vocab/Meanings:

GLOSS(ES)

(DH) Dominant Handshape:

(NDH) NonDominant Handshape:

(PO) Palm Orientation:

Movement:

Location (if not neutral):

NMS (if not neutral):

Looks like:

Variation(s):

Initialized Variation(s):

Specify if Regional:

Linguistic Register (if specific): FORMAL CONSULTATIVE INFORMAL INTIMATE

Other Vocab/Meanings:

GLOSS(ES)

(DH) <u>Dominant Handshape</u>:

(NDH) <u>NonDominant Handshape</u>:

  (PO) <u>Palm Orientation</u>:

    <u>Movement</u>:

    <u>Location</u> (if not neutral):

    <u>NMS</u> (if not neutral):

Looks like:

Variation(s):

Initialized Variation(s):

Specify if Regional:

<u>Linguistic Register</u> (if specific): FORMAL   CONSULTATIVE   INFORMAL   INTIMATE

Other Vocab/Meanings:

GLOSS(ES)

(DH) <u>Dominant Handshape</u>:

(NDH) <u>NonDominant Handshape</u>:

  (PO) <u>Palm Orientation</u>:

    <u>Movement</u>:

    <u>Location</u> (if not neutral):

    <u>NMS</u> (if not neutral):

Looks like:

Variation(s):

Initialized Variation(s):

Specify if Regional:

<u>Linguistic Register</u> (if specific): FORMAL   CONSULTATIVE   INFORMAL   INTIMATE

Other Vocab/Meanings:

GLOSS(ES)

(DH) <u>Dominant Handshape</u>:

(NDH) <u>NonDominant Handshape</u>:

  (PO) <u>Palm Orientation</u>:

    <u>Movement</u>:

    <u>Location</u> (if not neutral):

    <u>NMS</u> (if not neutral):

Looks like:

Variation(s):

Initialized Variation(s):

Specify if Regional:

<u>Linguistic Register</u> (if specific): FORMAL   CONSULTATIVE   INFORMAL   INTIMATE

Other Vocab/Meanings:

GLOSS(ES)

(DH) <u>Dominant Handshape</u>:

(NDH) <u>NonDominant Handshape</u>:

  (PO) <u>Palm Orientation</u>:

    <u>Movement</u>:

    <u>Location</u> (if not neutral):

    <u>NMS</u> (if not neutral):

Looks like:

Variation(s):

Initialized Variation(s):

Specify if Regional:

<u>Linguistic Register</u> (if specific): FORMAL   CONSULTATIVE   INFORMAL   INTIMATE

Other Vocab/Meanings:

GLOSS(ES)

(DH) <u>Dominant Handshape</u>:

(NDH) <u>NonDominant Handshape</u>:

  (PO) <u>Palm Orientation</u>:

    <u>Movement</u>:

    <u>Location</u> (if not neutral):

    <u>NMS</u> (if not neutral):

Looks like:

Variation(s):

Initialized Variation(s):

Specify if Regional:

<u>Linguistic Register</u> (if specific): FORMAL   CONSULTATIVE   INFORMAL   INTIMATE

Other Vocab/Meanings:

GLOSS(ES)

(DH) <u>Dominant Handshape</u>:

(NDH) <u>NonDominant Handshape</u>:

  (PO) <u>Palm Orientation</u>:

    <u>Movement</u>:

    <u>Location</u> (if not neutral):

    <u>NMS</u> (if not neutral):

Looks like:

Variation(s):

Initialized Variation(s):

Specify if Regional:

<u>Linguistic Register</u> (if specific): FORMAL   CONSULTATIVE   INFORMAL   INTIMATE

Other Vocab/Meanings:

GLOSS(ES)

(DH) <u>Dominant Handshape</u>:

(NDH) <u>NonDominant Handshape</u>:

(PO) <u>Palm Orientation</u>:

<u>Movement</u>:

<u>Location</u> (if not neutral):

<u>NMS</u> (if not neutral):

Looks like:

Variation(s):

Initialized Variation(s):

Specify if Regional:

Linguistic Register (if specific): FORMAL   CONSULTATIVE   INFORMAL   INTIMATE

Other Vocab/Meanings:

GLOSS(ES)

(DH) <u>Dominant Handshape</u>:

(NDH) <u>NonDominant Handshape</u>:

(PO) <u>Palm Orientation</u>:

<u>Movement</u>:

<u>Location</u> (if not neutral):

<u>NMS</u> (if not neutral):

Looks like:

Variation(s):

Initialized Variation(s):

Specify if Regional:

Linguistic Register (if specific): FORMAL   CONSULTATIVE   INFORMAL   INTIMATE

Other Vocab/Meanings:

GLOSS(ES)

(DH) <u>Dominant Handshape</u>:

(NDH) <u>NonDominant Handshape</u>:

(PO) <u>Palm Orientation</u>:

<u>Movement</u>:

<u>Location</u> (if not neutral):

<u>NMS</u> (if not neutral):

Looks like:

Variation(s):

Initialized Variation(s):

Specify if Regional:

Linguistic Register (if specific): FORMAL   CONSULTATIVE   INFORMAL   INTIMATE

Other Vocab/Meanings:

GLOSS(ES)

(DH) <u>Dominant Handshape</u>:

(NDH) <u>NonDominant Handshape</u>:

(PO) <u>Palm Orientation</u>:

<u>Movement</u>:

<u>Location</u> (if not neutral):

<u>NMS</u> (if not neutral):

Looks like:

Variation(s):

Initialized Variation(s):

Specify if Regional:

Linguistic Register (if specific): FORMAL   CONSULTATIVE   INFORMAL   INTIMATE

Other Vocab/Meanings:

GLOSS(ES)

(DH) <u>Dominant Handshape</u>:

(NDH) <u>NonDominant Handshape</u>:

(PO) <u>Palm Orientation</u>:

<u>Movement</u>:

<u>Location</u> (if not neutral):

<u>NMS</u> (if not neutral):

Looks like:

Variation(s):

Initialized Variation(s):

Specify if Regional:

Linguistic Register (if specific): FORMAL   CONSULTATIVE   INFORMAL   INTIMATE

Other Vocab/Meanings:

GLOSS(ES)

(DH) <u>Dominant Handshape</u>:

(NDH) <u>NonDominant Handshape</u>:

(PO) <u>Palm Orientation</u>:

<u>Movement</u>:

<u>Location</u> (if not neutral):

<u>NMS</u> (if not neutral):

Looks like:

Variation(s):

Initialized Variation(s):

Specify if Regional:

Linguistic Register (if specific): FORMAL   CONSULTATIVE   INFORMAL   INTIMATE

Other Vocab/Meanings:

GLOSS(ES)

(DH) Dominant Handshape:

(NDH) NonDominant Handshape:

(PO) Palm Orientation:

Movement:

Location (if not neutral):

NMS (if not neutral):

Looks like:

Variation(s):

Initialized Variation(s):

Specify if Regional:

Linguistic Register (if specific): FORMAL CONSULTATIVE INFORMAL INTIMATE

Other Vocab/Meanings:

GLOSS(ES)

(DH) Dominant Handshape:

(NDH) NonDominant Handshape:

(PO) Palm Orientation:

Movement:

Location (if not neutral):

NMS (if not neutral):

Looks like:

Variation(s):

Initialized Variation(s):

Specify if Regional:

Linguistic Register (if specific): FORMAL CONSULTATIVE INFORMAL INTIMATE

Other Vocab/Meanings:

GLOSS(ES)

(DH) Dominant Handshape:

(NDH) NonDominant Handshape:

(PO) Palm Orientation:

Movement:

Location (if not neutral):

NMS (if not neutral):

Looks like:

Variation(s):

Initialized Variation(s):

Specify if Regional:

Linguistic Register (if specific): FORMAL CONSULTATIVE INFORMAL INTIMATE

Other Vocab/Meanings:

GLOSS(ES)

(DH) Dominant Handshape:

(NDH) NonDominant Handshape:

(PO) Palm Orientation:

Movement:

Location (if not neutral):

NMS (if not neutral):

Looks like:

Variation(s):

Initialized Variation(s):

Specify if Regional:

Linguistic Register (if specific): FORMAL CONSULTATIVE INFORMAL INTIMATE

Other Vocab/Meanings:

GLOSS(ES)

(DH) Dominant Handshape:

(NDH) NonDominant Handshape:

(PO) Palm Orientation:

Movement:

Location (if not neutral):

NMS (if not neutral):

Looks like:

Variation(s):

Initialized Variation(s):

Specify if Regional:

Linguistic Register (if specific): FORMAL CONSULTATIVE INFORMAL INTIMATE

Other Vocab/Meanings:

GLOSS(ES)

(DH) Dominant Handshape:

(NDH) NonDominant Handshape:

(PO) Palm Orientation:

Movement:

Location (if not neutral):

NMS (if not neutral):

Looks like:

Variation(s):

Initialized Variation(s):

Specify if Regional:

Linguistic Register (if specific): FORMAL CONSULTATIVE INFORMAL INTIMATE

Other Vocab/Meanings:

GLOSS(ES)

(DH) Dominant Handshape:

(NDH) NonDominant Handshape:

(PO) Palm Orientation:

Movement:

Location (if not neutral):

NMS (if not neutral):

Looks like:

Variation(s):

Initialized Variation(s):

Specify if Regional:

Linguistic Register (if specific): FORMAL CONSULTATIVE INFORMAL INTIMATE

Other Vocab/Meanings:

GLOSS(ES)

(DH) Dominant Handshape:

(NDH) NonDominant Handshape:

(PO) Palm Orientation:

Movement:

Location (if not neutral):

NMS (if not neutral):

Looks like:

Variation(s):

Initialized Variation(s):

Specify if Regional:

Linguistic Register (if specific): FORMAL CONSULTATIVE INFORMAL INTIMATE

Other Vocab/Meanings:

GLOSS(ES)

(DH) Dominant Handshape:

(NDH) NonDominant Handshape:

(PO) Palm Orientation:

Movement:

Location (if not neutral):

NMS (if not neutral):

Looks like:

Variation(s):

Initialized Variation(s):

Specify if Regional:

Linguistic Register (if specific): FORMAL CONSULTATIVE INFORMAL INTIMATE

Other Vocab/Meanings:

GLOSS(ES)

(DH) Dominant Handshape:

(NDH) NonDominant Handshape:

(PO) Palm Orientation:

Movement:

Location (if not neutral):

NMS (if not neutral):

Looks like:

Variation(s):

Initialized Variation(s):

Specify if Regional:

Linguistic Register (if specific): FORMAL CONSULTATIVE INFORMAL INTIMATE

Other Vocab/Meanings:

GLOSS(ES)

(DH) Dominant Handshape:

(NDH) NonDominant Handshape:

(PO) Palm Orientation:

Movement:

Location (if not neutral):

NMS (if not neutral):

Looks like:

Variation(s):

Initialized Variation(s):

Specify if Regional:

Linguistic Register (if specific): FORMAL CONSULTATIVE INFORMAL INTIMATE

Other Vocab/Meanings:

GLOSS(ES)

(DH) Dominant Handshape:

(NDH) NonDominant Handshape:

(PO) Palm Orientation:

Movement:

Location (if not neutral):

NMS (if not neutral):

Looks like:

Variation(s):

Initialized Variation(s):

Specify if Regional:

Linguistic Register (if specific): FORMAL CONSULTATIVE INFORMAL INTIMATE

Other Vocab/Meanings:

GLOSS(ES)

(DH) <u>Dominant Handshape</u>:

(NDH) <u>NonDominant Handshape</u>:

   (PO) <u>Palm Orientation</u>:

      <u>Movement</u>:

     <u>Location</u> (if not neutral):

      <u>NMS</u> (if not neutral):

Looks like:

Variation(s):

Initialized Variation(s):

Specify if Regional:

Linguistic Register (if specific): FORMAL CONSULTATIVE INFORMAL INTIMATE

Other Vocab/Meanings:

GLOSS(ES)

(DH) <u>Dominant Handshape</u>:

(NDH) <u>NonDominant Handshape</u>:

   (PO) <u>Palm Orientation</u>:

      <u>Movement</u>:

     <u>Location</u> (if not neutral):

      <u>NMS</u> (if not neutral):

Looks like:

Variation(s):

Initialized Variation(s):

Specify if Regional:

Linguistic Register (if specific): FORMAL CONSULTATIVE INFORMAL INTIMATE

Other Vocab/Meanings:

GLOSS(ES)

(DH) <u>Dominant Handshape</u>:

(NDH) <u>NonDominant Handshape</u>:

   (PO) <u>Palm Orientation</u>:

      <u>Movement</u>:

     <u>Location</u> (if not neutral):

      <u>NMS</u> (if not neutral):

Looks like:

Variation(s):

Initialized Variation(s):

Specify if Regional:

Linguistic Register (if specific): FORMAL CONSULTATIVE INFORMAL INTIMATE

Other Vocab/Meanings:

GLOSS(ES)

(DH) <u>Dominant Handshape</u>:

(NDH) <u>NonDominant Handshape</u>:

   (PO) <u>Palm Orientation</u>:

      <u>Movement</u>:

     <u>Location</u> (if not neutral):

      <u>NMS</u> (if not neutral):

Looks like:

Variation(s):

Initialized Variation(s):

Specify if Regional:

Linguistic Register (if specific): FORMAL CONSULTATIVE INFORMAL INTIMATE

Other Vocab/Meanings:

GLOSS(ES)

(DH) <u>Dominant Handshape</u>:

(NDH) <u>NonDominant Handshape</u>:

   (PO) <u>Palm Orientation</u>:

      <u>Movement</u>:

     <u>Location</u> (if not neutral):

      <u>NMS</u> (if not neutral):

Looks like:

Variation(s):

Initialized Variation(s):

Specify if Regional:

Linguistic Register (if specific): FORMAL CONSULTATIVE INFORMAL INTIMATE

Other Vocab/Meanings:

GLOSS(ES)

(DH) <u>Dominant Handshape</u>:

(NDH) <u>NonDominant Handshape</u>:

   (PO) <u>Palm Orientation</u>:

      <u>Movement</u>:

     <u>Location</u> (if not neutral):

      <u>NMS</u> (if not neutral):

Looks like:

Variation(s):

Initialized Variation(s):

Specify if Regional:

Linguistic Register (if specific): FORMAL CONSULTATIVE INFORMAL INTIMATE

Other Vocab/Meanings:

GLOSS(ES)

(DH) Dominant Handshape:

(NDH) NonDominant Handshape:

(PO) Palm Orientation:

Movement:

Location (if not neutral):

NMS (if not neutral):

Looks like:

Variation(s):

Initialized Variation(s):

Specify if Regional:

Linguistic Register (if specific): FORMAL CONSULTATIVE INFORMAL INTIMATE

Other Vocab/Meanings:

GLOSS(ES)

(DH) Dominant Handshape:

(NDH) NonDominant Handshape:

(PO) Palm Orientation:

Movement:

Location (if not neutral):

NMS (if not neutral):

Looks like:

Variation(s):

Initialized Variation(s):

Specify if Regional:

Linguistic Register (if specific): FORMAL CONSULTATIVE INFORMAL INTIMATE

Other Vocab/Meanings:

GLOSS(ES)

(DH) Dominant Handshape:

(NDH) NonDominant Handshape:

(PO) Palm Orientation:

Movement:

Location (if not neutral):

NMS (if not neutral):

Looks like:

Variation(s):

Initialized Variation(s):

Specify if Regional:

Linguistic Register (if specific): FORMAL CONSULTATIVE INFORMAL INTIMATE

Other Vocab/Meanings:

GLOSS(ES)

(DH) Dominant Handshape:

(NDH) NonDominant Handshape:

(PO) Palm Orientation:

Movement:

Location (if not neutral):

NMS (if not neutral):

Looks like:

Variation(s):

Initialized Variation(s):

Specify if Regional:

Linguistic Register (if specific): FORMAL CONSULTATIVE INFORMAL INTIMATE

Other Vocab/Meanings:

GLOSS(ES)

(DH) Dominant Handshape:

(NDH) NonDominant Handshape:

(PO) Palm Orientation:

Movement:

Location (if not neutral):

NMS (if not neutral):

Looks like:

Variation(s):

Initialized Variation(s):

Specify if Regional:

Linguistic Register (if specific): FORMAL CONSULTATIVE INFORMAL INTIMATE

Other Vocab/Meanings:

GLOSS(ES)

(DH) Dominant Handshape:

(NDH) NonDominant Handshape:

(PO) Palm Orientation:

Movement:

Location (if not neutral):

NMS (if not neutral):

Looks like:

Variation(s):

Initialized Variation(s):

Specify if Regional:

Linguistic Register (if specific): FORMAL CONSULTATIVE INFORMAL INTIMATE

Other Vocab/Meanings:

GLOSS(ES)

(DH) Dominant Handshape:

(NDH) NonDominant Handshape:

(PO) Palm Orientation:

Movement:

Location (if not neutral):

NMS (if not neutral):

Looks like:

Variation(s):

Initialized Variation(s):

Specify if Regional:

Linguistic Register (if specific): FORMAL CONSULTATIVE INFORMAL INTIMATE

Other Vocab/Meanings:

GLOSS(ES)

(DH) Dominant Handshape:

(NDH) NonDominant Handshape:

(PO) Palm Orientation:

Movement:

Location (if not neutral):

NMS (if not neutral):

Looks like:

Variation(s):

Initialized Variation(s):

Specify if Regional:

Linguistic Register (if specific): FORMAL CONSULTATIVE INFORMAL INTIMATE

Other Vocab/Meanings:

GLOSS(ES)

(DH) Dominant Handshape:

(NDH) NonDominant Handshape:

(PO) Palm Orientation:

Movement:

Location (if not neutral):

NMS (if not neutral):

Looks like:

Variation(s):

Initialized Variation(s):

Specify if Regional:

Linguistic Register (if specific): FORMAL CONSULTATIVE INFORMAL INTIMATE

Other Vocab/Meanings:

GLOSS(ES)

(DH) Dominant Handshape:

(NDH) NonDominant Handshape:

(PO) Palm Orientation:

Movement:

Location (if not neutral):

NMS (if not neutral):

Looks like:

Variation(s):

Initialized Variation(s):

Specify if Regional:

Linguistic Register (if specific): FORMAL CONSULTATIVE INFORMAL INTIMATE

Other Vocab/Meanings:

GLOSS(ES)

(DH) Dominant Handshape:

(NDH) NonDominant Handshape:

(PO) Palm Orientation:

Movement:

Location (if not neutral):

NMS (if not neutral):

Looks like:

Variation(s):

Initialized Variation(s):

Specify if Regional:

Linguistic Register (if specific): FORMAL CONSULTATIVE INFORMAL INTIMATE

Other Vocab/Meanings:

GLOSS(ES)

(DH) Dominant Handshape:

(NDH) NonDominant Handshape:

(PO) Palm Orientation:

Movement:

Location (if not neutral):

NMS (if not neutral):

Looks like:

Variation(s):

Initialized Variation(s):

Specify if Regional:

Linguistic Register (if specific): FORMAL CONSULTATIVE INFORMAL INTIMATE

Other Vocab/Meanings:

GLOSS(ES)

(DH) <u>Dominant Handshape</u>:

(NDH) <u>NonDominant Handshape</u>:

(PO) <u>Palm Orientation</u>:

<u>Movement</u>:

<u>Location</u> (if not neutral):

<u>NMS</u> (if not neutral):

Looks like:

Variation(s):

Initialized Variation(s):

Specify if Regional:

Linguistic Register (if specific): FORMAL CONSULTATIVE INFORMAL INTIMATE

Other Vocab/Meanings:

GLOSS(ES)

(DH) <u>Dominant Handshape</u>:

(NDH) <u>NonDominant Handshape</u>:

(PO) <u>Palm Orientation</u>:

<u>Movement</u>:

<u>Location</u> (if not neutral):

<u>NMS</u> (if not neutral):

Looks like:

Variation(s):

Initialized Variation(s):

Specify if Regional:

Linguistic Register (if specific): FORMAL CONSULTATIVE INFORMAL INTIMATE

Other Vocab/Meanings:

GLOSS(ES)

(DH) <u>Dominant Handshape</u>:

(NDH) <u>NonDominant Handshape</u>:

(PO) <u>Palm Orientation</u>:

<u>Movement</u>:

<u>Location</u> (if not neutral):

<u>NMS</u> (if not neutral):

Looks like:

Variation(s):

Initialized Variation(s):

Specify if Regional:

Linguistic Register (if specific): FORMAL CONSULTATIVE INFORMAL INTIMATE

Other Vocab/Meanings:

GLOSS(ES)

(DH) <u>Dominant Handshape</u>:

(NDH) <u>NonDominant Handshape</u>:

(PO) <u>Palm Orientation</u>:

<u>Movement</u>:

<u>Location</u> (if not neutral):

<u>NMS</u> (if not neutral):

Looks like:

Variation(s):

Initialized Variation(s):

Specify if Regional:

Linguistic Register (if specific): FORMAL CONSULTATIVE INFORMAL INTIMATE

Other Vocab/Meanings:

GLOSS(ES)

(DH) <u>Dominant Handshape</u>:

(NDH) <u>NonDominant Handshape</u>:

(PO) <u>Palm Orientation</u>:

<u>Movement</u>:

<u>Location</u> (if not neutral):

<u>NMS</u> (if not neutral):

Looks like:

Variation(s):

Initialized Variation(s):

Specify if Regional:

Linguistic Register (if specific): FORMAL CONSULTATIVE INFORMAL INTIMATE

Other Vocab/Meanings:

GLOSS(ES)

(DH) <u>Dominant Handshape</u>:

(NDH) <u>NonDominant Handshape</u>:

(PO) <u>Palm Orientation</u>:

<u>Movement</u>:

<u>Location</u> (if not neutral):

<u>NMS</u> (if not neutral):

Looks like:

Variation(s):

Initialized Variation(s):

Specify if Regional:

Linguistic Register (if specific): FORMAL CONSULTATIVE INFORMAL INTIMATE

Other Vocab/Meanings:

GLOSS(ES)

(DH) Dominant Handshape:

(NDH) NonDominant Handshape:

(PO) Palm Orientation:

Movement:

Location (if not neutral):

NMS (if not neutral):

Looks like:

Variation(s):

Initialized Variation(s):

Specify if Regional:

Linguistic Register (if specific): FORMAL CONSULTATIVE INFORMAL INTIMATE

Other Vocab/Meanings:

GLOSS(ES)

(DH) Dominant Handshape:

(NDH) NonDominant Handshape:

(PO) Palm Orientation:

Movement:

Location (if not neutral):

NMS (if not neutral):

Looks like:

Variation(s):

Initialized Variation(s):

Specify if Regional:

Linguistic Register (if specific): FORMAL CONSULTATIVE INFORMAL INTIMATE

Other Vocab/Meanings:

GLOSS(ES)

(DH) Dominant Handshape:

(NDH) NonDominant Handshape:

(PO) Palm Orientation:

Movement:

Location (if not neutral):

NMS (if not neutral):

Looks like:

Variation(s):

Initialized Variation(s):

Specify if Regional:

Linguistic Register (if specific): FORMAL CONSULTATIVE INFORMAL INTIMATE

Other Vocab/Meanings:

GLOSS(ES)

(DH) Dominant Handshape:

(NDH) NonDominant Handshape:

(PO) Palm Orientation:

Movement:

Location (if not neutral):

NMS (if not neutral):

Looks like:

Variation(s):

Initialized Variation(s):

Specify if Regional:

Linguistic Register (if specific): FORMAL CONSULTATIVE INFORMAL INTIMATE

Other Vocab/Meanings:

GLOSS(ES)

(DH) Dominant Handshape:

(NDH) NonDominant Handshape:

(PO) Palm Orientation:

Movement:

Location (if not neutral):

NMS (if not neutral):

Looks like:

Variation(s):

Initialized Variation(s):

Specify if Regional:

Linguistic Register (if specific): FORMAL CONSULTATIVE INFORMAL INTIMATE

Other Vocab/Meanings:

GLOSS(ES)

(DH) Dominant Handshape:

(NDH) NonDominant Handshape:

(PO) Palm Orientation:

Movement:

Location (if not neutral):

NMS (if not neutral):

Looks like:

Variation(s):

Initialized Variation(s):

Specify if Regional:

Linguistic Register (if specific): FORMAL CONSULTATIVE INFORMAL INTIMATE

Other Vocab/Meanings:

GLOSS(ES)

(DH) <u>Dominant Handshape</u>:

(NDH) <u>NonDominant Handshape</u>:

(PO) <u>Palm Orientation</u>:

<u>Movement</u>:

<u>Location</u> (if not neutral):

<u>NMS</u> (if not neutral):

Looks like:

Variation(s):

Initialized Variation(s):

Specify if Regional:

Linguistic Register (if specific): FORMAL   CONSULTATIVE   INFORMAL   INTIMATE

Other Vocab/Meanings:

GLOSS(ES)

(DH) <u>Dominant Handshape</u>:

(NDH) <u>NonDominant Handshape</u>:

(PO) <u>Palm Orientation</u>:

<u>Movement</u>:

<u>Location</u> (if not neutral):

<u>NMS</u> (if not neutral):

Looks like:

Variation(s):

Initialized Variation(s):

Specify if Regional:

Linguistic Register (if specific): FORMAL   CONSULTATIVE   INFORMAL   INTIMATE

Other Vocab/Meanings:

GLOSS(ES)

(DH) <u>Dominant Handshape</u>:

(NDH) <u>NonDominant Handshape</u>:

(PO) <u>Palm Orientation</u>:

<u>Movement</u>:

<u>Location</u> (if not neutral):

<u>NMS</u> (if not neutral):

Looks like:

Variation(s):

Initialized Variation(s):

Specify if Regional:

Linguistic Register (if specific): FORMAL   CONSULTATIVE   INFORMAL   INTIMATE

Other Vocab/Meanings:

GLOSS(ES)

(DH) <u>Dominant Handshape</u>:

(NDH) <u>NonDominant Handshape</u>:

(PO) <u>Palm Orientation</u>:

<u>Movement</u>:

<u>Location</u> (if not neutral):

<u>NMS</u> (if not neutral):

Looks like:

Variation(s):

Initialized Variation(s):

Specify if Regional:

Linguistic Register (if specific): FORMAL   CONSULTATIVE   INFORMAL   INTIMATE

Other Vocab/Meanings:

GLOSS(ES)

(DH) <u>Dominant Handshape</u>:

(NDH) <u>NonDominant Handshape</u>:

(PO) <u>Palm Orientation</u>:

<u>Movement</u>:

<u>Location</u> (if not neutral):

<u>NMS</u> (if not neutral):

Looks like:

Variation(s):

Initialized Variation(s):

Specify if Regional:

Linguistic Register (if specific): FORMAL   CONSULTATIVE   INFORMAL   INTIMATE

Other Vocab/Meanings:

GLOSS(ES)

(DH) <u>Dominant Handshape</u>:

(NDH) <u>NonDominant Handshape</u>:

(PO) <u>Palm Orientation</u>:

<u>Movement</u>:

<u>Location</u> (if not neutral):

<u>NMS</u> (if not neutral):

Looks like:

Variation(s):

Initialized Variation(s):

Specify if Regional:

Linguistic Register (if specific): FORMAL   CONSULTATIVE   INFORMAL   INTIMATE

Other Vocab/Meanings:

GLOSS(ES)

(DH) Dominant Handshape:

(NDH) NonDominant Handshape:

(PO) Palm Orientation:

Movement:

Location (if not neutral):

NMS (if not neutral):

Looks like:

Variation(s):

Initialized Variation(s):

Specify if Regional:

Linguistic Register (if specific): FORMAL CONSULTATIVE INFORMAL INTIMATE

Other Vocab/Meanings:

GLOSS(ES)

(DH) Dominant Handshape:

(NDH) NonDominant Handshape:

(PO) Palm Orientation:

Movement:

Location (if not neutral):

NMS (if not neutral):

Looks like:

Variation(s):

Initialized Variation(s):

Specify if Regional:

Linguistic Register (if specific): FORMAL CONSULTATIVE INFORMAL INTIMATE

Other Vocab/Meanings:

GLOSS(ES)

(DH) Dominant Handshape:

(NDH) NonDominant Handshape:

(PO) Palm Orientation:

Movement:

Location (if not neutral):

NMS (if not neutral):

Looks like:

Variation(s):

Initialized Variation(s):

Specify if Regional:

Linguistic Register (if specific): FORMAL CONSULTATIVE INFORMAL INTIMATE

Other Vocab/Meanings:

GLOSS(ES)

(DH) Dominant Handshape:

(NDH) NonDominant Handshape:

(PO) Palm Orientation:

Movement:

Location (if not neutral):

NMS (if not neutral):

Looks like:

Variation(s):

Initialized Variation(s):

Specify if Regional:

Linguistic Register (if specific): FORMAL CONSULTATIVE INFORMAL INTIMATE

Other Vocab/Meanings:

GLOSS(ES)

(DH) Dominant Handshape:

(NDH) NonDominant Handshape:

(PO) Palm Orientation:

Movement:

Location (if not neutral):

NMS (if not neutral):

Looks like:

Variation(s):

Initialized Variation(s):

Specify if Regional:

Linguistic Register (if specific): FORMAL CONSULTATIVE INFORMAL INTIMATE

Other Vocab/Meanings:

GLOSS(ES)

(DH) Dominant Handshape:

(NDH) NonDominant Handshape:

(PO) Palm Orientation:

Movement:

Location (if not neutral):

NMS (if not neutral):

Looks like:

Variation(s):

Initialized Variation(s):

Specify if Regional:

Linguistic Register (if specific): FORMAL CONSULTATIVE INFORMAL INTIMATE

Other Vocab/Meanings:

GLOSS(ES)

(DH) <u>Dominant Handshape</u>:

(NDH) <u>NonDominant Handshape</u>:

(PO) <u>Palm Orientation</u>:

<u>Movement</u>:

<u>Location</u> (if not neutral):

<u>NMS</u> (if not neutral):

Looks like:

Variation(s):

Initialized Variation(s):

Specify if Regional:

Linguistic Register (if specific): FORMAL CONSULTATIVE INFORMAL INTIMATE

Other Vocab/Meanings:

GLOSS(ES)

(DH) <u>Dominant Handshape</u>:

(NDH) <u>NonDominant Handshape</u>:

(PO) <u>Palm Orientation</u>:

<u>Movement</u>:

<u>Location</u> (if not neutral):

<u>NMS</u> (if not neutral):

Looks like:

Variation(s):

Initialized Variation(s):

Specify if Regional:

Linguistic Register (if specific): FORMAL CONSULTATIVE INFORMAL INTIMATE

Other Vocab/Meanings:

GLOSS(ES)

(DH) <u>Dominant Handshape</u>:

(NDH) <u>NonDominant Handshape</u>:

(PO) <u>Palm Orientation</u>:

<u>Movement</u>:

<u>Location</u> (if not neutral):

<u>NMS</u> (if not neutral):

Looks like:

Variation(s):

Initialized Variation(s):

Specify if Regional:

Linguistic Register (if specific): FORMAL CONSULTATIVE INFORMAL INTIMATE

Other Vocab/Meanings:

GLOSS(ES)

(DH) <u>Dominant Handshape</u>:

(NDH) <u>NonDominant Handshape</u>:

(PO) <u>Palm Orientation</u>:

<u>Movement</u>:

<u>Location</u> (if not neutral):

<u>NMS</u> (if not neutral):

Looks like:

Variation(s):

Initialized Variation(s):

Specify if Regional:

Linguistic Register (if specific): FORMAL CONSULTATIVE INFORMAL INTIMATE

Other Vocab/Meanings:

GLOSS(ES)

(DH) <u>Dominant Handshape</u>:

(NDH) <u>NonDominant Handshape</u>:

(PO) <u>Palm Orientation</u>:

<u>Movement</u>:

<u>Location</u> (if not neutral):

<u>NMS</u> (if not neutral):

Looks like:

Variation(s):

Initialized Variation(s):

Specify if Regional:

Linguistic Register (if specific): FORMAL CONSULTATIVE INFORMAL INTIMATE

Other Vocab/Meanings:

GLOSS(ES)

(DH) <u>Dominant Handshape</u>:

(NDH) <u>NonDominant Handshape</u>:

(PO) <u>Palm Orientation</u>:

<u>Movement</u>:

<u>Location</u> (if not neutral):

<u>NMS</u> (if not neutral):

Looks like:

Variation(s):

Initialized Variation(s):

Specify if Regional:

Linguistic Register (if specific): FORMAL CONSULTATIVE INFORMAL INTIMATE

Other Vocab/Meanings:

GLOSS(ES)

(DH) <u>Dominant Handshape</u>:

(NDH) <u>NonDominant Handshape</u>:

(PO) <u>Palm Orientation</u>:

<u>Movement</u>:

<u>Location</u> (if not neutral):

<u>NMS</u> (if not neutral):

Looks like:

Variation(s):

Initialized Variation(s):

Specify if Regional:

Linguistic Register (if specific): FORMAL   CONSULTATIVE   INFORMAL   INTIMATE

Other Vocab/Meanings:

GLOSS(ES)

(DH) <u>Dominant Handshape</u>:

(NDH) <u>NonDominant Handshape</u>:

(PO) <u>Palm Orientation</u>:

<u>Movement</u>:

<u>Location</u> (if not neutral):

<u>NMS</u> (if not neutral):

Looks like:

Variation(s):

Initialized Variation(s):

Specify if Regional:

Linguistic Register (if specific): FORMAL   CONSULTATIVE   INFORMAL   INTIMATE

Other Vocab/Meanings:

GLOSS(ES)

(DH) <u>Dominant Handshape</u>:

(NDH) <u>NonDominant Handshape</u>:

(PO) <u>Palm Orientation</u>:

<u>Movement</u>:

<u>Location</u> (if not neutral):

<u>NMS</u> (if not neutral):

Looks like:

Variation(s):

Initialized Variation(s):

Specify if Regional:

Linguistic Register (if specific): FORMAL   CONSULTATIVE   INFORMAL   INTIMATE

Other Vocab/Meanings:

GLOSS(ES)

(DH) <u>Dominant Handshape</u>:

(NDH) <u>NonDominant Handshape</u>:

(PO) <u>Palm Orientation</u>:

<u>Movement</u>:

<u>Location</u> (if not neutral):

<u>NMS</u> (if not neutral):

Looks like:

Variation(s):

Initialized Variation(s):

Specify if Regional:

Linguistic Register (if specific): FORMAL   CONSULTATIVE   INFORMAL   INTIMATE

Other Vocab/Meanings:

GLOSS(ES)

(DH) <u>Dominant Handshape</u>:

(NDH) <u>NonDominant Handshape</u>:

(PO) <u>Palm Orientation</u>:

<u>Movement</u>:

<u>Location</u> (if not neutral):

<u>NMS</u> (if not neutral):

Looks like:

Variation(s):

Initialized Variation(s):

Specify if Regional:

Linguistic Register (if specific): FORMAL   CONSULTATIVE   INFORMAL   INTIMATE

Other Vocab/Meanings:

GLOSS(ES)

(DH) <u>Dominant Handshape</u>:

(NDH) <u>NonDominant Handshape</u>:

(PO) <u>Palm Orientation</u>:

<u>Movement</u>:

<u>Location</u> (if not neutral):

<u>NMS</u> (if not neutral):

Looks like:

Variation(s):

Initialized Variation(s):

Specify if Regional:

Linguistic Register (if specific): FORMAL   CONSULTATIVE   INFORMAL   INTIMATE

Other Vocab/Meanings:

GLOSS(ES)

(DH) <u>Dominant Handshape</u>:

(NDH) <u>NonDominant Handshape</u>:

(PO) <u>Palm Orientation</u>:

<u>Movement</u>:

<u>Location</u> (if not neutral):

<u>NMS</u> (if not neutral):

Looks like:

Variation(s):

Initialized Variation(s):

Specify if Regional:

Linguistic **Register** (if specific): FORMAL   CONSULTATIVE   INFORMAL   INTIMATE

Other Vocab/Meanings:

GLOSS(ES)

(DH) <u>Dominant Handshape</u>:

(NDH) <u>NonDominant Handshape</u>:

(PO) <u>Palm Orientation</u>:

<u>Movement</u>:

<u>Location</u> (if not neutral):

<u>NMS</u> (if not neutral):

Looks like:

Variation(s):

Initialized Variation(s):

Specify if Regional:

Linguistic **Register** (if specific): FORMAL   CONSULTATIVE   INFORMAL   INTIMATE

Other Vocab/Meanings:

GLOSS(ES)

(DH) <u>Dominant Handshape</u>:

(NDH) <u>NonDominant Handshape</u>:

(PO) <u>Palm Orientation</u>:

<u>Movement</u>:

<u>Location</u> (if not neutral):

<u>NMS</u> (if not neutral):

Looks like:

Variation(s):

Initialized Variation(s):

Specify if Regional:

Linguistic **Register** (if specific): FORMAL   CONSULTATIVE   INFORMAL   INTIMATE

Other Vocab/Meanings:

GLOSS(ES)

(DH) <u>Dominant Handshape</u>:

(NDH) <u>NonDominant Handshape</u>:

(PO) <u>Palm Orientation</u>:

<u>Movement</u>:

<u>Location</u> (if not neutral):

<u>NMS</u> (if not neutral):

Looks like:

Variation(s):

Initialized Variation(s):

Specify if Regional:

Linguistic **Register** (if specific): FORMAL   CONSULTATIVE   INFORMAL   INTIMATE

Other Vocab/Meanings:

GLOSS(ES)

(DH) <u>Dominant Handshape</u>:

(NDH) <u>NonDominant Handshape</u>:

(PO) <u>Palm Orientation</u>:

<u>Movement</u>:

<u>Location</u> (if not neutral):

<u>NMS</u> (if not neutral):

Looks like:

Variation(s):

Initialized Variation(s):

Specify if Regional:

Linguistic **Register** (if specific): FORMAL   CONSULTATIVE   INFORMAL   INTIMATE

Other Vocab/Meanings:

GLOSS(ES)

(DH) <u>Dominant Handshape</u>:

(NDH) <u>NonDominant Handshape</u>:

(PO) <u>Palm Orientation</u>:

<u>Movement</u>:

<u>Location</u> (if not neutral):

<u>NMS</u> (if not neutral):

Looks like:

Variation(s):

Initialized Variation(s):

Specify if Regional:

Linguistic **Register** (if specific): FORMAL   CONSULTATIVE   INFORMAL   INTIMATE

Other Vocab/Meanings:

GLOSS(ES)

(DH) Dominant Handshape:

(NDH) NonDominant Handshape:

(PO) Palm Orientation:

Movement:

Location (if not neutral):

NMS (if not neutral):

Looks like:

Variation(s):

Initialized Variation(s):

Specify if Regional:

Linguistic Register (if specific): FORMAL CONSULTATIVE INFORMAL INTIMATE

Other Vocab/Meanings:

GLOSS(ES)

(DH) Dominant Handshape:

(NDH) NonDominant Handshape:

(PO) Palm Orientation:

Movement:

Location (if not neutral):

NMS (if not neutral):

Looks like:

Variation(s):

Initialized Variation(s):

Specify if Regional:

Linguistic Register (if specific): FORMAL CONSULTATIVE INFORMAL INTIMATE

Other Vocab/Meanings:

GLOSS(ES)

(DH) Dominant Handshape:

(NDH) NonDominant Handshape:

(PO) Palm Orientation:

Movement:

Location (if not neutral):

NMS (if not neutral):

Looks like:

Variation(s):

Initialized Variation(s):

Specify if Regional:

Linguistic Register (if specific): FORMAL CONSULTATIVE INFORMAL INTIMATE

Other Vocab/Meanings:

GLOSS(ES)

(DH) Dominant Handshape:

(NDH) NonDominant Handshape:

(PO) Palm Orientation:

Movement:

Location (if not neutral):

NMS (if not neutral):

Looks like:

Variation(s):

Initialized Variation(s):

Specify if Regional:

Linguistic Register (if specific): FORMAL CONSULTATIVE INFORMAL INTIMATE

Other Vocab/Meanings:

GLOSS(ES)

(DH) Dominant Handshape:

(NDH) NonDominant Handshape:

(PO) Palm Orientation:

Movement:

Location (if not neutral):

NMS (if not neutral):

Looks like:

Variation(s):

Initialized Variation(s):

Specify if Regional:

Linguistic Register (if specific): FORMAL CONSULTATIVE INFORMAL INTIMATE

Other Vocab/Meanings:

GLOSS(ES)

(DH) Dominant Handshape:

(NDH) NonDominant Handshape:

(PO) Palm Orientation:

Movement:

Location (if not neutral):

NMS (if not neutral):

Looks like:

Variation(s):

Initialized Variation(s):

Specify if Regional:

Linguistic Register (if specific): FORMAL CONSULTATIVE INFORMAL INTIMATE

Other Vocab/Meanings:

GLOSS(ES)

(DH) <u>Dominant Handshape</u>:

(NDH) <u>NonDominant Handshape</u>:

(PO) <u>Palm Orientation</u>:

<u>Movement</u>:

<u>Location</u> (if not neutral):

<u>NMS</u> (if not neutral):

Looks like:

Variation(s):

Initialized Variation(s):

Specify if Regional:

Linguistic Register (if specific): FORMAL CONSULTATIVE INFORMAL INTIMATE

Other Vocab/Meanings:

GLOSS(ES)

(DH) <u>Dominant Handshape</u>:

(NDH) <u>NonDominant Handshape</u>:

(PO) <u>Palm Orientation</u>:

<u>Movement</u>:

<u>Location</u> (if not neutral):

<u>NMS</u> (if not neutral):

Looks like:

Variation(s):

Initialized Variation(s):

Specify if Regional:

Linguistic Register (if specific): FORMAL CONSULTATIVE INFORMAL INTIMATE

Other Vocab/Meanings:

GLOSS(ES)

(DH) <u>Dominant Handshape</u>:

(NDH) <u>NonDominant Handshape</u>:

(PO) <u>Palm Orientation</u>:

<u>Movement</u>:

<u>Location</u> (if not neutral):

<u>NMS</u> (if not neutral):

Looks like:

Variation(s):

Initialized Variation(s):

Specify if Regional:

Linguistic Register (if specific): FORMAL CONSULTATIVE INFORMAL INTIMATE

Other Vocab/Meanings:

GLOSS(ES)

(DH) <u>Dominant Handshape</u>:

(NDH) <u>NonDominant Handshape</u>:

(PO) <u>Palm Orientation</u>:

<u>Movement</u>:

<u>Location</u> (if not neutral):

<u>NMS</u> (if not neutral):

Looks like:

Variation(s):

Initialized Variation(s):

Specify if Regional:

Linguistic Register (if specific): FORMAL CONSULTATIVE INFORMAL INTIMATE

Other Vocab/Meanings:

GLOSS(ES)

(DH) <u>Dominant Handshape</u>:

(NDH) <u>NonDominant Handshape</u>:

(PO) <u>Palm Orientation</u>:

<u>Movement</u>:

<u>Location</u> (if not neutral):

<u>NMS</u> (if not neutral):

Looks like:

Variation(s):

Initialized Variation(s):

Specify if Regional:

Linguistic Register (if specific): FORMAL CONSULTATIVE INFORMAL INTIMATE

Other Vocab/Meanings:

GLOSS(ES)

(DH) <u>Dominant Handshape</u>:

(NDH) <u>NonDominant Handshape</u>:

(PO) <u>Palm Orientation</u>:

<u>Movement</u>:

<u>Location</u> (if not neutral):

<u>NMS</u> (if not neutral):

Looks like:

Variation(s):

Initialized Variation(s):

Specify if Regional:

Linguistic Register (if specific): FORMAL CONSULTATIVE INFORMAL INTIMATE

Other Vocab/Meanings:

GLOSS(ES)

(DH) Dominant Handshape:

(NDH) NonDominant Handshape:

(PO) Palm Orientation:

Movement:

Location (if not neutral):

NMS (if not neutral):

Looks like:

Variation(s):

Initialized Variation(s):

Specify if Regional:

Linguistic Register (if specific): FORMAL CONSULTATIVE INFORMAL INTIMATE

Other Vocab/Meanings:

GLOSS(ES)

(DH) Dominant Handshape:

(NDH) NonDominant Handshape:

(PO) Palm Orientation:

Movement:

Location (if not neutral):

NMS (if not neutral):

Looks like:

Variation(s):

Initialized Variation(s):

Specify if Regional:

Linguistic Register (if specific): FORMAL CONSULTATIVE INFORMAL INTIMATE

Other Vocab/Meanings:

GLOSS(ES)

(DH) Dominant Handshape:

(NDH) NonDominant Handshape:

(PO) Palm Orientation:

Movement:

Location (if not neutral):

NMS (if not neutral):

Looks like:

Variation(s):

Initialized Variation(s):

Specify if Regional:

Linguistic Register (if specific): FORMAL CONSULTATIVE INFORMAL INTIMATE

Other Vocab/Meanings:

GLOSS(ES)

(DH) Dominant Handshape:

(NDH) NonDominant Handshape:

(PO) Palm Orientation:

Movement:

Location (if not neutral):

NMS (if not neutral):

Looks like:

Variation(s):

Initialized Variation(s):

Specify if Regional:

Linguistic Register (if specific): FORMAL CONSULTATIVE INFORMAL INTIMATE

Other Vocab/Meanings:

GLOSS(ES)

(DH) Dominant Handshape:

(NDH) NonDominant Handshape:

(PO) Palm Orientation:

Movement:

Location (if not neutral):

NMS (if not neutral):

Looks like:

Variation(s):

Initialized Variation(s):

Specify if Regional:

Linguistic Register (if specific): FORMAL CONSULTATIVE INFORMAL INTIMATE

Other Vocab/Meanings:

GLOSS(ES)

(DH) Dominant Handshape:

(NDH) NonDominant Handshape:

(PO) Palm Orientation:

Movement:

Location (if not neutral):

NMS (if not neutral):

Looks like:

Variation(s):

Initialized Variation(s):

Specify if Regional:

Linguistic Register (if specific): FORMAL CONSULTATIVE INFORMAL INTIMATE

Other Vocab/Meanings:

GLOSS(ES)

(DH) <u>Dominant Handshape</u>:

(NDH) <u>NonDominant Handshape</u>:

(PO) <u>Palm Orientation</u>:

<u>Movement</u>:

<u>Location</u> (if not neutral):

<u>NMS</u> (if not neutral):

Looks like:

Variation(s):

Initialized Variation(s):

Specify if Regional:

Linguistic Register (if specific): FORMAL CONSULTATIVE INFORMAL INTIMATE

Other Vocab/Meanings:

GLOSS(ES)

(DH) <u>Dominant Handshape</u>:

(NDH) <u>NonDominant Handshape</u>:

(PO) <u>Palm Orientation</u>:

<u>Movement</u>:

<u>Location</u> (if not neutral):

<u>NMS</u> (if not neutral):

Looks like:

Variation(s):

Initialized Variation(s):

Specify if Regional:

Linguistic Register (if specific): FORMAL CONSULTATIVE INFORMAL INTIMATE

Other Vocab/Meanings:

GLOSS(ES)

(DH) <u>Dominant Handshape</u>:

(NDH) <u>NonDominant Handshape</u>:

(PO) <u>Palm Orientation</u>:

<u>Movement</u>:

<u>Location</u> (if not neutral):

<u>NMS</u> (if not neutral):

Looks like:

Variation(s):

Initialized Variation(s):

Specify if Regional:

Linguistic Register (if specific): FORMAL CONSULTATIVE INFORMAL INTIMATE

Other Vocab/Meanings:

GLOSS(ES)

(DH) <u>Dominant Handshape</u>:

(NDH) <u>NonDominant Handshape</u>:

(PO) <u>Palm Orientation</u>:

<u>Movement</u>:

<u>Location</u> (if not neutral):

<u>NMS</u> (if not neutral):

Looks like:

Variation(s):

Initialized Variation(s):

Specify if Regional:

Linguistic Register (if specific): FORMAL CONSULTATIVE INFORMAL INTIMATE

Other Vocab/Meanings:

GLOSS(ES)

(DH) <u>Dominant Handshape</u>:

(NDH) <u>NonDominant Handshape</u>:

(PO) <u>Palm Orientation</u>:

<u>Movement</u>:

<u>Location</u> (if not neutral):

<u>NMS</u> (if not neutral):

Looks like:

Variation(s):

Initialized Variation(s):

Specify if Regional:

Linguistic Register (if specific): FORMAL CONSULTATIVE INFORMAL INTIMATE

Other Vocab/Meanings:

GLOSS(ES)

(DH) <u>Dominant Handshape</u>:

(NDH) <u>NonDominant Handshape</u>:

(PO) <u>Palm Orientation</u>:

<u>Movement</u>:

<u>Location</u> (if not neutral):

<u>NMS</u> (if not neutral):

Looks like:

Variation(s):

Initialized Variation(s):

Specify if Regional:

Linguistic Register (if specific): FORMAL CONSULTATIVE INFORMAL INTIMATE

Other Vocab/Meanings:

GLOSS(ES)

(DH) Dominant Handshape:

(NDH) NonDominant Handshape:

(PO) Palm Orientation:

Movement:

Location (if not neutral):

NMS (if not neutral):

Looks like:

Variation(s):

Initialized Variation(s):

Specify if Regional:

Linguistic Register (if specific): FORMAL CONSULTATIVE INFORMAL INTIMATE

Other Vocab/Meanings:

GLOSS(ES)

(DH) Dominant Handshape:

(NDH) NonDominant Handshape:

(PO) Palm Orientation:

Movement:

Location (if not neutral):

NMS (if not neutral):

Looks like:

Variation(s):

Initialized Variation(s):

Specify if Regional:

Linguistic Register (if specific): FORMAL CONSULTATIVE INFORMAL INTIMATE

Other Vocab/Meanings:

GLOSS(ES)

(DH) Dominant Handshape:

(NDH) NonDominant Handshape:

(PO) Palm Orientation:

Movement:

Location (if not neutral):

NMS (if not neutral):

Looks like:

Variation(s):

Initialized Variation(s):

Specify if Regional:

Linguistic Register (if specific): FORMAL CONSULTATIVE INFORMAL INTIMATE

Other Vocab/Meanings:

GLOSS(ES)

(DH) Dominant Handshape:

(NDH) NonDominant Handshape:

(PO) Palm Orientation:

Movement:

Location (if not neutral):

NMS (if not neutral):

Looks like:

Variation(s):

Initialized Variation(s):

Specify if Regional:

Linguistic Register (if specific): FORMAL CONSULTATIVE INFORMAL INTIMATE

Other Vocab/Meanings:

GLOSS(ES)

(DH) Dominant Handshape:

(NDH) NonDominant Handshape:

(PO) Palm Orientation:

Movement:

Location (if not neutral):

NMS (if not neutral):

Looks like:

Variation(s):

Initialized Variation(s):

Specify if Regional:

Linguistic Register (if specific): FORMAL CONSULTATIVE INFORMAL INTIMATE

Other Vocab/Meanings:

GLOSS(ES)

(DH) Dominant Handshape:

(NDH) NonDominant Handshape:

(PO) Palm Orientation:

Movement:

Location (if not neutral):

NMS (if not neutral):

Looks like:

Variation(s):

Initialized Variation(s):

Specify if Regional:

Linguistic Register (if specific): FORMAL CONSULTATIVE INFORMAL INTIMATE

Other Vocab/Meanings:

GLOSS(ES)

(DH) <u>Dominant Handshape</u>:

(NDH) <u>NonDominant Handshape</u>:

(PO) <u>Palm Orientation</u>:

<u>Movement</u>:

<u>Location</u> (if not neutral):

<u>NMS</u> (if not neutral):

Looks like:

Variation(s):

Initialized Variation(s):

Specify if Regional:

Linguistic Register (if specific): FORMAL CONSULTATIVE INFORMAL INTIMATE

Other Vocab/Meanings:

GLOSS(ES)

(DH) <u>Dominant Handshape</u>:

(NDH) <u>NonDominant Handshape</u>:

(PO) <u>Palm Orientation</u>:

<u>Movement</u>:

<u>Location</u> (if not neutral):

<u>NMS</u> (if not neutral):

Looks like:

Variation(s):

Initialized Variation(s):

Specify if Regional:

Linguistic Register (if specific): FORMAL CONSULTATIVE INFORMAL INTIMATE

Other Vocab/Meanings:

GLOSS(ES)

(DH) <u>Dominant Handshape</u>:

(NDH) <u>NonDominant Handshape</u>:

(PO) <u>Palm Orientation</u>:

<u>Movement</u>:

<u>Location</u> (if not neutral):

<u>NMS</u> (if not neutral):

Looks like:

Variation(s):

Initialized Variation(s):

Specify if Regional:

Linguistic Register (if specific): FORMAL CONSULTATIVE INFORMAL INTIMATE

Other Vocab/Meanings:

GLOSS(ES)

(DH) <u>Dominant Handshape</u>:

(NDH) <u>NonDominant Handshape</u>:

(PO) <u>Palm Orientation</u>:

<u>Movement</u>:

<u>Location</u> (if not neutral):

<u>NMS</u> (if not neutral):

Looks like:

Variation(s):

Initialized Variation(s):

Specify if Regional:

Linguistic Register (if specific): FORMAL CONSULTATIVE INFORMAL INTIMATE

Other Vocab/Meanings:

GLOSS(ES)

(DH) <u>Dominant Handshape</u>:

(NDH) <u>NonDominant Handshape</u>:

(PO) <u>Palm Orientation</u>:

<u>Movement</u>:

<u>Location</u> (if not neutral):

<u>NMS</u> (if not neutral):

Looks like:

Variation(s):

Initialized Variation(s):

Specify if Regional:

Linguistic Register (if specific): FORMAL CONSULTATIVE INFORMAL INTIMATE

Other Vocab/Meanings:

GLOSS(ES)

(DH) <u>Dominant Handshape</u>:

(NDH) <u>NonDominant Handshape</u>:

(PO) <u>Palm Orientation</u>:

<u>Movement</u>:

<u>Location</u> (if not neutral):

<u>NMS</u> (if not neutral):

Looks like:

Variation(s):

Initialized Variation(s):

Specify if Regional:

Linguistic Register (if specific): FORMAL CONSULTATIVE INFORMAL INTIMATE

Other Vocab/Meanings:

GLOSS(ES)

(DH) Dominant Handshape:

(NDH) NonDominant Handshape:

(PO) Palm Orientation:

Movement:

Location (if not neutral):

NMS (if not neutral):

Looks like:

Variation(s):

Initialized Variation(s):

Specify if Regional:

Linguistic Register (if specific): FORMAL CONSULTATIVE INFORMAL INTIMATE

Other Vocab/Meanings:

GLOSS(ES)

(DH) Dominant Handshape:

(NDH) NonDominant Handshape:

(PO) Palm Orientation:

Movement:

Location (if not neutral):

NMS (if not neutral):

Looks like:

Variation(s):

Initialized Variation(s):

Specify if Regional:

Linguistic Register (if specific): FORMAL CONSULTATIVE INFORMAL INTIMATE

Other Vocab/Meanings:

GLOSS(ES)

(DH) Dominant Handshape:

(NDH) NonDominant Handshape:

(PO) Palm Orientation:

Movement:

Location (if not neutral):

NMS (if not neutral):

Looks like:

Variation(s):

Initialized Variation(s):

Specify if Regional:

Linguistic Register (if specific): FORMAL CONSULTATIVE INFORMAL INTIMATE

Other Vocab/Meanings:

GLOSS(ES)

(DH) Dominant Handshape:

(NDH) NonDominant Handshape:

(PO) Palm Orientation:

Movement:

Location (if not neutral):

NMS (if not neutral):

Looks like:

Variation(s):

Initialized Variation(s):

Specify if Regional:

Linguistic Register (if specific): FORMAL CONSULTATIVE INFORMAL INTIMATE

Other Vocab/Meanings:

GLOSS(ES)

(DH) Dominant Handshape:

(NDH) NonDominant Handshape:

(PO) Palm Orientation:

Movement:

Location (if not neutral):

NMS (if not neutral):

Looks like:

Variation(s):

Initialized Variation(s):

Specify if Regional:

Linguistic Register (if specific): FORMAL CONSULTATIVE INFORMAL INTIMATE

Other Vocab/Meanings:

GLOSS(ES)

(DH) Dominant Handshape:

(NDH) NonDominant Handshape:

(PO) Palm Orientation:

Movement:

Location (if not neutral):

NMS (if not neutral):

Looks like:

Variation(s):

Initialized Variation(s):

Specify if Regional:

Linguistic Register (if specific): FORMAL CONSULTATIVE INFORMAL INTIMATE

Other Vocab/Meanings:

GLOSS(ES)

(DH) <u>Dominant Handshape</u>:

(NDH) <u>NonDominant Handshape</u>:

(PO) <u>Palm Orientation</u>:

<u>Movement</u>:

<u>Location</u> (if not neutral):

<u>NMS</u> (if not neutral):

Looks like:

Variation(s):

Initialized Variation(s):

Specify if Regional:

Linguistic Register (if specific): FORMAL   CONSULTATIVE   INFORMAL   INTIMATE

Other Vocab/Meanings:

GLOSS(ES)

(DH) <u>Dominant Handshape</u>:

(NDH) <u>NonDominant Handshape</u>:

(PO) <u>Palm Orientation</u>:

<u>Movement</u>:

<u>Location</u> (if not neutral):

<u>NMS</u> (if not neutral):

Looks like:

Variation(s):

Initialized Variation(s):

Specify if Regional:

Linguistic Register (if specific): FORMAL   CONSULTATIVE   INFORMAL   INTIMATE

Other Vocab/Meanings:

GLOSS(ES)

(DH) <u>Dominant Handshape</u>:

(NDH) <u>NonDominant Handshape</u>:

(PO) <u>Palm Orientation</u>:

<u>Movement</u>:

<u>Location</u> (if not neutral):

<u>NMS</u> (if not neutral):

Looks like:

Variation(s):

Initialized Variation(s):

Specify if Regional:

Linguistic Register (if specific): FORMAL   CONSULTATIVE   INFORMAL   INTIMATE

Other Vocab/Meanings:

GLOSS(ES)

(DH) <u>Dominant Handshape</u>:

(NDH) <u>NonDominant Handshape</u>:

(PO) <u>Palm Orientation</u>:

<u>Movement</u>:

<u>Location</u> (if not neutral):

<u>NMS</u> (if not neutral):

Looks like:

Variation(s):

Initialized Variation(s):

Specify if Regional:

Linguistic Register (if specific): FORMAL   CONSULTATIVE   INFORMAL   INTIMATE

Other Vocab/Meanings:

GLOSS(ES)

(DH) <u>Dominant Handshape</u>:

(NDH) <u>NonDominant Handshape</u>:

(PO) <u>Palm Orientation</u>:

<u>Movement</u>:

<u>Location</u> (if not neutral):

<u>NMS</u> (if not neutral):

Looks like:

Variation(s):

Initialized Variation(s):

Specify if Regional:

Linguistic Register (if specific): FORMAL   CONSULTATIVE   INFORMAL   INTIMATE

Other Vocab/Meanings:

GLOSS(ES)

(DH) <u>Dominant Handshape</u>:

(NDH) <u>NonDominant Handshape</u>:

(PO) <u>Palm Orientation</u>:

<u>Movement</u>:

<u>Location</u> (if not neutral):

<u>NMS</u> (if not neutral):

Looks like:

Variation(s):

Initialized Variation(s):

Specify if Regional:

Linguistic Register (if specific): FORMAL   CONSULTATIVE   INFORMAL   INTIMATE

Other Vocab/Meanings:

GLOSS(ES)

(DH) <u>Dominant Handshape</u>:

(NDH) <u>NonDominant Handshape</u>:

(PO) <u>Palm Orientation</u>:

<u>Movement</u>:

<u>Location</u> (if not neutral):

<u>NMS</u> (if not neutral):

Looks like:

Variation(s):

Initialized Variation(s):

Specify if Regional:

Linguistic Register (if specific): FORMAL CONSULTATIVE INFORMAL INTIMATE

Other Vocab/Meanings:

GLOSS(ES)

(DH) <u>Dominant Handshape</u>:

(NDH) <u>NonDominant Handshape</u>:

(PO) <u>Palm Orientation</u>:

<u>Movement</u>:

<u>Location</u> (if not neutral):

<u>NMS</u> (if not neutral):

Looks like:

Variation(s):

Initialized Variation(s):

Specify if Regional:

Linguistic Register (if specific): FORMAL CONSULTATIVE INFORMAL INTIMATE

Other Vocab/Meanings:

GLOSS(ES)

(DH) <u>Dominant Handshape</u>:

(NDH) <u>NonDominant Handshape</u>:

(PO) <u>Palm Orientation</u>:

<u>Movement</u>:

<u>Location</u> (if not neutral):

<u>NMS</u> (if not neutral):

Looks like:

Variation(s):

Initialized Variation(s):

Specify if Regional:

Linguistic Register (if specific): FORMAL CONSULTATIVE INFORMAL INTIMATE

Other Vocab/Meanings:

GLOSS(ES)

(DH) <u>Dominant Handshape</u>:

(NDH) <u>NonDominant Handshape</u>:

(PO) <u>Palm Orientation</u>:

<u>Movement</u>:

<u>Location</u> (if not neutral):

<u>NMS</u> (if not neutral):

Looks like:

Variation(s):

Initialized Variation(s):

Specify if Regional:

Linguistic Register (if specific): FORMAL CONSULTATIVE INFORMAL INTIMATE

Other Vocab/Meanings:

GLOSS(ES)

(DH) <u>Dominant Handshape</u>:

(NDH) <u>NonDominant Handshape</u>:

(PO) <u>Palm Orientation</u>:

<u>Movement</u>:

<u>Location</u> (if not neutral):

<u>NMS</u> (if not neutral):

Looks like:

Variation(s):

Initialized Variation(s):

Specify if Regional:

Linguistic Register (if specific): FORMAL CONSULTATIVE INFORMAL INTIMATE

Other Vocab/Meanings:

GLOSS(ES)

(DH) <u>Dominant Handshape</u>:

(NDH) <u>NonDominant Handshape</u>:

(PO) <u>Palm Orientation</u>:

<u>Movement</u>:

<u>Location</u> (if not neutral):

<u>NMS</u> (if not neutral):

Looks like:

Variation(s):

Initialized Variation(s):

Specify if Regional:

Linguistic Register (if specific): FORMAL CONSULTATIVE INFORMAL INTIMATE

Other Vocab/Meanings:

GLOSS(ES)

(DH) Dominant Handshape:

(NDH) NonDominant Handshape:

(PO) Palm Orientation:

Movement:

Location (if not neutral):

NMS (if not neutral):

Looks like:

Variation(s):

Initialized Variation(s):

Specify if Regional:

Linguistic Register (if specific): FORMAL CONSULTATIVE INFORMAL INTIMATE

Other Vocab/Meanings:

GLOSS(ES)

(DH) Dominant Handshape:

(NDH) NonDominant Handshape:

(PO) Palm Orientation:

Movement:

Location (if not neutral):

NMS (if not neutral):

Looks like:

Variation(s):

Initialized Variation(s):

Specify if Regional:

Linguistic Register (if specific): FORMAL CONSULTATIVE INFORMAL INTIMATE

Other Vocab/Meanings:

GLOSS(ES)

(DH) Dominant Handshape:

(NDH) NonDominant Handshape:

(PO) Palm Orientation:

Movement:

Location (if not neutral):

NMS (if not neutral):

Looks like:

Variation(s):

Initialized Variation(s):

Specify if Regional:

Linguistic Register (if specific): FORMAL CONSULTATIVE INFORMAL INTIMATE

Other Vocab/Meanings:

GLOSS(ES)

(DH) Dominant Handshape:

(NDH) NonDominant Handshape:

(PO) Palm Orientation:

Movement:

Location (if not neutral):

NMS (if not neutral):

Looks like:

Variation(s):

Initialized Variation(s):

Specify if Regional:

Linguistic Register (if specific): FORMAL CONSULTATIVE INFORMAL INTIMATE

Other Vocab/Meanings:

GLOSS(ES)

(DH) Dominant Handshape:

(NDH) NonDominant Handshape:

(PO) Palm Orientation:

Movement:

Location (if not neutral):

NMS (if not neutral):

Looks like:

Variation(s):

Initialized Variation(s):

Specify if Regional:

Linguistic Register (if specific): FORMAL CONSULTATIVE INFORMAL INTIMATE

Other Vocab/Meanings:

GLOSS(ES)

(DH) Dominant Handshape:

(NDH) NonDominant Handshape:

(PO) Palm Orientation:

Movement:

Location (if not neutral):

NMS (if not neutral):

Looks like:

Variation(s):

Initialized Variation(s):

Specify if Regional:

Linguistic Register (if specific): FORMAL CONSULTATIVE INFORMAL INTIMATE

Other Vocab/Meanings:

GLOSS(ES)

(DH) <u>Dominant Handshape</u>:

(NDH) <u>NonDominant Handshape</u>:

(PO) <u>Palm Orientation</u>:

<u>Movement</u>:

<u>Location</u> (if not neutral):

<u>NMS</u> (if not neutral):

Looks like:

Variation(s):

Initialized Variation(s):

Specify if Regional:

Linguistic Register (if specific): FORMAL CONSULTATIVE INFORMAL INTIMATE

Other Vocab/Meanings:

GLOSS(ES)

(DH) <u>Dominant Handshape</u>:

(NDH) <u>NonDominant Handshape</u>:

(PO) <u>Palm Orientation</u>:

<u>Movement</u>:

<u>Location</u> (if not neutral):

<u>NMS</u> (if not neutral):

Looks like:

Variation(s):

Initialized Variation(s):

Specify if Regional:

Linguistic Register (if specific): FORMAL CONSULTATIVE INFORMAL INTIMATE

Other Vocab/Meanings:

GLOSS(ES)

(DH) <u>Dominant Handshape</u>:

(NDH) <u>NonDominant Handshape</u>:

(PO) <u>Palm Orientation</u>:

<u>Movement</u>:

<u>Location</u> (if not neutral):

<u>NMS</u> (if not neutral):

Looks like:

Variation(s):

Initialized Variation(s):

Specify if Regional:

Linguistic Register (if specific): FORMAL CONSULTATIVE INFORMAL INTIMATE

Other Vocab/Meanings:

GLOSS(ES)

(DH) <u>Dominant Handshape</u>:

(NDH) <u>NonDominant Handshape</u>:

(PO) <u>Palm Orientation</u>:

<u>Movement</u>:

<u>Location</u> (if not neutral):

<u>NMS</u> (if not neutral):

Looks like:

Variation(s):

Initialized Variation(s):

Specify if Regional:

Linguistic Register (if specific): FORMAL CONSULTATIVE INFORMAL INTIMATE

Other Vocab/Meanings:

GLOSS(ES)

(DH) <u>Dominant Handshape</u>:

(NDH) <u>NonDominant Handshape</u>:

(PO) <u>Palm Orientation</u>:

<u>Movement</u>:

<u>Location</u> (if not neutral):

<u>NMS</u> (if not neutral):

Looks like:

Variation(s):

Initialized Variation(s):

Specify if Regional:

Linguistic Register (if specific): FORMAL CONSULTATIVE INFORMAL INTIMATE

Other Vocab/Meanings:

GLOSS(ES)

(DH) <u>Dominant Handshape</u>:

(NDH) <u>NonDominant Handshape</u>:

(PO) <u>Palm Orientation</u>:

<u>Movement</u>:

<u>Location</u> (if not neutral):

<u>NMS</u> (if not neutral):

Looks like:

Variation(s):

Initialized Variation(s):

Specify if Regional:

Linguistic Register (if specific): FORMAL CONSULTATIVE INFORMAL INTIMATE

Other Vocab/Meanings:

GLOSS(ES)

 (DH) <u>Dominant Handshape</u>:

(NDH) <u>NonDominant Handshape</u>:

 (PO) <u>Palm Orientation</u>:

  <u>Movement</u>:

  <u>Location</u> (if not neutral):

  <u>NMS</u> (if not neutral):

 Looks like:

 Variation(s):

Initialized Variation(s):

 Specify if Regional:

 Linguistic Register (if specific): Formal Consultative Informal Intimate

Other Vocab/Meanings:

GLOSS(ES)

 (DH) <u>Dominant Handshape</u>:

(NDH) <u>NonDominant Handshape</u>:

 (PO) <u>Palm Orientation</u>:

  <u>Movement</u>:

  <u>Location</u> (if not neutral):

  <u>NMS</u> (if not neutral):

 Looks like:

 Variation(s):

Initialized Variation(s):

 Specify if Regional:

 Linguistic Register (if specific): Formal Consultative Informal Intimate

Other Vocab/Meanings:

GLOSS(ES)

 (DH) <u>Dominant Handshape</u>:

(NDH) <u>NonDominant Handshape</u>:

 (PO) <u>Palm Orientation</u>:

  <u>Movement</u>:

  <u>Location</u> (if not neutral):

  <u>NMS</u> (if not neutral):

 Looks like:

 Variation(s):

Initialized Variation(s):

 Specify if Regional:

 Linguistic Register (if specific): Formal Consultative Informal Intimate

Other Vocab/Meanings:

GLOSS(ES)

 (DH) <u>Dominant Handshape</u>:

(NDH) <u>NonDominant Handshape</u>:

 (PO) <u>Palm Orientation</u>:

  <u>Movement</u>:

  <u>Location</u> (if not neutral):

  <u>NMS</u> (if not neutral):

 Looks like:

 Variation(s):

Initialized Variation(s):

 Specify if Regional:

 Linguistic Register (if specific): Formal Consultative Informal Intimate

Other Vocab/Meanings:

GLOSS(ES)

 (DH) <u>Dominant Handshape</u>:

(NDH) <u>NonDominant Handshape</u>:

 (PO) <u>Palm Orientation</u>:

  <u>Movement</u>:

  <u>Location</u> (if not neutral):

  <u>NMS</u> (if not neutral):

 Looks like:

 Variation(s):

Initialized Variation(s):

 Specify if Regional:

 Linguistic Register (if specific): Formal Consultative Informal Intimate

Other Vocab/Meanings:

GLOSS(ES)

 (DH) <u>Dominant Handshape</u>:

(NDH) <u>NonDominant Handshape</u>:

 (PO) <u>Palm Orientation</u>:

  <u>Movement</u>:

  <u>Location</u> (if not neutral):

  <u>NMS</u> (if not neutral):

 Looks like:

 Variation(s):

Initialized Variation(s):

 Specify if Regional:

 Linguistic Register (if specific): Formal Consultative Informal Intimate

Other Vocab/Meanings:

GLOSS(ES)

(DH) Dominant Handshape:

(NDH) NonDominant Handshape:

(PO) Palm Orientation:

Movement:

Location (if not neutral):

NMS (if not neutral):

Looks like:

Variation(s):

Initialized Variation(s):

Specify if Regional:

Linguistic Register (if specific): FORMAL CONSULTATIVE INFORMAL INTIMATE

Other Vocab/Meanings:

GLOSS(ES)

(DH) Dominant Handshape:

(NDH) NonDominant Handshape:

(PO) Palm Orientation:

Movement:

Location (if not neutral):

NMS (if not neutral):

Looks like:

Variation(s):

Initialized Variation(s):

Specify if Regional:

Linguistic Register (if specific): FORMAL CONSULTATIVE INFORMAL INTIMATE

Other Vocab/Meanings:

GLOSS(ES)

(DH) Dominant Handshape:

(NDH) NonDominant Handshape:

(PO) Palm Orientation:

Movement:

Location (if not neutral):

NMS (if not neutral):

Looks like:

Variation(s):

Initialized Variation(s):

Specify if Regional:

Linguistic Register (if specific): FORMAL CONSULTATIVE INFORMAL INTIMATE

Other Vocab/Meanings:

GLOSS(ES)

(DH) Dominant Handshape:

(NDH) NonDominant Handshape:

(PO) Palm Orientation:

Movement:

Location (if not neutral):

NMS (if not neutral):

Looks like:

Variation(s):

Initialized Variation(s):

Specify if Regional:

Linguistic Register (if specific): FORMAL CONSULTATIVE INFORMAL INTIMATE

Other Vocab/Meanings:

GLOSS(ES)

(DH) Dominant Handshape:

(NDH) NonDominant Handshape:

(PO) Palm Orientation:

Movement:

Location (if not neutral):

NMS (if not neutral):

Looks like:

Variation(s):

Initialized Variation(s):

Specify if Regional:

Linguistic Register (if specific): FORMAL CONSULTATIVE INFORMAL INTIMATE

Other Vocab/Meanings:

GLOSS(ES)

(DH) Dominant Handshape:

(NDH) NonDominant Handshape:

(PO) Palm Orientation:

Movement:

Location (if not neutral):

NMS (if not neutral):

Looks like:

Variation(s):

Initialized Variation(s):

Specify if Regional:

Linguistic Register (if specific): FORMAL CONSULTATIVE INFORMAL INTIMATE

Other Vocab/Meanings:

GLOSS(ES)

(DH) <u>Dominant Handshape</u>:

(NDH) <u>NonDominant Handshape</u>:

(PO) <u>Palm Orientation</u>:

<u>Movement</u>:

<u>Location</u> (if not neutral):

<u>NMS</u> (if not neutral):

Looks like:

Variation(s):

Initialized Variation(s):

Specify if Regional:

Linguistic Register (if specific): FORMAL CONSULTATIVE INFORMAL INTIMATE

Other Vocab/Meanings:

GLOSS(ES)

(DH) <u>Dominant Handshape</u>:

(NDH) <u>NonDominant Handshape</u>:

(PO) <u>Palm Orientation</u>:

<u>Movement</u>:

<u>Location</u> (if not neutral):

<u>NMS</u> (if not neutral):

Looks like:

Variation(s):

Initialized Variation(s):

Specify if Regional:

Linguistic Register (if specific): FORMAL CONSULTATIVE INFORMAL INTIMATE

Other Vocab/Meanings:

GLOSS(ES)

(DH) <u>Dominant Handshape</u>:

(NDH) <u>NonDominant Handshape</u>:

(PO) <u>Palm Orientation</u>:

<u>Movement</u>:

<u>Location</u> (if not neutral):

<u>NMS</u> (if not neutral):

Looks like:

Variation(s):

Initialized Variation(s):

Specify if Regional:

Linguistic Register (if specific): FORMAL CONSULTATIVE INFORMAL INTIMATE

Other Vocab/Meanings:

GLOSS(ES)

(DH) <u>Dominant Handshape</u>:

(NDH) <u>NonDominant Handshape</u>:

(PO) <u>Palm Orientation</u>:

<u>Movement</u>:

<u>Location</u> (if not neutral):

<u>NMS</u> (if not neutral):

Looks like:

Variation(s):

Initialized Variation(s):

Specify if Regional:

Linguistic Register (if specific): FORMAL CONSULTATIVE INFORMAL INTIMATE

Other Vocab/Meanings:

GLOSS(ES)

(DH) <u>Dominant Handshape</u>:

(NDH) <u>NonDominant Handshape</u>:

(PO) <u>Palm Orientation</u>:

<u>Movement</u>:

<u>Location</u> (if not neutral):

<u>NMS</u> (if not neutral):

Looks like:

Variation(s):

Initialized Variation(s):

Specify if Regional:

Linguistic Register (if specific): FORMAL CONSULTATIVE INFORMAL INTIMATE

Other Vocab/Meanings:

GLOSS(ES)

(DH) <u>Dominant Handshape</u>:

(NDH) <u>NonDominant Handshape</u>:

(PO) <u>Palm Orientation</u>:

<u>Movement</u>:

<u>Location</u> (if not neutral):

<u>NMS</u> (if not neutral):

Looks like:

Variation(s):

Initialized Variation(s):

Specify if Regional:

Linguistic Register (if specific): FORMAL CONSULTATIVE INFORMAL INTIMATE

Other Vocab/Meanings:

GLOSS(ES)

(DH) <u>Dominant Handshape</u>:

(NDH) <u>NonDominant Handshape</u>:

(PO) <u>Palm Orientation</u>:

<u>Movement</u>:

<u>Location</u> (if not neutral):

<u>NMS</u> (if not neutral):

Looks like:

Variation(s):

Initialized Variation(s):

Specify if Regional:

Linguistic Register (if specific): FORMAL CONSULTATIVE INFORMAL INTIMATE

Other Vocab/Meanings:

GLOSS(ES)

(DH) <u>Dominant Handshape</u>:

(NDH) <u>NonDominant Handshape</u>:

(PO) <u>Palm Orientation</u>:

<u>Movement</u>:

<u>Location</u> (if not neutral):

<u>NMS</u> (if not neutral):

Looks like:

Variation(s):

Initialized Variation(s):

Specify if Regional:

Linguistic Register (if specific): FORMAL CONSULTATIVE INFORMAL INTIMATE

Other Vocab/Meanings:

GLOSS(ES)

(DH) <u>Dominant Handshape</u>:

(NDH) <u>NonDominant Handshape</u>:

(PO) <u>Palm Orientation</u>:

<u>Movement</u>:

<u>Location</u> (if not neutral):

<u>NMS</u> (if not neutral):

Looks like:

Variation(s):

Initialized Variation(s):

Specify if Regional:

Linguistic Register (if specific): FORMAL CONSULTATIVE INFORMAL INTIMATE

Other Vocab/Meanings:

GLOSS(ES)

(DH) <u>Dominant Handshape</u>:

(NDH) <u>NonDominant Handshape</u>:

(PO) <u>Palm Orientation</u>:

<u>Movement</u>:

<u>Location</u> (if not neutral):

<u>NMS</u> (if not neutral):

Looks like:

Variation(s):

Initialized Variation(s):

Specify if Regional:

Linguistic Register (if specific): FORMAL CONSULTATIVE INFORMAL INTIMATE

Other Vocab/Meanings:

GLOSS(ES)

(DH) <u>Dominant Handshape</u>:

(NDH) <u>NonDominant Handshape</u>:

(PO) <u>Palm Orientation</u>:

<u>Movement</u>:

<u>Location</u> (if not neutral):

<u>NMS</u> (if not neutral):

Looks like:

Variation(s):

Initialized Variation(s):

Specify if Regional:

Linguistic Register (if specific): FORMAL CONSULTATIVE INFORMAL INTIMATE

Other Vocab/Meanings:

GLOSS(ES)

(DH) <u>Dominant Handshape</u>:

(NDH) <u>NonDominant Handshape</u>:

(PO) <u>Palm Orientation</u>:

<u>Movement</u>:

<u>Location</u> (if not neutral):

<u>NMS</u> (if not neutral):

Looks like:

Variation(s):

Initialized Variation(s):

Specify if Regional:

Linguistic Register (if specific): FORMAL CONSULTATIVE INFORMAL INTIMATE

Other Vocab/Meanings:

GLOSS(ES)

(DH) <u>Dominant Handshape</u>:

(NDH) <u>NonDominant Handshape</u>:

(PO) <u>Palm Orientation</u>:

<u>Movement</u>:

<u>Location</u> (if not neutral):

<u>NMS</u> (if not neutral):

Looks like:

Variation(s):

Initialized Variation(s):

Specify if Regional:

Linguistic Register (if specific): FORMAL CONSULTATIVE INFORMAL INTIMATE

Other Vocab/Meanings:

GLOSS(ES)

(DH) <u>Dominant Handshape</u>:

(NDH) <u>NonDominant Handshape</u>:

(PO) <u>Palm Orientation</u>:

<u>Movement</u>:

<u>Location</u> (if not neutral):

<u>NMS</u> (if not neutral):

Looks like:

Variation(s):

Initialized Variation(s):

Specify if Regional:

Linguistic Register (if specific): FORMAL CONSULTATIVE INFORMAL INTIMATE

Other Vocab/Meanings:

GLOSS(ES)

(DH) <u>Dominant Handshape</u>:

(NDH) <u>NonDominant Handshape</u>:

(PO) <u>Palm Orientation</u>:

<u>Movement</u>:

<u>Location</u> (if not neutral):

<u>NMS</u> (if not neutral):

Looks like:

Variation(s):

Initialized Variation(s):

Specify if Regional:

Linguistic Register (if specific): FORMAL CONSULTATIVE INFORMAL INTIMATE

Other Vocab/Meanings:

GLOSS(ES)

(DH) <u>Dominant Handshape</u>:

(NDH) <u>NonDominant Handshape</u>:

(PO) <u>Palm Orientation</u>:

<u>Movement</u>:

<u>Location</u> (if not neutral):

<u>NMS</u> (if not neutral):

Looks like:

Variation(s):

Initialized Variation(s):

Specify if Regional:

Linguistic Register (if specific): FORMAL CONSULTATIVE INFORMAL INTIMATE

Other Vocab/Meanings:

GLOSS(ES)

(DH) <u>Dominant Handshape</u>:

(NDH) <u>NonDominant Handshape</u>:

(PO) <u>Palm Orientation</u>:

<u>Movement</u>:

<u>Location</u> (if not neutral):

<u>NMS</u> (if not neutral):

Looks like:

Variation(s):

Initialized Variation(s):

Specify if Regional:

Linguistic Register (if specific): FORMAL CONSULTATIVE INFORMAL INTIMATE

Other Vocab/Meanings:

GLOSS(ES)

(DH) <u>Dominant Handshape</u>:

(NDH) <u>NonDominant Handshape</u>:

(PO) <u>Palm Orientation</u>:

<u>Movement</u>:

<u>Location</u> (if not neutral):

<u>NMS</u> (if not neutral):

Looks like:

Variation(s):

Initialized Variation(s):

Specify if Regional:

Linguistic Register (if specific): FORMAL CONSULTATIVE INFORMAL INTIMATE

Other Vocab/Meanings:

GLOSS(ES)

(DH) Dominant Handshape:

(NDH) NonDominant Handshape:

(PO) Palm Orientation:

Movement:

Location (if not neutral):

NMS (if not neutral):

Looks like:

Variation(s):

Initialized Variation(s):

Specify if Regional:

Linguistic Register (if specific): FORMAL CONSULTATIVE INFORMAL INTIMATE

Other Vocab/Meanings:

GLOSS(ES)

(DH) Dominant Handshape:

(NDH) NonDominant Handshape:

(PO) Palm Orientation:

Movement:

Location (if not neutral):

NMS (if not neutral):

Looks like:

Variation(s):

Initialized Variation(s):

Specify if Regional:

Linguistic Register (if specific): FORMAL CONSULTATIVE INFORMAL INTIMATE

Other Vocab/Meanings:

GLOSS(ES)

(DH) Dominant Handshape:

(NDH) NonDominant Handshape:

(PO) Palm Orientation:

Movement:

Location (if not neutral):

NMS (if not neutral):

Looks like:

Variation(s):

Initialized Variation(s):

Specify if Regional:

Linguistic Register (if specific): FORMAL CONSULTATIVE INFORMAL INTIMATE

Other Vocab/Meanings:

GLOSS(ES)

(DH) Dominant Handshape:

(NDH) NonDominant Handshape:

(PO) Palm Orientation:

Movement:

Location (if not neutral):

NMS (if not neutral):

Looks like:

Variation(s):

Initialized Variation(s):

Specify if Regional:

Linguistic Register (if specific): FORMAL CONSULTATIVE INFORMAL INTIMATE

Other Vocab/Meanings:

GLOSS(ES)

(DH) Dominant Handshape:

(NDH) NonDominant Handshape:

(PO) Palm Orientation:

Movement:

Location (if not neutral):

NMS (if not neutral):

Looks like:

Variation(s):

Initialized Variation(s):

Specify if Regional:

Linguistic Register (if specific): FORMAL CONSULTATIVE INFORMAL INTIMATE

Other Vocab/Meanings:

GLOSS(ES)

(DH) Dominant Handshape:

(NDH) NonDominant Handshape:

(PO) Palm Orientation:

Movement:

Location (if not neutral):

NMS (if not neutral):

Looks like:

Variation(s):

Initialized Variation(s):

Specify if Regional:

Linguistic Register (if specific): FORMAL CONSULTATIVE INFORMAL INTIMATE

Other Vocab/Meanings:

GLOSS(ES)

(DH) <u>Dominant Handshape</u>:

(NDH) <u>NonDominant Handshape</u>:

(PO) <u>Palm Orientation</u>:

<u>Movement</u>:

<u>Location</u> (if not neutral):

<u>NMS</u> (if not neutral):

Looks like:

Variation(s):

Initialized Variation(s):

Specify if Regional:

<u>Linguistic Register</u> (if specific): FORMAL CONSULTATIVE INFORMAL INTIMATE

Other Vocab/Meanings:

GLOSS(ES)

(DH) <u>Dominant Handshape</u>:

(NDH) <u>NonDominant Handshape</u>:

(PO) <u>Palm Orientation</u>:

<u>Movement</u>:

<u>Location</u> (if not neutral):

<u>NMS</u> (if not neutral):

Looks like:

Variation(s):

Initialized Variation(s):

Specify if Regional:

<u>Linguistic Register</u> (if specific): FORMAL CONSULTATIVE INFORMAL INTIMATE

Other Vocab/Meanings:

GLOSS(ES)

(DH) <u>Dominant Handshape</u>:

(NDH) <u>NonDominant Handshape</u>:

(PO) <u>Palm Orientation</u>:

<u>Movement</u>:

<u>Location</u> (if not neutral):

<u>NMS</u> (if not neutral):

Looks like:

Variation(s):

Initialized Variation(s):

Specify if Regional:

<u>Linguistic Register</u> (if specific): FORMAL CONSULTATIVE INFORMAL INTIMATE

Other Vocab/Meanings:

GLOSS(ES)

(DH) <u>Dominant Handshape</u>:

(NDH) <u>NonDominant Handshape</u>:

(PO) <u>Palm Orientation</u>:

<u>Movement</u>:

<u>Location</u> (if not neutral):

<u>NMS</u> (if not neutral):

Looks like:

Variation(s):

Initialized Variation(s):

Specify if Regional:

<u>Linguistic Register</u> (if specific): FORMAL CONSULTATIVE INFORMAL INTIMATE

Other Vocab/Meanings:

GLOSS(ES)

(DH) <u>Dominant Handshape</u>:

(NDH) <u>NonDominant Handshape</u>:

(PO) <u>Palm Orientation</u>:

<u>Movement</u>:

<u>Location</u> (if not neutral):

<u>NMS</u> (if not neutral):

Looks like:

Variation(s):

Initialized Variation(s):

Specify if Regional:

<u>Linguistic Register</u> (if specific): FORMAL CONSULTATIVE INFORMAL INTIMATE

Other Vocab/Meanings:

GLOSS(ES)

(DH) <u>Dominant Handshape</u>:

(NDH) <u>NonDominant Handshape</u>:

(PO) <u>Palm Orientation</u>:

<u>Movement</u>:

<u>Location</u> (if not neutral):

<u>NMS</u> (if not neutral):

Looks like:

Variation(s):

Initialized Variation(s):

Specify if Regional:

<u>Linguistic Register</u> (if specific): FORMAL CONSULTATIVE INFORMAL INTIMATE

Other Vocab/Meanings:

GLOSS(ES)

(DH) <u>Dominant Handshape</u>:

(NDH) <u>NonDominant Handshape</u>:

   (PO) <u>Palm Orientation</u>:

     <u>Movement</u>:

    <u>Location</u> (if not neutral):

     <u>NMS</u> (if not neutral):

  Looks like:

  Variation(s):

Initialized Variation(s):

 Specify if Regional:

Linguistic Register (if specific): FORMAL CONSULTATIVE INFORMAL INTIMATE

Other Vocab/Meanings:

GLOSS(ES)

(DH) <u>Dominant Handshape</u>:

(NDH) <u>NonDominant Handshape</u>:

   (PO) <u>Palm Orientation</u>:

     <u>Movement</u>:

    <u>Location</u> (if not neutral):

     <u>NMS</u> (if not neutral):

  Looks like:

  Variation(s):

Initialized Variation(s):

 Specify if Regional:

Linguistic Register (if specific): FORMAL CONSULTATIVE INFORMAL INTIMATE

Other Vocab/Meanings:

GLOSS(ES)

(DH) <u>Dominant Handshape</u>:

(NDH) <u>NonDominant Handshape</u>:

   (PO) <u>Palm Orientation</u>:

     <u>Movement</u>:

    <u>Location</u> (if not neutral):

     <u>NMS</u> (if not neutral):

  Looks like:

  Variation(s):

Initialized Variation(s):

 Specify if Regional:

Linguistic Register (if specific): FORMAL CONSULTATIVE INFORMAL INTIMATE

Other Vocab/Meanings:

GLOSS(ES)

(DH) <u>Dominant Handshape</u>:

(NDH) <u>NonDominant Handshape</u>:

   (PO) <u>Palm Orientation</u>:

     <u>Movement</u>:

    <u>Location</u> (if not neutral):

     <u>NMS</u> (if not neutral):

  Looks like:

  Variation(s):

Initialized Variation(s):

 Specify if Regional:

Linguistic Register (if specific): FORMAL CONSULTATIVE INFORMAL INTIMATE

Other Vocab/Meanings:

GLOSS(ES)

(DH) <u>Dominant Handshape</u>:

(NDH) <u>NonDominant Handshape</u>:

   (PO) <u>Palm Orientation</u>:

     <u>Movement</u>:

    <u>Location</u> (if not neutral):

     <u>NMS</u> (if not neutral):

  Looks like:

  Variation(s):

Initialized Variation(s):

 Specify if Regional:

Linguistic Register (if specific): FORMAL CONSULTATIVE INFORMAL INTIMATE

Other Vocab/Meanings:

GLOSS(ES)

(DH) <u>Dominant Handshape</u>:

(NDH) <u>NonDominant Handshape</u>:

   (PO) <u>Palm Orientation</u>:

     <u>Movement</u>:

    <u>Location</u> (if not neutral):

     <u>NMS</u> (if not neutral):

  Looks like:

  Variation(s):

Initialized Variation(s):

 Specify if Regional:

Linguistic Register (if specific): FORMAL CONSULTATIVE INFORMAL INTIMATE

Other Vocab/Meanings:

GLOSS(ES)

(DH) <u>Dominant Handshape</u>:

(NDH) <u>NonDominant Handshape</u>:

(PO) <u>Palm Orientation</u>:

<u>Movement</u>:

<u>Location</u> (if not neutral):

<u>NMS</u> (if not neutral):

Looks like:

Variation(s):

Initialized Variation(s):

Specify if Regional:

Linguistic Register (if specific): FORMAL   CONSULTATIVE   INFORMAL   INTIMATE

Other Vocab/Meanings:

GLOSS(ES)

(DH) <u>Dominant Handshape</u>:

(NDH) <u>NonDominant Handshape</u>:

(PO) <u>Palm Orientation</u>:

<u>Movement</u>:

<u>Location</u> (if not neutral):

<u>NMS</u> (if not neutral):

Looks like:

Variation(s):

Initialized Variation(s):

Specify if Regional:

Linguistic Register (if specific): FORMAL   CONSULTATIVE   INFORMAL   INTIMATE

Other Vocab/Meanings:

GLOSS(ES)

(DH) <u>Dominant Handshape</u>:

(NDH) <u>NonDominant Handshape</u>:

(PO) <u>Palm Orientation</u>:

<u>Movement</u>:

<u>Location</u> (if not neutral):

<u>NMS</u> (if not neutral):

Looks like:

Variation(s):

Initialized Variation(s):

Specify if Regional:

Linguistic Register (if specific): FORMAL   CONSULTATIVE   INFORMAL   INTIMATE

Other Vocab/Meanings:

GLOSS(ES)

(DH) <u>Dominant Handshape</u>:

(NDH) <u>NonDominant Handshape</u>:

(PO) <u>Palm Orientation</u>:

<u>Movement</u>:

<u>Location</u> (if not neutral):

<u>NMS</u> (if not neutral):

Looks like:

Variation(s):

Initialized Variation(s):

Specify if Regional:

Linguistic Register (if specific): FORMAL   CONSULTATIVE   INFORMAL   INTIMATE

Other Vocab/Meanings:

GLOSS(ES)

(DH) <u>Dominant Handshape</u>:

(NDH) <u>NonDominant Handshape</u>:

(PO) <u>Palm Orientation</u>:

<u>Movement</u>:

<u>Location</u> (if not neutral):

<u>NMS</u> (if not neutral):

Looks like:

Variation(s):

Initialized Variation(s):

Specify if Regional:

Linguistic Register (if specific): FORMAL   CONSULTATIVE   INFORMAL   INTIMATE

Other Vocab/Meanings:

GLOSS(ES)

(DH) <u>Dominant Handshape</u>:

(NDH) <u>NonDominant Handshape</u>:

(PO) <u>Palm Orientation</u>:

<u>Movement</u>:

<u>Location</u> (if not neutral):

<u>NMS</u> (if not neutral):

Looks like:

Variation(s):

Initialized Variation(s):

Specify if Regional:

Linguistic Register (if specific): FORMAL   CONSULTATIVE   INFORMAL   INTIMATE

Other Vocab/Meanings:

GLOSS(ES)

(DH) Dominant Handshape:

(NDH) NonDominant Handshape:

(PO) Palm Orientation:

Movement:

Location (if not neutral):

NMS (if not neutral):

Looks like:

Variation(s):

Initialized Variation(s):

Specify if Regional:

Linguistic Register (if specific): FORMAL CONSULTATIVE INFORMAL INTIMATE

Other Vocab/Meanings:

GLOSS(ES)

(DH) Dominant Handshape:

(NDH) NonDominant Handshape:

(PO) Palm Orientation:

Movement:

Location (if not neutral):

NMS (if not neutral):

Looks like:

Variation(s):

Initialized Variation(s):

Specify if Regional:

Linguistic Register (if specific): FORMAL CONSULTATIVE INFORMAL INTIMATE

Other Vocab/Meanings:

GLOSS(ES)

(DH) Dominant Handshape:

(NDH) NonDominant Handshape:

(PO) Palm Orientation:

Movement:

Location (if not neutral):

NMS (if not neutral):

Looks like:

Variation(s):

Initialized Variation(s):

Specify if Regional:

Linguistic Register (if specific): FORMAL CONSULTATIVE INFORMAL INTIMATE

Other Vocab/Meanings:

GLOSS(ES)

(DH) Dominant Handshape:

(NDH) NonDominant Handshape:

(PO) Palm Orientation:

Movement:

Location (if not neutral):

NMS (if not neutral):

Looks like:

Variation(s):

Initialized Variation(s):

Specify if Regional:

Linguistic Register (if specific): FORMAL CONSULTATIVE INFORMAL INTIMATE

Other Vocab/Meanings:

GLOSS(ES)

(DH) Dominant Handshape:

(NDH) NonDominant Handshape:

(PO) Palm Orientation:

Movement:

Location (if not neutral):

NMS (if not neutral):

Looks like:

Variation(s):

Initialized Variation(s):

Specify if Regional:

Linguistic Register (if specific): FORMAL CONSULTATIVE INFORMAL INTIMATE

Other Vocab/Meanings:

GLOSS(ES)

(DH) Dominant Handshape:

(NDH) NonDominant Handshape:

(PO) Palm Orientation:

Movement:

Location (if not neutral):

NMS (if not neutral):

Looks like:

Variation(s):

Initialized Variation(s):

Specify if Regional:

Linguistic Register (if specific): FORMAL CONSULTATIVE INFORMAL INTIMATE

Other Vocab/Meanings:

GLOSS(ES)

(DH) <u>Dominant Handshape</u>:

(NDH) <u>NonDominant Handshape</u>:

(PO) <u>Palm Orientation</u>:

<u>Movement</u>:

<u>Location</u> (if not neutral):

<u>NMS</u> (if not neutral):

Looks like:

Variation(s):

Initialized Variation(s):

Specify if Regional:

Linguistic Register (if specific): FORMAL CONSULTATIVE INFORMAL INTIMATE

Other Vocab/Meanings:

GLOSS(ES)

(DH) <u>Dominant Handshape</u>:

(NDH) <u>NonDominant Handshape</u>:

(PO) <u>Palm Orientation</u>:

<u>Movement</u>:

<u>Location</u> (if not neutral):

<u>NMS</u> (if not neutral):

Looks like:

Variation(s):

Initialized Variation(s):

Specify if Regional:

Linguistic Register (if specific): FORMAL CONSULTATIVE INFORMAL INTIMATE

Other Vocab/Meanings:

GLOSS(ES)

(DH) <u>Dominant Handshape</u>:

(NDH) <u>NonDominant Handshape</u>:

(PO) <u>Palm Orientation</u>:

<u>Movement</u>:

<u>Location</u> (if not neutral):

<u>NMS</u> (if not neutral):

Looks like:

Variation(s):

Initialized Variation(s):

Specify if Regional:

Linguistic Register (if specific): FORMAL CONSULTATIVE INFORMAL INTIMATE

Other Vocab/Meanings:

GLOSS(ES)

(DH) <u>Dominant Handshape</u>:

(NDH) <u>NonDominant Handshape</u>:

(PO) <u>Palm Orientation</u>:

<u>Movement</u>:

<u>Location</u> (if not neutral):

<u>NMS</u> (if not neutral):

Looks like:

Variation(s):

Initialized Variation(s):

Specify if Regional:

Linguistic Register (if specific): FORMAL CONSULTATIVE INFORMAL INTIMATE

Other Vocab/Meanings:

GLOSS(ES)

(DH) <u>Dominant Handshape</u>:

(NDH) <u>NonDominant Handshape</u>:

(PO) <u>Palm Orientation</u>:

<u>Movement</u>:

<u>Location</u> (if not neutral):

<u>NMS</u> (if not neutral):

Looks like:

Variation(s):

Initialized Variation(s):

Specify if Regional:

Linguistic Register (if specific): FORMAL CONSULTATIVE INFORMAL INTIMATE

Other Vocab/Meanings:

GLOSS(ES)

(DH) <u>Dominant Handshape</u>:

(NDH) <u>NonDominant Handshape</u>:

(PO) <u>Palm Orientation</u>:

<u>Movement</u>:

<u>Location</u> (if not neutral):

<u>NMS</u> (if not neutral):

Looks like:

Variation(s):

Initialized Variation(s):

Specify if Regional:

Linguistic Register (if specific): FORMAL CONSULTATIVE INFORMAL INTIMATE

Other Vocab/Meanings:

GLOSS(ES)

(DH) <u>Dominant Handshape</u>:

(NDH) <u>NonDominant Handshape</u>:

(PO) <u>Palm Orientation</u>:

<u>Movement</u>:

<u>Location</u> (if not neutral):

<u>NMS</u> (if not neutral):

Looks like:

Variation(s):

Initialized Variation(s):

Specify if Regional:

Linguistic Register (if specific): FORMAL CONSULTATIVE INFORMAL INTIMATE

Other Vocab/Meanings:

GLOSS(ES)

(DH) <u>Dominant Handshape</u>:

(NDH) <u>NonDominant Handshape</u>:

(PO) <u>Palm Orientation</u>:

<u>Movement</u>:

<u>Location</u> (if not neutral):

<u>NMS</u> (if not neutral):

Looks like:

Variation(s):

Initialized Variation(s):

Specify if Regional:

Linguistic Register (if specific): FORMAL CONSULTATIVE INFORMAL INTIMATE

Other Vocab/Meanings:

GLOSS(ES)

(DH) <u>Dominant Handshape</u>:

(NDH) <u>NonDominant Handshape</u>:

(PO) <u>Palm Orientation</u>:

<u>Movement</u>:

<u>Location</u> (if not neutral):

<u>NMS</u> (if not neutral):

Looks like:

Variation(s):

Initialized Variation(s):

Specify if Regional:

Linguistic Register (if specific): FORMAL CONSULTATIVE INFORMAL INTIMATE

Other Vocab/Meanings:

GLOSS(ES)

(DH) <u>Dominant Handshape</u>:

(NDH) <u>NonDominant Handshape</u>:

(PO) <u>Palm Orientation</u>:

<u>Movement</u>:

<u>Location</u> (if not neutral):

<u>NMS</u> (if not neutral):

Looks like:

Variation(s):

Initialized Variation(s):

Specify if Regional:

Linguistic Register (if specific): FORMAL CONSULTATIVE INFORMAL INTIMATE

Other Vocab/Meanings:

GLOSS(ES)

(DH) <u>Dominant Handshape</u>:

(NDH) <u>NonDominant Handshape</u>:

(PO) <u>Palm Orientation</u>:

<u>Movement</u>:

<u>Location</u> (if not neutral):

<u>NMS</u> (if not neutral):

Looks like:

Variation(s):

Initialized Variation(s):

Specify if Regional:

Linguistic Register (if specific): FORMAL CONSULTATIVE INFORMAL INTIMATE

Other Vocab/Meanings:

GLOSS(ES)

(DH) <u>Dominant Handshape</u>:

(NDH) <u>NonDominant Handshape</u>:

(PO) <u>Palm Orientation</u>:

<u>Movement</u>:

<u>Location</u> (if not neutral):

<u>NMS</u> (if not neutral):

Looks like:

Variation(s):

Initialized Variation(s):

Specify if Regional:

Linguistic Register (if specific): FORMAL CONSULTATIVE INFORMAL INTIMATE

Other Vocab/Meanings:

GLOSS(ES)

(DH) <u>Dominant Handshape</u>:

(NDH) <u>NonDominant Handshape</u>:

(PO) <u>Palm Orientation</u>:

<u>Movement</u>:

<u>Location</u> (if not neutral):

<u>NMS</u> (if not neutral):

Looks like:

Variation(s):

Initialized Variation(s):

Specify if Regional:

Linguistic Register (if specific): FORMAL CONSULTATIVE INFORMAL INTIMATE

Other Vocab/Meanings:

GLOSS(ES)

(DH) <u>Dominant Handshape</u>:

(NDH) <u>NonDominant Handshape</u>:

(PO) <u>Palm Orientation</u>:

<u>Movement</u>:

<u>Location</u> (if not neutral):

<u>NMS</u> (if not neutral):

Looks like:

Variation(s):

Initialized Variation(s):

Specify if Regional:

Linguistic Register (if specific): FORMAL CONSULTATIVE INFORMAL INTIMATE

Other Vocab/Meanings:

GLOSS(ES)

(DH) <u>Dominant Handshape</u>:

(NDH) <u>NonDominant Handshape</u>:

(PO) <u>Palm Orientation</u>:

<u>Movement</u>:

<u>Location</u> (if not neutral):

<u>NMS</u> (if not neutral):

Looks like:

Variation(s):

Initialized Variation(s):

Specify if Regional:

Linguistic Register (if specific): FORMAL CONSULTATIVE INFORMAL INTIMATE

Other Vocab/Meanings:

GLOSS(ES)

(DH) <u>Dominant Handshape</u>:

(NDH) <u>NonDominant Handshape</u>:

(PO) <u>Palm Orientation</u>:

<u>Movement</u>:

<u>Location</u> (if not neutral):

<u>NMS</u> (if not neutral):

Looks like:

Variation(s):

Initialized Variation(s):

Specify if Regional:

Linguistic Register (if specific): FORMAL CONSULTATIVE INFORMAL INTIMATE

Other Vocab/Meanings:

GLOSS(ES)

(DH) <u>Dominant Handshape</u>:

(NDH) <u>NonDominant Handshape</u>:

(PO) <u>Palm Orientation</u>:

<u>Movement</u>:

<u>Location</u> (if not neutral):

<u>NMS</u> (if not neutral):

Looks like:

Variation(s):

Initialized Variation(s):

Specify if Regional:

Linguistic Register (if specific): FORMAL CONSULTATIVE INFORMAL INTIMATE

Other Vocab/Meanings:

GLOSS(ES)

(DH) <u>Dominant Handshape</u>:

(NDH) <u>NonDominant Handshape</u>:

(PO) <u>Palm Orientation</u>:

<u>Movement</u>:

<u>Location</u> (if not neutral):

<u>NMS</u> (if not neutral):

Looks like:

Variation(s):

Initialized Variation(s):

Specify if Regional:

Linguistic Register (if specific): FORMAL CONSULTATIVE INFORMAL INTIMATE

Other Vocab/Meanings:

GLOSS(ES)

(DH) <u>Dominant Handshape</u>:

(NDH) <u>NonDominant Handshape</u>:

(PO) <u>Palm Orientation</u>:

<u>Movement</u>:

<u>Location</u> (if not neutral):

<u>NMS</u> (if not neutral):

Looks like:

Variation(s):

Initialized Variation(s):

Specify if Regional:

Linguistic Register (if specific): FORMAL CONSULTATIVE INFORMAL INTIMATE

Other Vocab/Meanings:

GLOSS(ES)

(DH) <u>Dominant Handshape</u>:

(NDH) <u>NonDominant Handshape</u>:

(PO) <u>Palm Orientation</u>:

<u>Movement</u>:

<u>Location</u> (if not neutral):

<u>NMS</u> (if not neutral):

Looks like:

Variation(s):

Initialized Variation(s):

Specify if Regional:

Linguistic Register (if specific): FORMAL CONSULTATIVE INFORMAL INTIMATE

Other Vocab/Meanings:

GLOSS(ES)

(DH) <u>Dominant Handshape</u>:

(NDH) <u>NonDominant Handshape</u>:

(PO) <u>Palm Orientation</u>:

<u>Movement</u>:

<u>Location</u> (if not neutral):

<u>NMS</u> (if not neutral):

Looks like:

Variation(s):

Initialized Variation(s):

Specify if Regional:

Linguistic Register (if specific): FORMAL CONSULTATIVE INFORMAL INTIMATE

Other Vocab/Meanings:

GLOSS(ES)

(DH) <u>Dominant Handshape</u>:

(NDH) <u>NonDominant Handshape</u>:

(PO) <u>Palm Orientation</u>:

<u>Movement</u>:

<u>Location</u> (if not neutral):

<u>NMS</u> (if not neutral):

Looks like:

Variation(s):

Initialized Variation(s):

Specify if Regional:

Linguistic Register (if specific): FORMAL CONSULTATIVE INFORMAL INTIMATE

Other Vocab/Meanings:

GLOSS(ES)

(DH) <u>Dominant Handshape</u>:

(NDH) <u>NonDominant Handshape</u>:

(PO) <u>Palm Orientation</u>:

<u>Movement</u>:

<u>Location</u> (if not neutral):

<u>NMS</u> (if not neutral):

Looks like:

Variation(s):

Initialized Variation(s):

Specify if Regional:

Linguistic Register (if specific): FORMAL CONSULTATIVE INFORMAL INTIMATE

Other Vocab/Meanings:

GLOSS(ES)

(DH) <u>Dominant Handshape</u>:

(NDH) <u>NonDominant Handshape</u>:

(PO) <u>Palm Orientation</u>:

<u>Movement</u>:

<u>Location</u> (if not neutral):

<u>NMS</u> (if not neutral):

Looks like:

Variation(s):

Initialized Variation(s):

Specify if Regional:

Linguistic Register (if specific): FORMAL CONSULTATIVE INFORMAL INTIMATE

Other Vocab/Meanings:

GLOSS(ES)

(DH) Dominant Handshape:

(NDH) NonDominant Handshape:

(PO) Palm Orientation:

Movement:

Location (if not neutral):

NMS (if not neutral):

Looks like:

Variation(s):

Initialized Variation(s):

Specify if Regional:

Linguistic Register (if specific): FORMAL CONSULTATIVE INFORMAL INTIMATE

Other Vocab/Meanings:

GLOSS(ES)

(DH) Dominant Handshape:

(NDH) NonDominant Handshape:

(PO) Palm Orientation:

Movement:

Location (if not neutral):

NMS (if not neutral):

Looks like:

Variation(s):

Initialized Variation(s):

Specify if Regional:

Linguistic Register (if specific): FORMAL CONSULTATIVE INFORMAL INTIMATE

Other Vocab/Meanings:

GLOSS(ES)

(DH) Dominant Handshape:

(NDH) NonDominant Handshape:

(PO) Palm Orientation:

Movement:

Location (if not neutral):

NMS (if not neutral):

Looks like:

Variation(s):

Initialized Variation(s):

Specify if Regional:

Linguistic Register (if specific): FORMAL CONSULTATIVE INFORMAL INTIMATE

Other Vocab/Meanings:

GLOSS(ES)

(DH) Dominant Handshape:

(NDH) NonDominant Handshape:

(PO) Palm Orientation:

Movement:

Location (if not neutral):

NMS (if not neutral):

Looks like:

Variation(s):

Initialized Variation(s):

Specify if Regional:

Linguistic Register (if specific): FORMAL CONSULTATIVE INFORMAL INTIMATE

Other Vocab/Meanings:

GLOSS(ES)

(DH) Dominant Handshape:

(NDH) NonDominant Handshape:

(PO) Palm Orientation:

Movement:

Location (if not neutral):

NMS (if not neutral):

Looks like:

Variation(s):

Initialized Variation(s):

Specify if Regional:

Linguistic Register (if specific): FORMAL CONSULTATIVE INFORMAL INTIMATE

Other Vocab/Meanings:

GLOSS(ES)

(DH) Dominant Handshape:

(NDH) NonDominant Handshape:

(PO) Palm Orientation:

Movement:

Location (if not neutral):

NMS (if not neutral):

Looks like:

Variation(s):

Initialized Variation(s):

Specify if Regional:

Linguistic Register (if specific): FORMAL CONSULTATIVE INFORMAL INTIMATE

Other Vocab/Meanings:

GLOSS(ES)

(DH) <u>Dominant Handshape</u>:

(NDH) <u>NonDominant Handshape</u>:

(PO) <u>Palm Orientation</u>:

<u>Movement</u>:

<u>Location</u> (if not neutral):

<u>NMS</u> (if not neutral):

Looks like:

Variation(s):

Initialized Variation(s):

Specify if Regional:

Linguistic Register (if specific): FORMAL CONSULTATIVE INFORMAL INTIMATE

Other Vocab/Meanings:

GLOSS(ES)

(DH) <u>Dominant Handshape</u>:

(NDH) <u>NonDominant Handshape</u>:

(PO) <u>Palm Orientation</u>:

<u>Movement</u>:

<u>Location</u> (if not neutral):

<u>NMS</u> (if not neutral):

Looks like:

Variation(s):

Initialized Variation(s):

Specify if Regional:

Linguistic Register (if specific): FORMAL CONSULTATIVE INFORMAL INTIMATE

Other Vocab/Meanings:

GLOSS(ES)

(DH) <u>Dominant Handshape</u>:

(NDH) <u>NonDominant Handshape</u>:

(PO) <u>Palm Orientation</u>:

<u>Movement</u>:

<u>Location</u> (if not neutral):

<u>NMS</u> (if not neutral):

Looks like:

Variation(s):

Initialized Variation(s):

Specify if Regional:

Linguistic Register (if specific): FORMAL CONSULTATIVE INFORMAL INTIMATE

Other Vocab/Meanings:

GLOSS(ES)

(DH) <u>Dominant Handshape</u>:

(NDH) <u>NonDominant Handshape</u>:

(PO) <u>Palm Orientation</u>:

<u>Movement</u>:

<u>Location</u> (if not neutral):

<u>NMS</u> (if not neutral):

Looks like:

Variation(s):

Initialized Variation(s):

Specify if Regional:

Linguistic Register (if specific): FORMAL CONSULTATIVE INFORMAL INTIMATE

Other Vocab/Meanings:

GLOSS(ES)

(DH) <u>Dominant Handshape</u>:

(NDH) <u>NonDominant Handshape</u>:

(PO) <u>Palm Orientation</u>:

<u>Movement</u>:

<u>Location</u> (if not neutral):

<u>NMS</u> (if not neutral):

Looks like:

Variation(s):

Initialized Variation(s):

Specify if Regional:

Linguistic Register (if specific): FORMAL CONSULTATIVE INFORMAL INTIMATE

Other Vocab/Meanings:

GLOSS(ES)

(DH) <u>Dominant Handshape</u>:

(NDH) <u>NonDominant Handshape</u>:

(PO) <u>Palm Orientation</u>:

<u>Movement</u>:

<u>Location</u> (if not neutral):

<u>NMS</u> (if not neutral):

Looks like:

Variation(s):

Initialized Variation(s):

Specify if Regional:

Linguistic Register (if specific): FORMAL CONSULTATIVE INFORMAL INTIMATE

Other Vocab/Meanings:

GLOSS(ES)

(DH) Dominant Handshape:

(NDH) NonDominant Handshape:

(PO) Palm Orientation:

Movement:

Location (if not neutral):

NMS (if not neutral):

Looks like:

Variation(s):

Initialized Variation(s):

Specify if Regional:

Linguistic Register (if specific): FORMAL CONSULTATIVE INFORMAL INTIMATE

Other Vocab/Meanings:

GLOSS(ES)

(DH) Dominant Handshape:

(NDH) NonDominant Handshape:

(PO) Palm Orientation:

Movement:

Location (if not neutral):

NMS (if not neutral):

Looks like:

Variation(s):

Initialized Variation(s):

Specify if Regional:

Linguistic Register (if specific): FORMAL CONSULTATIVE INFORMAL INTIMATE

Other Vocab/Meanings:

GLOSS(ES)

(DH) Dominant Handshape:

(NDH) NonDominant Handshape:

(PO) Palm Orientation:

Movement:

Location (if not neutral):

NMS (if not neutral):

Looks like:

Variation(s):

Initialized Variation(s):

Specify if Regional:

Linguistic Register (if specific): FORMAL CONSULTATIVE INFORMAL INTIMATE

Other Vocab/Meanings:

GLOSS(ES)

(DH) Dominant Handshape:

(NDH) NonDominant Handshape:

(PO) Palm Orientation:

Movement:

Location (if not neutral):

NMS (if not neutral):

Looks like:

Variation(s):

Initialized Variation(s):

Specify if Regional:

Linguistic Register (if specific): FORMAL CONSULTATIVE INFORMAL INTIMATE

Other Vocab/Meanings:

GLOSS(ES)

(DH) Dominant Handshape:

(NDH) NonDominant Handshape:

(PO) Palm Orientation:

Movement:

Location (if not neutral):

NMS (if not neutral):

Looks like:

Variation(s):

Initialized Variation(s):

Specify if Regional:

Linguistic Register (if specific): FORMAL CONSULTATIVE INFORMAL INTIMATE

Other Vocab/Meanings:

GLOSS(ES)

(DH) Dominant Handshape:

(NDH) NonDominant Handshape:

(PO) Palm Orientation:

Movement:

Location (if not neutral):

NMS (if not neutral):

Looks like:

Variation(s):

Initialized Variation(s):

Specify if Regional:

Linguistic Register (if specific): FORMAL CONSULTATIVE INFORMAL INTIMATE

Other Vocab/Meanings:

GLOSS(ES)

(DH) Dominant Handshape:

(NDH) NonDominant Handshape:

(PO) Palm Orientation:

Movement:

Location (if not neutral):

NMS (if not neutral):

Looks like:

Variation(s):

Initialized Variation(s):

Specify if Regional:

Linguistic Register (if specific): FORMAL CONSULTATIVE INFORMAL INTIMATE

Other Vocab/Meanings:

GLOSS(ES)

(DH) Dominant Handshape:

(NDH) NonDominant Handshape:

(PO) Palm Orientation:

Movement:

Location (if not neutral):

NMS (if not neutral):

Looks like:

Variation(s):

Initialized Variation(s):

Specify if Regional:

Linguistic Register (if specific): FORMAL CONSULTATIVE INFORMAL INTIMATE

Other Vocab/Meanings:

GLOSS(ES)

(DH) Dominant Handshape:

(NDH) NonDominant Handshape:

(PO) Palm Orientation:

Movement:

Location (if not neutral):

NMS (if not neutral):

Looks like:

Variation(s):

Initialized Variation(s):

Specify if Regional:

Linguistic Register (if specific): FORMAL CONSULTATIVE INFORMAL INTIMATE

Other Vocab/Meanings:

GLOSS(ES)

(DH) Dominant Handshape:

(NDH) NonDominant Handshape:

(PO) Palm Orientation:

Movement:

Location (if not neutral):

NMS (if not neutral):

Looks like:

Variation(s):

Initialized Variation(s):

Specify if Regional:

Linguistic Register (if specific): FORMAL CONSULTATIVE INFORMAL INTIMATE

Other Vocab/Meanings:

GLOSS(ES)

(DH) Dominant Handshape:

(NDH) NonDominant Handshape:

(PO) Palm Orientation:

Movement:

Location (if not neutral):

NMS (if not neutral):

Looks like:

Variation(s):

Initialized Variation(s):

Specify if Regional:

Linguistic Register (if specific): FORMAL CONSULTATIVE INFORMAL INTIMATE

Other Vocab/Meanings:

GLOSS(ES)

(DH) Dominant Handshape:

(NDH) NonDominant Handshape:

(PO) Palm Orientation:

Movement:

Location (if not neutral):

NMS (if not neutral):

Looks like:

Variation(s):

Initialized Variation(s):

Specify if Regional:

Linguistic Register (if specific): FORMAL CONSULTATIVE INFORMAL INTIMATE

Other Vocab/Meanings:

GLOSS(ES)

(DH) Dominant Handshape:

(NDH) NonDominant Handshape:

(PO) Palm Orientation:

Movement:

Location (if not neutral):

NMS (if not neutral):

Looks like:

Variation(s):

Initialized Variation(s):

Specify if Regional:

Linguistic Register (if specific): FORMAL CONSULTATIVE INFORMAL INTIMATE

Other Vocab/Meanings:

GLOSS(ES)

(DH) Dominant Handshape:

(NDH) NonDominant Handshape:

(PO) Palm Orientation:

Movement:

Location (if not neutral):

NMS (if not neutral):

Looks like:

Variation(s):

Initialized Variation(s):

Specify if Regional:

Linguistic Register (if specific): FORMAL CONSULTATIVE INFORMAL INTIMATE

Other Vocab/Meanings:

GLOSS(ES)

(DH) Dominant Handshape:

(NDH) NonDominant Handshape:

(PO) Palm Orientation:

Movement:

Location (if not neutral):

NMS (if not neutral):

Looks like:

Variation(s):

Initialized Variation(s):

Specify if Regional:

Linguistic Register (if specific): FORMAL CONSULTATIVE INFORMAL INTIMATE

Other Vocab/Meanings:

GLOSS(ES)

(DH) Dominant Handshape:

(NDH) NonDominant Handshape:

(PO) Palm Orientation:

Movement:

Location (if not neutral):

NMS (if not neutral):

Looks like:

Variation(s):

Initialized Variation(s):

Specify if Regional:

Linguistic Register (if specific): FORMAL CONSULTATIVE INFORMAL INTIMATE

Other Vocab/Meanings:

GLOSS(ES)

(DH) Dominant Handshape:

(NDH) NonDominant Handshape:

(PO) Palm Orientation:

Movement:

Location (if not neutral):

NMS (if not neutral):

Looks like:

Variation(s):

Initialized Variation(s):

Specify if Regional:

Linguistic Register (if specific): FORMAL CONSULTATIVE INFORMAL INTIMATE

Other Vocab/Meanings:

GLOSS(ES)

(DH) Dominant Handshape:

(NDH) NonDominant Handshape:

(PO) Palm Orientation:

Movement:

Location (if not neutral):

NMS (if not neutral):

Looks like:

Variation(s):

Initialized Variation(s):

Specify if Regional:

Linguistic Register (if specific): FORMAL CONSULTATIVE INFORMAL INTIMATE

Other Vocab/Meanings:

GLOSS(ES)

(DH) Dominant Handshape:

(NDH) NonDominant Handshape:

(PO) Palm Orientation:

Movement:

Location (if not neutral):

NMS (if not neutral):

Looks like:

Variation(s):

Initialized Variation(s):

Specify if Regional:

Linguistic Register (if specific): FORMAL CONSULTATIVE INFORMAL INTIMATE

Other Vocab/Meanings:

GLOSS(ES)

(DH) Dominant Handshape:

(NDH) NonDominant Handshape:

(PO) Palm Orientation:

Movement:

Location (if not neutral):

NMS (if not neutral):

Looks like:

Variation(s):

Initialized Variation(s):

Specify if Regional:

Linguistic Register (if specific): FORMAL CONSULTATIVE INFORMAL INTIMATE

Other Vocab/Meanings:

GLOSS(ES)

(DH) Dominant Handshape:

(NDH) NonDominant Handshape:

(PO) Palm Orientation:

Movement:

Location (if not neutral):

NMS (if not neutral):

Looks like:

Variation(s):

Initialized Variation(s):

Specify if Regional:

Linguistic Register (if specific): FORMAL CONSULTATIVE INFORMAL INTIMATE

Other Vocab/Meanings:

GLOSS(ES)

(DH) Dominant Handshape:

(NDH) NonDominant Handshape:

(PO) Palm Orientation:

Movement:

Location (if not neutral):

NMS (if not neutral):

Looks like:

Variation(s):

Initialized Variation(s):

Specify if Regional:

Linguistic Register (if specific): FORMAL CONSULTATIVE INFORMAL INTIMATE

Other Vocab/Meanings:

GLOSS(ES)

(DH) Dominant Handshape:

(NDH) NonDominant Handshape:

(PO) Palm Orientation:

Movement:

Location (if not neutral):

NMS (if not neutral):

Looks like:

Variation(s):

Initialized Variation(s):

Specify if Regional:

Linguistic Register (if specific): FORMAL CONSULTATIVE INFORMAL INTIMATE

Other Vocab/Meanings:

GLOSS(ES)

(DH) Dominant Handshape:

(NDH) NonDominant Handshape:

(PO) Palm Orientation:

Movement:

Location (if not neutral):

NMS (if not neutral):

Looks like:

Variation(s):

Initialized Variation(s):

Specify if Regional:

Linguistic Register (if specific): FORMAL CONSULTATIVE INFORMAL INTIMATE

Other Vocab/Meanings:

GLOSS(ES)

(DH) <u>Dominant Handshape</u>:

(NDH) <u>NonDominant Handshape</u>:

(PO) <u>Palm Orientation</u>:

<u>Movement</u>:

<u>Location</u> (if not neutral):

<u>NMS</u> (if not neutral):

Looks like:

Variation(s):

Initialized Variation(s):

Specify if Regional:

Linguistic Register (if specific): FORMAL CONSULTATIVE INFORMAL INTIMATE

Other Vocab/Meanings:

GLOSS(ES)

(DH) <u>Dominant Handshape</u>:

(NDH) <u>NonDominant Handshape</u>:

(PO) <u>Palm Orientation</u>:

<u>Movement</u>:

<u>Location</u> (if not neutral):

<u>NMS</u> (if not neutral):

Looks like:

Variation(s):

Initialized Variation(s):

Specify if Regional:

Linguistic Register (if specific): FORMAL CONSULTATIVE INFORMAL INTIMATE

Other Vocab/Meanings:

GLOSS(ES)

(DH) <u>Dominant Handshape</u>:

(NDH) <u>NonDominant Handshape</u>:

(PO) <u>Palm Orientation</u>:

<u>Movement</u>:

<u>Location</u> (if not neutral):

<u>NMS</u> (if not neutral):

Looks like:

Variation(s):

Initialized Variation(s):

Specify if Regional:

Linguistic Register (if specific): FORMAL CONSULTATIVE INFORMAL INTIMATE

Other Vocab/Meanings:

GLOSS(ES)

(DH) <u>Dominant Handshape</u>:

(NDH) <u>NonDominant Handshape</u>:

(PO) <u>Palm Orientation</u>:

<u>Movement</u>:

<u>Location</u> (if not neutral):

<u>NMS</u> (if not neutral):

Looks like:

Variation(s):

Initialized Variation(s):

Specify if Regional:

Linguistic Register (if specific): FORMAL CONSULTATIVE INFORMAL INTIMATE

Other Vocab/Meanings:

GLOSS(ES)

(DH) <u>Dominant Handshape</u>:

(NDH) <u>NonDominant Handshape</u>:

(PO) <u>Palm Orientation</u>:

<u>Movement</u>:

<u>Location</u> (if not neutral):

<u>NMS</u> (if not neutral):

Looks like:

Variation(s):

Initialized Variation(s):

Specify if Regional:

Linguistic Register (if specific): FORMAL CONSULTATIVE INFORMAL INTIMATE

Other Vocab/Meanings:

GLOSS(ES)

(DH) <u>Dominant Handshape</u>:

(NDH) <u>NonDominant Handshape</u>:

(PO) <u>Palm Orientation</u>:

<u>Movement</u>:

<u>Location</u> (if not neutral):

<u>NMS</u> (if not neutral):

Looks like:

Variation(s):

Initialized Variation(s):

Specify if Regional:

Linguistic Register (if specific): FORMAL CONSULTATIVE INFORMAL INTIMATE

Other Vocab/Meanings:

GLOSS(ES)

(DH) Dominant Handshape:

(NDH) NonDominant Handshape:

(PO) Palm Orientation:

Movement:

Location (if not neutral):

NMS (if not neutral):

Looks like:

Variation(s):

Initialized Variation(s):

Specify if Regional:

Linguistic Register (if specific): FORMAL   CONSULTATIVE   INFORMAL   INTIMATE

Other Vocab/Meanings:

GLOSS(ES)

(DH) Dominant Handshape:

(NDH) NonDominant Handshape:

(PO) Palm Orientation:

Movement:

Location (if not neutral):

NMS (if not neutral):

Looks like:

Variation(s):

Initialized Variation(s):

Specify if Regional:

Linguistic Register (if specific): FORMAL   CONSULTATIVE   INFORMAL   INTIMATE

Other Vocab/Meanings:

GLOSS(ES)

(DH) Dominant Handshape:

(NDH) NonDominant Handshape:

(PO) Palm Orientation:

Movement:

Location (if not neutral):

NMS (if not neutral):

Looks like:

Variation(s):

Initialized Variation(s):

Specify if Regional:

Linguistic Register (if specific): FORMAL   CONSULTATIVE   INFORMAL   INTIMATE

Other Vocab/Meanings:

GLOSS(ES)

(DH) Dominant Handshape:

(NDH) NonDominant Handshape:

(PO) Palm Orientation:

Movement:

Location (if not neutral):

NMS (if not neutral):

Looks like:

Variation(s):

Initialized Variation(s):

Specify if Regional:

Linguistic Register (if specific): FORMAL   CONSULTATIVE   INFORMAL   INTIMATE

Other Vocab/Meanings:

GLOSS(ES)

(DH) Dominant Handshape:

(NDH) NonDominant Handshape:

(PO) Palm Orientation:

Movement:

Location (if not neutral):

NMS (if not neutral):

Looks like:

Variation(s):

Initialized Variation(s):

Specify if Regional:

Linguistic Register (if specific): FORMAL   CONSULTATIVE   INFORMAL   INTIMATE

Other Vocab/Meanings:

GLOSS(ES)

(DH) Dominant Handshape:

(NDH) NonDominant Handshape:

(PO) Palm Orientation:

Movement:

Location (if not neutral):

NMS (if not neutral):

Looks like:

Variation(s):

Initialized Variation(s):

Specify if Regional:

Linguistic Register (if specific): FORMAL   CONSULTATIVE   INFORMAL   INTIMATE

Other Vocab/Meanings:

GLOSS(ES)

(DH) Dominant Handshape:

(NDH) NonDominant Handshape:

(PO) Palm Orientation:

Movement:

Location (if not neutral):

NMS (if not neutral):

Looks like:

Variation(s):

Initialized Variation(s):

Specify if Regional:

Linguistic Register (if specific): FORMAL CONSULTATIVE INFORMAL INTIMATE

Other Vocab/Meanings:

GLOSS(ES)

(DH) Dominant Handshape:

(NDH) NonDominant Handshape:

(PO) Palm Orientation:

Movement:

Location (if not neutral):

NMS (if not neutral):

Looks like:

Variation(s):

Initialized Variation(s):

Specify if Regional:

Linguistic Register (if specific): FORMAL CONSULTATIVE INFORMAL INTIMATE

Other Vocab/Meanings:

GLOSS(ES)

(DH) Dominant Handshape:

(NDH) NonDominant Handshape:

(PO) Palm Orientation:

Movement:

Location (if not neutral):

NMS (if not neutral):

Looks like:

Variation(s):

Initialized Variation(s):

Specify if Regional:

Linguistic Register (if specific): FORMAL CONSULTATIVE INFORMAL INTIMATE

Other Vocab/Meanings:

GLOSS(ES)

(DH) Dominant Handshape:

(NDH) NonDominant Handshape:

(PO) Palm Orientation:

Movement:

Location (if not neutral):

NMS (if not neutral):

Looks like:

Variation(s):

Initialized Variation(s):

Specify if Regional:

Linguistic Register (if specific): FORMAL CONSULTATIVE INFORMAL INTIMATE

Other Vocab/Meanings:

GLOSS(ES)

(DH) Dominant Handshape:

(NDH) NonDominant Handshape:

(PO) Palm Orientation:

Movement:

Location (if not neutral):

NMS (if not neutral):

Looks like:

Variation(s):

Initialized Variation(s):

Specify if Regional:

Linguistic Register (if specific): FORMAL CONSULTATIVE INFORMAL INTIMATE

Other Vocab/Meanings:

GLOSS(ES)

(DH) Dominant Handshape:

(NDH) NonDominant Handshape:

(PO) Palm Orientation:

Movement:

Location (if not neutral):

NMS (if not neutral):

Looks like:

Variation(s):

Initialized Variation(s):

Specify if Regional:

Linguistic Register (if specific): FORMAL CONSULTATIVE INFORMAL INTIMATE

Other Vocab/Meanings:

GLOSS(ES)

(DH) Dominant Handshape:

(NDH) NonDominant Handshape:

(PO) Palm Orientation:

Movement:

Location (if not neutral):

NMS (if not neutral):

Looks like:

Variation(s):

Initialized Variation(s):

Specify if Regional:

Linguistic Register (if specific): FORMAL CONSULTATIVE INFORMAL INTIMATE

Other Vocab/Meanings:

GLOSS(ES)

(DH) Dominant Handshape:

(NDH) NonDominant Handshape:

(PO) Palm Orientation:

Movement:

Location (if not neutral):

NMS (if not neutral):

Looks like:

Variation(s):

Initialized Variation(s):

Specify if Regional:

Linguistic Register (if specific): FORMAL CONSULTATIVE INFORMAL INTIMATE

Other Vocab/Meanings:

GLOSS(ES)

(DH) Dominant Handshape:

(NDH) NonDominant Handshape:

(PO) Palm Orientation:

Movement:

Location (if not neutral):

NMS (if not neutral):

Looks like:

Variation(s):

Initialized Variation(s):

Specify if Regional:

Linguistic Register (if specific): FORMAL CONSULTATIVE INFORMAL INTIMATE

Other Vocab/Meanings:

GLOSS(ES)

(DH) Dominant Handshape:

(NDH) NonDominant Handshape:

(PO) Palm Orientation:

Movement:

Location (if not neutral):

NMS (if not neutral):

Looks like:

Variation(s):

Initialized Variation(s):

Specify if Regional:

Linguistic Register (if specific): FORMAL CONSULTATIVE INFORMAL INTIMATE

Other Vocab/Meanings:

GLOSS(ES)

(DH) Dominant Handshape:

(NDH) NonDominant Handshape:

(PO) Palm Orientation:

Movement:

Location (if not neutral):

NMS (if not neutral):

Looks like:

Variation(s):

Initialized Variation(s):

Specify if Regional:

Linguistic Register (if specific): FORMAL CONSULTATIVE INFORMAL INTIMATE

Other Vocab/Meanings:

GLOSS(ES)

(DH) Dominant Handshape:

(NDH) NonDominant Handshape:

(PO) Palm Orientation:

Movement:

Location (if not neutral):

NMS (if not neutral):

Looks like:

Variation(s):

Initialized Variation(s):

Specify if Regional:

Linguistic Register (if specific): FORMAL CONSULTATIVE INFORMAL INTIMATE

Other Vocab/Meanings:

GLOSS(ES)

(DH) <u>Dominant Handshape</u>:

(NDH) <u>NonDominant Handshape</u>:

(PO) <u>Palm Orientation</u>:

<u>Movement</u>:

<u>Location</u> (if not neutral):

<u>NMS</u> (if not neutral):

Looks like:

Variation(s):

Initialized Variation(s):

Specify if Regional:

Linguistic **Register** (if specific): FORMAL   CONSULTATIVE   INFORMAL   INTIMATE

Other Vocab/Meanings:

GLOSS(ES)

(DH) <u>Dominant Handshape</u>:

(NDH) <u>NonDominant Handshape</u>:

(PO) <u>Palm Orientation</u>:

<u>Movement</u>:

<u>Location</u> (if not neutral):

<u>NMS</u> (if not neutral):

Looks like:

Variation(s):

Initialized Variation(s):

Specify if Regional:

Linguistic **Register** (if specific): FORMAL   CONSULTATIVE   INFORMAL   INTIMATE

Other Vocab/Meanings:

GLOSS(ES)

(DH) <u>Dominant Handshape</u>:

(NDH) <u>NonDominant Handshape</u>:

(PO) <u>Palm Orientation</u>:

<u>Movement</u>:

<u>Location</u> (if not neutral):

<u>NMS</u> (if not neutral):

Looks like:

Variation(s):

Initialized Variation(s):

Specify if Regional:

Linguistic **Register** (if specific): FORMAL   CONSULTATIVE   INFORMAL   INTIMATE

Other Vocab/Meanings:

GLOSS(ES)

(DH) <u>Dominant Handshape</u>:

(NDH) <u>NonDominant Handshape</u>:

(PO) <u>Palm Orientation</u>:

<u>Movement</u>:

<u>Location</u> (if not neutral):

<u>NMS</u> (if not neutral):

Looks like:

Variation(s):

Initialized Variation(s):

Specify if Regional:

Linguistic **Register** (if specific): FORMAL   CONSULTATIVE   INFORMAL   INTIMATE

Other Vocab/Meanings:

GLOSS(ES)

(DH) <u>Dominant Handshape</u>:

(NDH) <u>NonDominant Handshape</u>:

(PO) <u>Palm Orientation</u>:

<u>Movement</u>:

<u>Location</u> (if not neutral):

<u>NMS</u> (if not neutral):

Looks like:

Variation(s):

Initialized Variation(s):

Specify if Regional:

Linguistic **Register** (if specific): FORMAL   CONSULTATIVE   INFORMAL   INTIMATE

Other Vocab/Meanings:

GLOSS(ES)

(DH) <u>Dominant Handshape</u>:

(NDH) <u>NonDominant Handshape</u>:

(PO) <u>Palm Orientation</u>:

<u>Movement</u>:

<u>Location</u> (if not neutral):

<u>NMS</u> (if not neutral):

Looks like:

Variation(s):

Initialized Variation(s):

Specify if Regional:

Linguistic **Register** (if specific): FORMAL   CONSULTATIVE   INFORMAL   INTIMATE

Other Vocab/Meanings:

GLOSS(ES)

(DH) <u>Dominant Handshape</u>:

(NDH) <u>NonDominant Handshape</u>:

(PO) <u>Palm Orientation</u>:

<u>Movement</u>:

<u>Location</u> (if not neutral):

<u>NMS</u> (if not neutral):

Looks like:

Variation(s):

Initialized Variation(s):

Specify if Regional:

Linguistic Register (if specific): FORMAL CONSULTATIVE INFORMAL INTIMATE

Other Vocab/Meanings:

GLOSS(ES)

(DH) <u>Dominant Handshape</u>:

(NDH) <u>NonDominant Handshape</u>:

(PO) <u>Palm Orientation</u>:

<u>Movement</u>:

<u>Location</u> (if not neutral):

<u>NMS</u> (if not neutral):

Looks like:

Variation(s):

Initialized Variation(s):

Specify if Regional:

Linguistic Register (if specific): FORMAL CONSULTATIVE INFORMAL INTIMATE

Other Vocab/Meanings:

GLOSS(ES)

(DH) <u>Dominant Handshape</u>:

(NDH) <u>NonDominant Handshape</u>:

(PO) <u>Palm Orientation</u>:

<u>Movement</u>:

<u>Location</u> (if not neutral):

<u>NMS</u> (if not neutral):

Looks like:

Variation(s):

Initialized Variation(s):

Specify if Regional:

Linguistic Register (if specific): FORMAL CONSULTATIVE INFORMAL INTIMATE

Other Vocab/Meanings:

GLOSS(ES)

(DH) <u>Dominant Handshape</u>:

(NDH) <u>NonDominant Handshape</u>:

(PO) <u>Palm Orientation</u>:

<u>Movement</u>:

<u>Location</u> (if not neutral):

<u>NMS</u> (if not neutral):

Looks like:

Variation(s):

Initialized Variation(s):

Specify if Regional:

Linguistic Register (if specific): FORMAL CONSULTATIVE INFORMAL INTIMATE

Other Vocab/Meanings:

GLOSS(ES)

(DH) <u>Dominant Handshape</u>:

(NDH) <u>NonDominant Handshape</u>:

(PO) <u>Palm Orientation</u>:

<u>Movement</u>:

<u>Location</u> (if not neutral):

<u>NMS</u> (if not neutral):

Looks like:

Variation(s):

Initialized Variation(s):

Specify if Regional:

Linguistic Register (if specific): FORMAL CONSULTATIVE INFORMAL INTIMATE

Other Vocab/Meanings:

GLOSS(ES)

(DH) <u>Dominant Handshape</u>:

(NDH) <u>NonDominant Handshape</u>:

(PO) <u>Palm Orientation</u>:

<u>Movement</u>:

<u>Location</u> (if not neutral):

<u>NMS</u> (if not neutral):

Looks like:

Variation(s):

Initialized Variation(s):

Specify if Regional:

Linguistic Register (if specific): FORMAL CONSULTATIVE INFORMAL INTIMATE

Other Vocab/Meanings:

GLOSS(ES)

(DH) <u>Dominant Handshape</u>:

(NDH) <u>NonDominant Handshape</u>:

(PO) <u>Palm Orientation</u>:

<u>Movement</u>:

<u>Location</u> (if not neutral):

<u>NMS</u> (if not neutral):

Looks like:

Variation(s):

Initialized Variation(s):

Specify if Regional:

Linguistic Register (if specific): FORMAL CONSULTATIVE INFORMAL INTIMATE

Other Vocab/Meanings:

GLOSS(ES)

(DH) <u>Dominant Handshape</u>:

(NDH) <u>NonDominant Handshape</u>:

(PO) <u>Palm Orientation</u>:

<u>Movement</u>:

<u>Location</u> (if not neutral):

<u>NMS</u> (if not neutral):

Looks like:

Variation(s):

Initialized Variation(s):

Specify if Regional:

Linguistic Register (if specific): FORMAL CONSULTATIVE INFORMAL INTIMATE

Other Vocab/Meanings:

GLOSS(ES)

(DH) <u>Dominant Handshape</u>:

(NDH) <u>NonDominant Handshape</u>:

(PO) <u>Palm Orientation</u>:

<u>Movement</u>:

<u>Location</u> (if not neutral):

<u>NMS</u> (if not neutral):

Looks like:

Variation(s):

Initialized Variation(s):

Specify if Regional:

Linguistic Register (if specific): FORMAL CONSULTATIVE INFORMAL INTIMATE

Other Vocab/Meanings:

GLOSS(ES)

(DH) <u>Dominant Handshape</u>:

(NDH) <u>NonDominant Handshape</u>:

(PO) <u>Palm Orientation</u>:

<u>Movement</u>:

<u>Location</u> (if not neutral):

<u>NMS</u> (if not neutral):

Looks like:

Variation(s):

Initialized Variation(s):

Specify if Regional:

Linguistic Register (if specific): FORMAL CONSULTATIVE INFORMAL INTIMATE

Other Vocab/Meanings:

GLOSS(ES)

(DH) <u>Dominant Handshape</u>:

(NDH) <u>NonDominant Handshape</u>:

(PO) <u>Palm Orientation</u>:

<u>Movement</u>:

<u>Location</u> (if not neutral):

<u>NMS</u> (if not neutral):

Looks like:

Variation(s):

Initialized Variation(s):

Specify if Regional:

Linguistic Register (if specific): FORMAL CONSULTATIVE INFORMAL INTIMATE

Other Vocab/Meanings:

GLOSS(ES)

(DH) <u>Dominant Handshape</u>:

(NDH) <u>NonDominant Handshape</u>:

(PO) <u>Palm Orientation</u>:

<u>Movement</u>:

<u>Location</u> (if not neutral):

<u>NMS</u> (if not neutral):

Looks like:

Variation(s):

Initialized Variation(s):

Specify if Regional:

Linguistic Register (if specific): FORMAL CONSULTATIVE INFORMAL INTIMATE

Other Vocab/Meanings:

GLOSS(ES)

(DH) <u>Dominant Handshape</u>:

(NDH) <u>NonDominant Handshape</u>:

(PO) <u>Palm Orientation</u>:

<u>Movement</u>:

<u>Location</u> (if not neutral):

<u>NMS</u> (if not neutral):

Looks like:

Variation(s):

Initialized Variation(s):

Specify if Regional:

Linguistic Register (if specific): FORMAL   CONSULTATIVE   INFORMAL   INTIMATE

Other Vocab/Meanings:

GLOSS(ES)

(DH) <u>Dominant Handshape</u>:

(NDH) <u>NonDominant Handshape</u>:

(PO) <u>Palm Orientation</u>:

<u>Movement</u>:

<u>Location</u> (if not neutral):

<u>NMS</u> (if not neutral):

Looks like:

Variation(s):

Initialized Variation(s):

Specify if Regional:

Linguistic Register (if specific): FORMAL   CONSULTATIVE   INFORMAL   INTIMATE

Other Vocab/Meanings:

GLOSS(ES)

(DH) <u>Dominant Handshape</u>:

(NDH) <u>NonDominant Handshape</u>:

(PO) <u>Palm Orientation</u>:

<u>Movement</u>:

<u>Location</u> (if not neutral):

<u>NMS</u> (if not neutral):

Looks like:

Variation(s):

Initialized Variation(s):

Specify if Regional:

Linguistic Register (if specific): FORMAL   CONSULTATIVE   INFORMAL   INTIMATE

Other Vocab/Meanings:

GLOSS(ES)

(DH) <u>Dominant Handshape</u>:

(NDH) <u>NonDominant Handshape</u>:

(PO) <u>Palm Orientation</u>:

<u>Movement</u>:

<u>Location</u> (if not neutral):

<u>NMS</u> (if not neutral):

Looks like:

Variation(s):

Initialized Variation(s):

Specify if Regional:

Linguistic Register (if specific): FORMAL   CONSULTATIVE   INFORMAL   INTIMATE

Other Vocab/Meanings:

GLOSS(ES)

(DH) <u>Dominant Handshape</u>:

(NDH) <u>NonDominant Handshape</u>:

(PO) <u>Palm Orientation</u>:

<u>Movement</u>:

<u>Location</u> (if not neutral):

<u>NMS</u> (if not neutral):

Looks like:

Variation(s):

Initialized Variation(s):

Specify if Regional:

Linguistic Register (if specific): FORMAL   CONSULTATIVE   INFORMAL   INTIMATE

Other Vocab/Meanings:

GLOSS(ES)

(DH) <u>Dominant Handshape</u>:

(NDH) <u>NonDominant Handshape</u>:

(PO) <u>Palm Orientation</u>:

<u>Movement</u>:

<u>Location</u> (if not neutral):

<u>NMS</u> (if not neutral):

Looks like:

Variation(s):

Initialized Variation(s):

Specify if Regional:

Linguistic Register (if specific): FORMAL   CONSULTATIVE   INFORMAL   INTIMATE

Other Vocab/Meanings:

GLOSS(ES)

   (DH) <u>Dominant Handshape</u>:

(NDH) <u>NonDominant Handshape</u>:

   (PO) <u>Palm Orientation</u>:

      <u>Movement</u>:

     <u>Location</u> (if not neutral):

      <u>NMS</u> (if not neutral):

  Looks like:

  Variation(s):

Initialized Variation(s):

 Specify if Regional:

 Linguistic Register (if specific): FORMAL CONSULTATIVE INFORMAL INTIMATE

Other Vocab/Meanings:

GLOSS(ES)

   (DH) <u>Dominant Handshape</u>:

(NDH) <u>NonDominant Handshape</u>:

   (PO) <u>Palm Orientation</u>:

      <u>Movement</u>:

     <u>Location</u> (if not neutral):

      <u>NMS</u> (if not neutral):

  Looks like:

  Variation(s):

Initialized Variation(s):

 Specify if Regional:

 Linguistic Register (if specific): FORMAL CONSULTATIVE INFORMAL INTIMATE

Other Vocab/Meanings:

GLOSS(ES)

   (DH) <u>Dominant Handshape</u>:

(NDH) <u>NonDominant Handshape</u>:

   (PO) <u>Palm Orientation</u>:

      <u>Movement</u>:

     <u>Location</u> (if not neutral):

      <u>NMS</u> (if not neutral):

  Looks like:

  Variation(s):

Initialized Variation(s):

 Specify if Regional:

 Linguistic Register (if specific): FORMAL CONSULTATIVE INFORMAL INTIMATE

Other Vocab/Meanings:

GLOSS(ES)

   (DH) <u>Dominant Handshape</u>:

(NDH) <u>NonDominant Handshape</u>:

   (PO) <u>Palm Orientation</u>:

      <u>Movement</u>:

     <u>Location</u> (if not neutral):

      <u>NMS</u> (if not neutral):

  Looks like:

  Variation(s):

Initialized Variation(s):

 Specify if Regional:

 Linguistic Register (if specific): FORMAL CONSULTATIVE INFORMAL INTIMATE

Other Vocab/Meanings:

GLOSS(ES)

   (DH) <u>Dominant Handshape</u>:

(NDH) <u>NonDominant Handshape</u>:

   (PO) <u>Palm Orientation</u>:

      <u>Movement</u>:

     <u>Location</u> (if not neutral):

      <u>NMS</u> (if not neutral):

  Looks like:

  Variation(s):

Initialized Variation(s):

 Specify if Regional:

 Linguistic Register (if specific): FORMAL CONSULTATIVE INFORMAL INTIMATE

Other Vocab/Meanings:

GLOSS(ES)

   (DH) <u>Dominant Handshape</u>:

(NDH) <u>NonDominant Handshape</u>:

   (PO) <u>Palm Orientation</u>:

      <u>Movement</u>:

     <u>Location</u> (if not neutral):

      <u>NMS</u> (if not neutral):

  Looks like:

  Variation(s):

Initialized Variation(s):

 Specify if Regional:

 Linguistic Register (if specific): FORMAL CONSULTATIVE INFORMAL INTIMATE

Other Vocab/Meanings:

GLOSS(ES)

(DH) <u>Dominant Handshape</u>:

(NDH) <u>NonDominant Handshape</u>:

(PO) <u>Palm Orientation</u>:

<u>Movement</u>:

<u>Location</u> (if not neutral):

<u>NMS</u> (if not neutral):

Looks like:

Variation(s):

Initialized Variation(s):

Specify if Regional:

Linguistic Register (if specific): FORMAL CONSULTATIVE INFORMAL INTIMATE

Other Vocab/Meanings:

GLOSS(ES)

(DH) <u>Dominant Handshape</u>:

(NDH) <u>NonDominant Handshape</u>:

(PO) <u>Palm Orientation</u>:

<u>Movement</u>:

<u>Location</u> (if not neutral):

<u>NMS</u> (if not neutral):

Looks like:

Variation(s):

Initialized Variation(s):

Specify if Regional:

Linguistic Register (if specific): FORMAL CONSULTATIVE INFORMAL INTIMATE

Other Vocab/Meanings:

GLOSS(ES)

(DH) <u>Dominant Handshape</u>:

(NDH) <u>NonDominant Handshape</u>:

(PO) <u>Palm Orientation</u>:

<u>Movement</u>:

<u>Location</u> (if not neutral):

<u>NMS</u> (if not neutral):

Looks like:

Variation(s):

Initialized Variation(s):

Specify if Regional:

Linguistic Register (if specific): FORMAL CONSULTATIVE INFORMAL INTIMATE

Other Vocab/Meanings:

GLOSS(ES)

(DH) <u>Dominant Handshape</u>:

(NDH) <u>NonDominant Handshape</u>:

(PO) <u>Palm Orientation</u>:

<u>Movement</u>:

<u>Location</u> (if not neutral):

<u>NMS</u> (if not neutral):

Looks like:

Variation(s):

Initialized Variation(s):

Specify if Regional:

Linguistic Register (if specific): FORMAL CONSULTATIVE INFORMAL INTIMATE

Other Vocab/Meanings:

GLOSS(ES)

(DH) <u>Dominant Handshape</u>:

(NDH) <u>NonDominant Handshape</u>:

(PO) <u>Palm Orientation</u>:

<u>Movement</u>:

<u>Location</u> (if not neutral):

<u>NMS</u> (if not neutral):

Looks like:

Variation(s):

Initialized Variation(s):

Specify if Regional:

Linguistic Register (if specific): FORMAL CONSULTATIVE INFORMAL INTIMATE

Other Vocab/Meanings:

GLOSS(ES)

(DH) <u>Dominant Handshape</u>:

(NDH) <u>NonDominant Handshape</u>:

(PO) <u>Palm Orientation</u>:

<u>Movement</u>:

<u>Location</u> (if not neutral):

<u>NMS</u> (if not neutral):

Looks like:

Variation(s):

Initialized Variation(s):

Specify if Regional:

Linguistic Register (if specific): FORMAL CONSULTATIVE INFORMAL INTIMATE

Other Vocab/Meanings:

GLOSS(ES)

(DH) <u>Dominant Handshape</u>:

(NDH) <u>NonDominant Handshape</u>:

(PO) <u>Palm Orientation</u>:

<u>Movement</u>:

<u>Location</u> (if not neutral):

<u>NMS</u> (if not neutral):

Looks like:

Variation(s):

Initialized Variation(s):

Specify if Regional:

Linguistic Register (if specific): FORMAL CONSULTATIVE INFORMAL INTIMATE

Other Vocab/Meanings:

GLOSS(ES)

(DH) <u>Dominant Handshape</u>:

(NDH) <u>NonDominant Handshape</u>:

(PO) <u>Palm Orientation</u>:

<u>Movement</u>:

<u>Location</u> (if not neutral):

<u>NMS</u> (if not neutral):

Looks like:

Variation(s):

Initialized Variation(s):

Specify if Regional:

Linguistic Register (if specific): FORMAL CONSULTATIVE INFORMAL INTIMATE

Other Vocab/Meanings:

GLOSS(ES)

(DH) <u>Dominant Handshape</u>:

(NDH) <u>NonDominant Handshape</u>:

(PO) <u>Palm Orientation</u>:

<u>Movement</u>:

<u>Location</u> (if not neutral):

<u>NMS</u> (if not neutral):

Looks like:

Variation(s):

Initialized Variation(s):

Specify if Regional:

Linguistic Register (if specific): FORMAL CONSULTATIVE INFORMAL INTIMATE

Other Vocab/Meanings:

GLOSS(ES)

(DH) <u>Dominant Handshape</u>:

(NDH) <u>NonDominant Handshape</u>:

(PO) <u>Palm Orientation</u>:

<u>Movement</u>:

<u>Location</u> (if not neutral):

<u>NMS</u> (if not neutral):

Looks like:

Variation(s):

Initialized Variation(s):

Specify if Regional:

Linguistic Register (if specific): FORMAL CONSULTATIVE INFORMAL INTIMATE

Other Vocab/Meanings:

GLOSS(ES)

(DH) <u>Dominant Handshape</u>:

(NDH) <u>NonDominant Handshape</u>:

(PO) <u>Palm Orientation</u>:

<u>Movement</u>:

<u>Location</u> (if not neutral):

<u>NMS</u> (if not neutral):

Looks like:

Variation(s):

Initialized Variation(s):

Specify if Regional:

Linguistic Register (if specific): FORMAL CONSULTATIVE INFORMAL INTIMATE

Other Vocab/Meanings:

GLOSS(ES)

(DH) <u>Dominant Handshape</u>:

(NDH) <u>NonDominant Handshape</u>:

(PO) <u>Palm Orientation</u>:

<u>Movement</u>:

<u>Location</u> (if not neutral):

<u>NMS</u> (if not neutral):

Looks like:

Variation(s):

Initialized Variation(s):

Specify if Regional:

Linguistic Register (if specific): FORMAL CONSULTATIVE INFORMAL INTIMATE

Other Vocab/Meanings:

GLOSS(ES)

(DH) <u>Dominant Handshape</u>:

(NDH) <u>NonDominant Handshape</u>:

  (PO) <u>Palm Orientation</u>:

    <u>Movement</u>:

   <u>Location</u> (if not neutral):

    <u>NMS</u> (if not neutral):

 Looks like:

 Variation(s):

Initialized Variation(s):

 Specify if Regional:

Linguistic Register (if specific): Formal Consultative Informal Intimate

Other Vocab/Meanings:

GLOSS(ES)

(DH) <u>Dominant Handshape</u>:

(NDH) <u>NonDominant Handshape</u>:

  (PO) <u>Palm Orientation</u>:

    <u>Movement</u>:

   <u>Location</u> (if not neutral):

    <u>NMS</u> (if not neutral):

 Looks like:

 Variation(s):

Initialized Variation(s):

 Specify if Regional:

Linguistic Register (if specific): Formal Consultative Informal Intimate

Other Vocab/Meanings:

GLOSS(ES)

(DH) <u>Dominant Handshape</u>:

(NDH) <u>NonDominant Handshape</u>:

  (PO) <u>Palm Orientation</u>:

    <u>Movement</u>:

   <u>Location</u> (if not neutral):

    <u>NMS</u> (if not neutral):

 Looks like:

 Variation(s):

Initialized Variation(s):

 Specify if Regional:

Linguistic Register (if specific): Formal Consultative Informal Intimate

Other Vocab/Meanings:

GLOSS(ES)

(DH) <u>Dominant Handshape</u>:

(NDH) <u>NonDominant Handshape</u>:

  (PO) <u>Palm Orientation</u>:

    <u>Movement</u>:

   <u>Location</u> (if not neutral):

    <u>NMS</u> (if not neutral):

 Looks like:

 Variation(s):

Initialized Variation(s):

 Specify if Regional:

Linguistic Register (if specific): Formal Consultative Informal Intimate

Other Vocab/Meanings:

GLOSS(ES)

(DH) <u>Dominant Handshape</u>:

(NDH) <u>NonDominant Handshape</u>:

  (PO) <u>Palm Orientation</u>:

    <u>Movement</u>:

   <u>Location</u> (if not neutral):

    <u>NMS</u> (if not neutral):

 Looks like:

 Variation(s):

Initialized Variation(s):

 Specify if Regional:

Linguistic Register (if specific): Formal Consultative Informal Intimate

Other Vocab/Meanings:

GLOSS(ES)

(DH) <u>Dominant Handshape</u>:

(NDH) <u>NonDominant Handshape</u>:

  (PO) <u>Palm Orientation</u>:

    <u>Movement</u>:

   <u>Location</u> (if not neutral):

    <u>NMS</u> (if not neutral):

 Looks like:

 Variation(s):

Initialized Variation(s):

 Specify if Regional:

Linguistic Register (if specific): Formal Consultative Informal Intimate

Other Vocab/Meanings:

GLOSS(ES)

(DH) Dominant Handshape:

(NDH) NonDominant Handshape:

(PO) Palm Orientation:

Movement:

Location (if not neutral):

NMS (if not neutral):

Looks like:

Variation(s):

Initialized Variation(s):

Specify if Regional:

Linguistic Register (if specific): FORMAL   CONSULTATIVE   INFORMAL   INTIMATE

Other Vocab/Meanings:

GLOSS(ES)

(DH) Dominant Handshape:

(NDH) NonDominant Handshape:

(PO) Palm Orientation:

Movement:

Location (if not neutral):

NMS (if not neutral):

Looks like:

Variation(s):

Initialized Variation(s):

Specify if Regional:

Linguistic Register (if specific): FORMAL   CONSULTATIVE   INFORMAL   INTIMATE

Other Vocab/Meanings:

GLOSS(ES)

(DH) Dominant Handshape:

(NDH) NonDominant Handshape:

(PO) Palm Orientation:

Movement:

Location (if not neutral):

NMS (if not neutral):

Looks like:

Variation(s):

Initialized Variation(s):

Specify if Regional:

Linguistic Register (if specific): FORMAL   CONSULTATIVE   INFORMAL   INTIMATE

Other Vocab/Meanings:

GLOSS(ES)

(DH) Dominant Handshape:

(NDH) NonDominant Handshape:

(PO) Palm Orientation:

Movement:

Location (if not neutral):

NMS (if not neutral):

Looks like:

Variation(s):

Initialized Variation(s):

Specify if Regional:

Linguistic Register (if specific): FORMAL   CONSULTATIVE   INFORMAL   INTIMATE

Other Vocab/Meanings:

GLOSS(ES)

(DH) Dominant Handshape:

(NDH) NonDominant Handshape:

(PO) Palm Orientation:

Movement:

Location (if not neutral):

NMS (if not neutral):

Looks like:

Variation(s):

Initialized Variation(s):

Specify if Regional:

Linguistic Register (if specific): FORMAL   CONSULTATIVE   INFORMAL   INTIMATE

Other Vocab/Meanings:

GLOSS(ES)

(DH) Dominant Handshape:

(NDH) NonDominant Handshape:

(PO) Palm Orientation:

Movement:

Location (if not neutral):

NMS (if not neutral):

Looks like:

Variation(s):

Initialized Variation(s):

Specify if Regional:

Linguistic Register (if specific): FORMAL   CONSULTATIVE   INFORMAL   INTIMATE

Other Vocab/Meanings:

GLOSS(ES)

(DH) Dominant Handshape:

(NDH) NonDominant Handshape:

(PO) Palm Orientation:

Movement:

Location (if not neutral):

NMS (if not neutral):

Looks like:

Variation(s):

Initialized Variation(s):

Specify if Regional:

Linguistic Register (if specific): FORMAL CONSULTATIVE INFORMAL INTIMATE

Other Vocab/Meanings:

GLOSS(ES)

(DH) Dominant Handshape:

(NDH) NonDominant Handshape:

(PO) Palm Orientation:

Movement:

Location (if not neutral):

NMS (if not neutral):

Looks like:

Variation(s):

Initialized Variation(s):

Specify if Regional:

Linguistic Register (if specific): FORMAL CONSULTATIVE INFORMAL INTIMATE

Other Vocab/Meanings:

GLOSS(ES)

(DH) Dominant Handshape:

(NDH) NonDominant Handshape:

(PO) Palm Orientation:

Movement:

Location (if not neutral):

NMS (if not neutral):

Looks like:

Variation(s):

Initialized Variation(s):

Specify if Regional:

Linguistic Register (if specific): FORMAL CONSULTATIVE INFORMAL INTIMATE

Other Vocab/Meanings:

GLOSS(ES)

(DH) Dominant Handshape:

(NDH) NonDominant Handshape:

(PO) Palm Orientation:

Movement:

Location (if not neutral):

NMS (if not neutral):

Looks like:

Variation(s):

Initialized Variation(s):

Specify if Regional:

Linguistic Register (if specific): FORMAL CONSULTATIVE INFORMAL INTIMATE

Other Vocab/Meanings:

GLOSS(ES)

(DH) Dominant Handshape:

(NDH) NonDominant Handshape:

(PO) Palm Orientation:

Movement:

Location (if not neutral):

NMS (if not neutral):

Looks like:

Variation(s):

Initialized Variation(s):

Specify if Regional:

Linguistic Register (if specific): FORMAL CONSULTATIVE INFORMAL INTIMATE

Other Vocab/Meanings:

GLOSS(ES)

(DH) Dominant Handshape:

(NDH) NonDominant Handshape:

(PO) Palm Orientation:

Movement:

Location (if not neutral):

NMS (if not neutral):

Looks like:

Variation(s):

Initialized Variation(s):

Specify if Regional:

Linguistic Register (if specific): FORMAL CONSULTATIVE INFORMAL INTIMATE

Other Vocab/Meanings:

GLOSS(ES)

(DH) Dominant Handshape:

(NDH) NonDominant Handshape:

(PO) Palm Orientation:

Movement:

Location (if not neutral):

NMS (if not neutral):

Looks like:

Variation(s):

Initialized Variation(s):

Specify if Regional:

Linguistic Register (if specific): FORMAL CONSULTATIVE INFORMAL INTIMATE

Other Vocab/Meanings:

GLOSS(ES)

(DH) Dominant Handshape:

(NDH) NonDominant Handshape:

(PO) Palm Orientation:

Movement:

Location (if not neutral):

NMS (if not neutral):

Looks like:

Variation(s):

Initialized Variation(s):

Specify if Regional:

Linguistic Register (if specific): FORMAL CONSULTATIVE INFORMAL INTIMATE

Other Vocab/Meanings:

GLOSS(ES)

(DH) Dominant Handshape:

(NDH) NonDominant Handshape:

(PO) Palm Orientation:

Movement:

Location (if not neutral):

NMS (if not neutral):

Looks like:

Variation(s):

Initialized Variation(s):

Specify if Regional:

Linguistic Register (if specific): FORMAL CONSULTATIVE INFORMAL INTIMATE

Other Vocab/Meanings:

GLOSS(ES)

(DH) Dominant Handshape:

(NDH) NonDominant Handshape:

(PO) Palm Orientation:

Movement:

Location (if not neutral):

NMS (if not neutral):

Looks like:

Variation(s):

Initialized Variation(s):

Specify if Regional:

Linguistic Register (if specific): FORMAL CONSULTATIVE INFORMAL INTIMATE

Other Vocab/Meanings:

GLOSS(ES)

(DH) Dominant Handshape:

(NDH) NonDominant Handshape:

(PO) Palm Orientation:

Movement:

Location (if not neutral):

NMS (if not neutral):

Looks like:

Variation(s):

Initialized Variation(s):

Specify if Regional:

Linguistic Register (if specific): FORMAL CONSULTATIVE INFORMAL INTIMATE

Other Vocab/Meanings:

GLOSS(ES)

(DH) Dominant Handshape:

(NDH) NonDominant Handshape:

(PO) Palm Orientation:

Movement:

Location (if not neutral):

NMS (if not neutral):

Looks like:

Variation(s):

Initialized Variation(s):

Specify if Regional:

Linguistic Register (if specific): FORMAL CONSULTATIVE INFORMAL INTIMATE

Other Vocab/Meanings:

GLOSS(ES)

    (DH) <u>Dominant Handshape</u>:

(NDH) <u>NonDominant Handshape</u>:

    (PO) <u>Palm Orientation</u>:

      <u>Movement</u>:

      <u>Location</u> (if not neutral):

      <u>NMS</u> (if not neutral):

  Looks like:

  Variation(s):

Initialized Variation(s):

 Specify if Regional:

Linguistic Register (if specific): Formal Consultative Informal Intimate

Other Vocab/Meanings:

GLOSS(ES)

    (DH) <u>Dominant Handshape</u>:

(NDH) <u>NonDominant Handshape</u>:

    (PO) <u>Palm Orientation</u>:

      <u>Movement</u>:

      <u>Location</u> (if not neutral):

      <u>NMS</u> (if not neutral):

  Looks like:

  Variation(s):

Initialized Variation(s):

 Specify if Regional:

Linguistic Register (if specific): Formal Consultative Informal Intimate

Other Vocab/Meanings:

GLOSS(ES)

    (DH) <u>Dominant Handshape</u>:

(NDH) <u>NonDominant Handshape</u>:

    (PO) <u>Palm Orientation</u>:

      <u>Movement</u>:

      <u>Location</u> (if not neutral):

      <u>NMS</u> (if not neutral):

  Looks like:

  Variation(s):

Initialized Variation(s):

 Specify if Regional:

Linguistic Register (if specific): Formal Consultative Informal Intimate

Other Vocab/Meanings:

GLOSS(ES)

    (DH) <u>Dominant Handshape</u>:

(NDH) <u>NonDominant Handshape</u>:

    (PO) <u>Palm Orientation</u>:

      <u>Movement</u>:

      <u>Location</u> (if not neutral):

      <u>NMS</u> (if not neutral):

  Looks like:

  Variation(s):

Initialized Variation(s):

 Specify if Regional:

Linguistic Register (if specific): Formal Consultative Informal Intimate

Other Vocab/Meanings:

GLOSS(ES)

    (DH) <u>Dominant Handshape</u>:

(NDH) <u>NonDominant Handshape</u>:

    (PO) <u>Palm Orientation</u>:

      <u>Movement</u>:

      <u>Location</u> (if not neutral):

      <u>NMS</u> (if not neutral):

  Looks like:

  Variation(s):

Initialized Variation(s):

 Specify if Regional:

Linguistic Register (if specific): Formal Consultative Informal Intimate

Other Vocab/Meanings:

GLOSS(ES)

    (DH) <u>Dominant Handshape</u>:

(NDH) <u>NonDominant Handshape</u>:

    (PO) <u>Palm Orientation</u>:

      <u>Movement</u>:

      <u>Location</u> (if not neutral):

      <u>NMS</u> (if not neutral):

  Looks like:

  Variation(s):

Initialized Variation(s):

 Specify if Regional:

Linguistic Register (if specific): Formal Consultative Informal Intimate

Other Vocab/Meanings:

GLOSS(ES)

(DH) <u>Dominant Handshape</u>:

(NDH) <u>NonDominant Handshape</u>:

(PO) <u>Palm Orientation</u>:

<u>Movement</u>:

<u>Location</u> (if not neutral):

<u>NMS</u> (if not neutral):

Looks like:

Variation(s):

Initialized Variation(s):

Specify if Regional:

Linguistic Register (if specific): FORMAL CONSULTATIVE INFORMAL INTIMATE

Other Vocab/Meanings:

GLOSS(ES)

(DH) <u>Dominant Handshape</u>:

(NDH) <u>NonDominant Handshape</u>:

(PO) <u>Palm Orientation</u>:

<u>Movement</u>:

<u>Location</u> (if not neutral):

<u>NMS</u> (if not neutral):

Looks like:

Variation(s):

Initialized Variation(s):

Specify if Regional:

Linguistic Register (if specific): FORMAL CONSULTATIVE INFORMAL INTIMATE

Other Vocab/Meanings:

GLOSS(ES)

(DH) <u>Dominant Handshape</u>:

(NDH) <u>NonDominant Handshape</u>:

(PO) <u>Palm Orientation</u>:

<u>Movement</u>:

<u>Location</u> (if not neutral):

<u>NMS</u> (if not neutral):

Looks like:

Variation(s):

Initialized Variation(s):

Specify if Regional:

Linguistic Register (if specific): FORMAL CONSULTATIVE INFORMAL INTIMATE

Other Vocab/Meanings:

GLOSS(ES)

(DH) <u>Dominant Handshape</u>:

(NDH) <u>NonDominant Handshape</u>:

(PO) <u>Palm Orientation</u>:

<u>Movement</u>:

<u>Location</u> (if not neutral):

<u>NMS</u> (if not neutral):

Looks like:

Variation(s):

Initialized Variation(s):

Specify if Regional:

Linguistic Register (if specific): FORMAL CONSULTATIVE INFORMAL INTIMATE

Other Vocab/Meanings:

GLOSS(ES)

(DH) <u>Dominant Handshape</u>:

(NDH) <u>NonDominant Handshape</u>:

(PO) <u>Palm Orientation</u>:

<u>Movement</u>:

<u>Location</u> (if not neutral):

<u>NMS</u> (if not neutral):

Looks like:

Variation(s):

Initialized Variation(s):

Specify if Regional:

Linguistic Register (if specific): FORMAL CONSULTATIVE INFORMAL INTIMATE

Other Vocab/Meanings:

GLOSS(ES)

(DH) <u>Dominant Handshape</u>:

(NDH) <u>NonDominant Handshape</u>:

(PO) <u>Palm Orientation</u>:

<u>Movement</u>:

<u>Location</u> (if not neutral):

<u>NMS</u> (if not neutral):

Looks like:

Variation(s):

Initialized Variation(s):

Specify if Regional:

Linguistic Register (if specific): FORMAL CONSULTATIVE INFORMAL INTIMATE

Other Vocab/Meanings:

GLOSS(ES)

    (DH) <u>Dominant Handshape</u>:

(NDH) <u>NonDominant Handshape</u>:

    (PO) <u>Palm Orientation</u>:

        <u>Movement</u>:

        <u>Location</u> (if not neutral):

        <u>NMS</u> (if not neutral):

    Looks like:

    Variation(s):

Initialized Variation(s):

  Specify if Regional:

  Linguistic Register (if specific): Formal Consultative Informal Intimate

Other Vocab/Meanings:

GLOSS(ES)

    (DH) <u>Dominant Handshape</u>:

(NDH) <u>NonDominant Handshape</u>:

    (PO) <u>Palm Orientation</u>:

        <u>Movement</u>:

        <u>Location</u> (if not neutral):

        <u>NMS</u> (if not neutral):

    Looks like:

    Variation(s):

Initialized Variation(s):

  Specify if Regional:

  Linguistic Register (if specific): Formal Consultative Informal Intimate

Other Vocab/Meanings:

GLOSS(ES)

    (DH) <u>Dominant Handshape</u>:

(NDH) <u>NonDominant Handshape</u>:

    (PO) <u>Palm Orientation</u>:

        <u>Movement</u>:

        <u>Location</u> (if not neutral):

        <u>NMS</u> (if not neutral):

    Looks like:

    Variation(s):

Initialized Variation(s):

  Specify if Regional:

  Linguistic Register (if specific): Formal Consultative Informal Intimate

Other Vocab/Meanings:

GLOSS(ES)

    (DH) <u>Dominant Handshape</u>:

(NDH) <u>NonDominant Handshape</u>:

    (PO) <u>Palm Orientation</u>:

        <u>Movement</u>:

        <u>Location</u> (if not neutral):

        <u>NMS</u> (if not neutral):

    Looks like:

    Variation(s):

Initialized Variation(s):

  Specify if Regional:

  Linguistic Register (if specific): Formal Consultative Informal Intimate

Other Vocab/Meanings:

GLOSS(ES)

    (DH) <u>Dominant Handshape</u>:

(NDH) <u>NonDominant Handshape</u>:

    (PO) <u>Palm Orientation</u>:

        <u>Movement</u>:

        <u>Location</u> (if not neutral):

        <u>NMS</u> (if not neutral):

    Looks like:

    Variation(s):

Initialized Variation(s):

  Specify if Regional:

  Linguistic Register (if specific): Formal Consultative Informal Intimate

Other Vocab/Meanings:

GLOSS(ES)

    (DH) <u>Dominant Handshape</u>:

(NDH) <u>NonDominant Handshape</u>:

    (PO) <u>Palm Orientation</u>:

        <u>Movement</u>:

        <u>Location</u> (if not neutral):

        <u>NMS</u> (if not neutral):

    Looks like:

    Variation(s):

Initialized Variation(s):

  Specify if Regional:

  Linguistic Register (if specific): Formal Consultative Informal Intimate

Other Vocab/Meanings:

GLOSS(ES)

(DH) <u>Dominant Handshape</u>:

(NDH) <u>NonDominant Handshape</u>:

(PO) <u>Palm Orientation</u>:

<u>Movement</u>:

<u>Location</u> (if not neutral):

<u>NMS</u> (if not neutral):

Looks like:

Variation(s):

Initialized Variation(s):

Specify if Regional:

Linguistic Register (if specific): FORMAL CONSULTATIVE INFORMAL INTIMATE

Other Vocab/Meanings:

GLOSS(ES)

(DH) <u>Dominant Handshape</u>:

(NDH) <u>NonDominant Handshape</u>:

(PO) <u>Palm Orientation</u>:

<u>Movement</u>:

<u>Location</u> (if not neutral):

<u>NMS</u> (if not neutral):

Looks like:

Variation(s):

Initialized Variation(s):

Specify if Regional:

Linguistic Register (if specific): FORMAL CONSULTATIVE INFORMAL INTIMATE

Other Vocab/Meanings:

GLOSS(ES)

(DH) <u>Dominant Handshape</u>:

(NDH) <u>NonDominant Handshape</u>:

(PO) <u>Palm Orientation</u>:

<u>Movement</u>:

<u>Location</u> (if not neutral):

<u>NMS</u> (if not neutral):

Looks like:

Variation(s):

Initialized Variation(s):

Specify if Regional:

Linguistic Register (if specific): FORMAL CONSULTATIVE INFORMAL INTIMATE

Other Vocab/Meanings:

GLOSS(ES)

(DH) <u>Dominant Handshape</u>:

(NDH) <u>NonDominant Handshape</u>:

(PO) <u>Palm Orientation</u>:

<u>Movement</u>:

<u>Location</u> (if not neutral):

<u>NMS</u> (if not neutral):

Looks like:

Variation(s):

Initialized Variation(s):

Specify if Regional:

Linguistic Register (if specific): FORMAL CONSULTATIVE INFORMAL INTIMATE

Other Vocab/Meanings:

GLOSS(ES)

(DH) <u>Dominant Handshape</u>:

(NDH) <u>NonDominant Handshape</u>:

(PO) <u>Palm Orientation</u>:

<u>Movement</u>:

<u>Location</u> (if not neutral):

<u>NMS</u> (if not neutral):

Looks like:

Variation(s):

Initialized Variation(s):

Specify if Regional:

Linguistic Register (if specific): FORMAL CONSULTATIVE INFORMAL INTIMATE

Other Vocab/Meanings:

GLOSS(ES)

(DH) <u>Dominant Handshape</u>:

(NDH) <u>NonDominant Handshape</u>:

(PO) <u>Palm Orientation</u>:

<u>Movement</u>:

<u>Location</u> (if not neutral):

<u>NMS</u> (if not neutral):

Looks like:

Variation(s):

Initialized Variation(s):

Specify if Regional:

Linguistic Register (if specific): FORMAL CONSULTATIVE INFORMAL INTIMATE

Other Vocab/Meanings:

GLOSS(ES)

(DH) <u>Dominant Handshape</u>:

(NDH) <u>NonDominant Handshape</u>:

  (PO) <u>Palm Orientation</u>:

    <u>Movement</u>:

    <u>Location</u> (if not neutral):

    <u>NMS</u> (if not neutral):

  Looks like:

  Variation(s):

Initialized Variation(s):

  Specify if Regional:

  Linguistic Register (if specific): FORMAL CONSULTATIVE INFORMAL INTIMATE

Other Vocab/Meanings:

GLOSS(ES)

(DH) <u>Dominant Handshape</u>:

(NDH) <u>NonDominant Handshape</u>:

  (PO) <u>Palm Orientation</u>:

    <u>Movement</u>:

    <u>Location</u> (if not neutral):

    <u>NMS</u> (if not neutral):

  Looks like:

  Variation(s):

Initialized Variation(s):

  Specify if Regional:

  Linguistic Register (if specific): FORMAL CONSULTATIVE INFORMAL INTIMATE

Other Vocab/Meanings:

GLOSS(ES)

(DH) <u>Dominant Handshape</u>:

(NDH) <u>NonDominant Handshape</u>:

  (PO) <u>Palm Orientation</u>:

    <u>Movement</u>:

    <u>Location</u> (if not neutral):

    <u>NMS</u> (if not neutral):

  Looks like:

  Variation(s):

Initialized Variation(s):

  Specify if Regional:

  Linguistic Register (if specific): FORMAL CONSULTATIVE INFORMAL INTIMATE

Other Vocab/Meanings:

GLOSS(ES)

(DH) <u>Dominant Handshape</u>:

(NDH) <u>NonDominant Handshape</u>:

  (PO) <u>Palm Orientation</u>:

    <u>Movement</u>:

    <u>Location</u> (if not neutral):

    <u>NMS</u> (if not neutral):

  Looks like:

  Variation(s):

Initialized Variation(s):

  Specify if Regional:

  Linguistic Register (if specific): FORMAL CONSULTATIVE INFORMAL INTIMATE

Other Vocab/Meanings:

GLOSS(ES)

(DH) <u>Dominant Handshape</u>:

(NDH) <u>NonDominant Handshape</u>:

  (PO) <u>Palm Orientation</u>:

    <u>Movement</u>:

    <u>Location</u> (if not neutral):

    <u>NMS</u> (if not neutral):

  Looks like:

  Variation(s):

Initialized Variation(s):

  Specify if Regional:

  Linguistic Register (if specific): FORMAL CONSULTATIVE INFORMAL INTIMATE

Other Vocab/Meanings:

GLOSS(ES)

(DH) <u>Dominant Handshape</u>:

(NDH) <u>NonDominant Handshape</u>:

  (PO) <u>Palm Orientation</u>:

    <u>Movement</u>:

    <u>Location</u> (if not neutral):

    <u>NMS</u> (if not neutral):

  Looks like:

  Variation(s):

Initialized Variation(s):

  Specify if Regional:

  Linguistic Register (if specific): FORMAL CONSULTATIVE INFORMAL INTIMATE

Other Vocab/Meanings:

GLOSS(ES)

(DH) <u>Dominant Handshape</u>:

(NDH) <u>NonDominant Handshape:</u>

(PO) <u>Palm Orientation</u>:

<u>Movement</u>:

<u>Location</u> (if not neutral):

<u>NMS</u> (if not neutral):

Looks like:

Variation(s):

Initialized Variation(s):

Specify if Regional:

Linguistic Register (if specific): FORMAL CONSULTATIVE INFORMAL INTIMATE

Other Vocab/Meanings:

GLOSS(ES)

(DH) <u>Dominant Handshape</u>:

(NDH) <u>NonDominant Handshape:</u>

(PO) <u>Palm Orientation</u>:

<u>Movement</u>:

<u>Location</u> (if not neutral):

<u>NMS</u> (if not neutral):

Looks like:

Variation(s):

Initialized Variation(s):

Specify if Regional:

Linguistic Register (if specific): FORMAL CONSULTATIVE INFORMAL INTIMATE

Other Vocab/Meanings:

GLOSS(ES)

(DH) <u>Dominant Handshape</u>:

(NDH) <u>NonDominant Handshape:</u>

(PO) <u>Palm Orientation</u>:

<u>Movement</u>:

<u>Location</u> (if not neutral):

<u>NMS</u> (if not neutral):

Looks like:

Variation(s):

Initialized Variation(s):

Specify if Regional:

Linguistic Register (if specific): FORMAL CONSULTATIVE INFORMAL INTIMATE

Other Vocab/Meanings:

GLOSS(ES)

(DH) <u>Dominant Handshape</u>:

(NDH) <u>NonDominant Handshape:</u>

(PO) <u>Palm Orientation</u>:

<u>Movement</u>:

<u>Location</u> (if not neutral):

<u>NMS</u> (if not neutral):

Looks like:

Variation(s):

Initialized Variation(s):

Specify if Regional:

Linguistic Register (if specific): FORMAL CONSULTATIVE INFORMAL INTIMATE

Other Vocab/Meanings:

GLOSS(ES)

(DH) <u>Dominant Handshape</u>:

(NDH) <u>NonDominant Handshape:</u>

(PO) <u>Palm Orientation</u>:

<u>Movement</u>:

<u>Location</u> (if not neutral):

<u>NMS</u> (if not neutral):

Looks like:

Variation(s):

Initialized Variation(s):

Specify if Regional:

Linguistic Register (if specific): FORMAL CONSULTATIVE INFORMAL INTIMATE

Other Vocab/Meanings:

GLOSS(ES)

(DH) <u>Dominant Handshape</u>:

(NDH) <u>NonDominant Handshape:</u>

(PO) <u>Palm Orientation</u>:

<u>Movement</u>:

<u>Location</u> (if not neutral):

<u>NMS</u> (if not neutral):

Looks like:

Variation(s):

Initialized Variation(s):

Specify if Regional:

Linguistic Register (if specific): FORMAL CONSULTATIVE INFORMAL INTIMATE

Other Vocab/Meanings:

GLOSS(ES)

(DH) Dominant Handshape:

(NDH) NonDominant Handshape:

(PO) Palm Orientation:

Movement:

Location (if not neutral):

NMS (if not neutral):

Looks like:

Variation(s):

Initialized Variation(s):

Specify if Regional:

Linguistic Register (if specific): FORMAL CONSULTATIVE INFORMAL INTIMATE

Other Vocab/Meanings:

GLOSS(ES)

(DH) Dominant Handshape:

(NDH) NonDominant Handshape:

(PO) Palm Orientation:

Movement:

Location (if not neutral):

NMS (if not neutral):

Looks like:

Variation(s):

Initialized Variation(s):

Specify if Regional:

Linguistic Register (if specific): FORMAL CONSULTATIVE INFORMAL INTIMATE

Other Vocab/Meanings:

GLOSS(ES)

(DH) Dominant Handshape:

(NDH) NonDominant Handshape:

(PO) Palm Orientation:

Movement:

Location (if not neutral):

NMS (if not neutral):

Looks like:

Variation(s):

Initialized Variation(s):

Specify if Regional:

Linguistic Register (if specific): FORMAL CONSULTATIVE INFORMAL INTIMATE

Other Vocab/Meanings:

GLOSS(ES)

(DH) Dominant Handshape:

(NDH) NonDominant Handshape:

(PO) Palm Orientation:

Movement:

Location (if not neutral):

NMS (if not neutral):

Looks like:

Variation(s):

Initialized Variation(s):

Specify if Regional:

Linguistic Register (if specific): FORMAL CONSULTATIVE INFORMAL INTIMATE

Other Vocab/Meanings:

GLOSS(ES)

(DH) Dominant Handshape:

(NDH) NonDominant Handshape:

(PO) Palm Orientation:

Movement:

Location (if not neutral):

NMS (if not neutral):

Looks like:

Variation(s):

Initialized Variation(s):

Specify if Regional:

Linguistic Register (if specific): FORMAL CONSULTATIVE INFORMAL INTIMATE

Other Vocab/Meanings:

GLOSS(ES)

(DH) Dominant Handshape:

(NDH) NonDominant Handshape:

(PO) Palm Orientation:

Movement:

Location (if not neutral):

NMS (if not neutral):

Looks like:

Variation(s):

Initialized Variation(s):

Specify if Regional:

Linguistic Register (if specific): FORMAL CONSULTATIVE INFORMAL INTIMATE

Other Vocab/Meanings:

GLOSS(ES)

(DH) <u>Dominant Handshape</u>:

(NDH) <u>NonDominant Handshape</u>:

(PO) <u>Palm Orientation</u>:

<u>Movement</u>:

<u>Location</u> (if not neutral):

<u>NMS</u> (if not neutral):

Looks like:

Variation(s):

Initialized Variation(s):

Specify if Regional:

Linguistic Register (if specific): FORMAL CONSULTATIVE INFORMAL INTIMATE

Other Vocab/Meanings:

GLOSS(ES)

(DH) <u>Dominant Handshape</u>:

(NDH) <u>NonDominant Handshape</u>:

(PO) <u>Palm Orientation</u>:

<u>Movement</u>:

<u>Location</u> (if not neutral):

<u>NMS</u> (if not neutral):

Looks like:

Variation(s):

Initialized Variation(s):

Specify if Regional:

Linguistic Register (if specific): FORMAL CONSULTATIVE INFORMAL INTIMATE

Other Vocab/Meanings:

GLOSS(ES)

(DH) <u>Dominant Handshape</u>:

(NDH) <u>NonDominant Handshape</u>:

(PO) <u>Palm Orientation</u>:

<u>Movement</u>:

<u>Location</u> (if not neutral):

<u>NMS</u> (if not neutral):

Looks like:

Variation(s):

Initialized Variation(s):

Specify if Regional:

Linguistic Register (if specific): FORMAL CONSULTATIVE INFORMAL INTIMATE

Other Vocab/Meanings:

GLOSS(ES)

(DH) <u>Dominant Handshape</u>:

(NDH) <u>NonDominant Handshape</u>:

(PO) <u>Palm Orientation</u>:

<u>Movement</u>:

<u>Location</u> (if not neutral):

<u>NMS</u> (if not neutral):

Looks like:

Variation(s):

Initialized Variation(s):

Specify if Regional:

Linguistic Register (if specific): FORMAL CONSULTATIVE INFORMAL INTIMATE

Other Vocab/Meanings:

GLOSS(ES)

(DH) <u>Dominant Handshape</u>:

(NDH) <u>NonDominant Handshape</u>:

(PO) <u>Palm Orientation</u>:

<u>Movement</u>:

<u>Location</u> (if not neutral):

<u>NMS</u> (if not neutral):

Looks like:

Variation(s):

Initialized Variation(s):

Specify if Regional:

Linguistic Register (if specific): FORMAL CONSULTATIVE INFORMAL INTIMATE

Other Vocab/Meanings:

GLOSS(ES)

(DH) <u>Dominant Handshape</u>:

(NDH) <u>NonDominant Handshape</u>:

(PO) <u>Palm Orientation</u>:

<u>Movement</u>:

<u>Location</u> (if not neutral):

<u>NMS</u> (if not neutral):

Looks like:

Variation(s):

Initialized Variation(s):

Specify if Regional:

Linguistic Register (if specific): FORMAL CONSULTATIVE INFORMAL INTIMATE

Other Vocab/Meanings:

GLOSS(ES)

(DH) <u>Dominant Handshape</u>:

(NDH) <u>NonDominant Handshape</u>:

(PO) <u>Palm Orientation</u>:

<u>Movement</u>:

<u>Location</u> (if not neutral):

<u>NMS</u> (if not neutral):

Looks like:

Variation(s):

Initialized Variation(s):

Specify if Regional:

Linguistic Register (if specific): FORMAL CONSULTATIVE INFORMAL INTIMATE

Other Vocab/Meanings:

GLOSS(ES)

(DH) <u>Dominant Handshape</u>:

(NDH) <u>NonDominant Handshape</u>:

(PO) <u>Palm Orientation</u>:

<u>Movement</u>:

<u>Location</u> (if not neutral):

<u>NMS</u> (if not neutral):

Looks like:

Variation(s):

Initialized Variation(s):

Specify if Regional:

Linguistic Register (if specific): FORMAL CONSULTATIVE INFORMAL INTIMATE

Other Vocab/Meanings:

GLOSS(ES)

(DH) <u>Dominant Handshape</u>:

(NDH) <u>NonDominant Handshape</u>:

(PO) <u>Palm Orientation</u>:

<u>Movement</u>:

<u>Location</u> (if not neutral):

<u>NMS</u> (if not neutral):

Looks like:

Variation(s):

Initialized Variation(s):

Specify if Regional:

Linguistic Register (if specific): FORMAL CONSULTATIVE INFORMAL INTIMATE

Other Vocab/Meanings:

GLOSS(ES)

(DH) <u>Dominant Handshape</u>:

(NDH) <u>NonDominant Handshape</u>:

(PO) <u>Palm Orientation</u>:

<u>Movement</u>:

<u>Location</u> (if not neutral):

<u>NMS</u> (if not neutral):

Looks like:

Variation(s):

Initialized Variation(s):

Specify if Regional:

Linguistic Register (if specific): FORMAL CONSULTATIVE INFORMAL INTIMATE

Other Vocab/Meanings:

GLOSS(ES)

(DH) <u>Dominant Handshape</u>:

(NDH) <u>NonDominant Handshape</u>:

(PO) <u>Palm Orientation</u>:

<u>Movement</u>:

<u>Location</u> (if not neutral):

<u>NMS</u> (if not neutral):

Looks like:

Variation(s):

Initialized Variation(s):

Specify if Regional:

Linguistic Register (if specific): FORMAL CONSULTATIVE INFORMAL INTIMATE

Other Vocab/Meanings:

GLOSS(ES)

(DH) <u>Dominant Handshape</u>:

(NDH) <u>NonDominant Handshape</u>:

(PO) <u>Palm Orientation</u>:

<u>Movement</u>:

<u>Location</u> (if not neutral):

<u>NMS</u> (if not neutral):

Looks like:

Variation(s):

Initialized Variation(s):

Specify if Regional:

Linguistic Register (if specific): FORMAL CONSULTATIVE INFORMAL INTIMATE

Other Vocab/Meanings:

GLOSS(ES)

(DH) Dominant Handshape:

(NDH) NonDominant Handshape:

(PO) Palm Orientation:

Movement:

Location (if not neutral):

NMS (if not neutral):

Looks like:

Variation(s):

Initialized Variation(s):

Specify if Regional:

Linguistic Register (if specific): FORMAL   CONSULTATIVE   INFORMAL   INTIMATE

Other Vocab/Meanings:

GLOSS(ES)

(DH) Dominant Handshape:

(NDH) NonDominant Handshape:

(PO) Palm Orientation:

Movement:

Location (if not neutral):

NMS (if not neutral):

Looks like:

Variation(s):

Initialized Variation(s):

Specify if Regional:

Linguistic Register (if specific): FORMAL   CONSULTATIVE   INFORMAL   INTIMATE

Other Vocab/Meanings:

GLOSS(ES)

(DH) Dominant Handshape:

(NDH) NonDominant Handshape:

(PO) Palm Orientation:

Movement:

Location (if not neutral):

NMS (if not neutral):

Looks like:

Variation(s):

Initialized Variation(s):

Specify if Regional:

Linguistic Register (if specific): FORMAL   CONSULTATIVE   INFORMAL   INTIMATE

Other Vocab/Meanings:

GLOSS(ES)

(DH) Dominant Handshape:

(NDH) NonDominant Handshape:

(PO) Palm Orientation:

Movement:

Location (if not neutral):

NMS (if not neutral):

Looks like:

Variation(s):

Initialized Variation(s):

Specify if Regional:

Linguistic Register (if specific): FORMAL   CONSULTATIVE   INFORMAL   INTIMATE

Other Vocab/Meanings:

GLOSS(ES)

(DH) Dominant Handshape:

(NDH) NonDominant Handshape:

(PO) Palm Orientation:

Movement:

Location (if not neutral):

NMS (if not neutral):

Looks like:

Variation(s):

Initialized Variation(s):

Specify if Regional:

Linguistic Register (if specific): FORMAL   CONSULTATIVE   INFORMAL   INTIMATE

Other Vocab/Meanings:

GLOSS(ES)

(DH) Dominant Handshape:

(NDH) NonDominant Handshape:

(PO) Palm Orientation:

Movement:

Location (if not neutral):

NMS (if not neutral):

Looks like:

Variation(s):

Initialized Variation(s):

Specify if Regional:

Linguistic Register (if specific): FORMAL   CONSULTATIVE   INFORMAL   INTIMATE

Other Vocab/Meanings:

GLOSS(ES)

(DH) Dominant Handshape:

(NDH) NonDominant Handshape:

(PO) Palm Orientation:

Movement:

Location (if not neutral):

NMS (if not neutral):

Looks like:

Variation(s):

Initialized Variation(s):

Specify if Regional:

Linguistic Register (if specific): FORMAL CONSULTATIVE INFORMAL INTIMATE

Other Vocab/Meanings:

GLOSS(ES)

(DH) Dominant Handshape:

(NDH) NonDominant Handshape:

(PO) Palm Orientation:

Movement:

Location (if not neutral):

NMS (if not neutral):

Looks like:

Variation(s):

Initialized Variation(s):

Specify if Regional:

Linguistic Register (if specific): FORMAL CONSULTATIVE INFORMAL INTIMATE

Other Vocab/Meanings:

GLOSS(ES)

(DH) Dominant Handshape:

(NDH) NonDominant Handshape:

(PO) Palm Orientation:

Movement:

Location (if not neutral):

NMS (if not neutral):

Looks like:

Variation(s):

Initialized Variation(s):

Specify if Regional:

Linguistic Register (if specific): FORMAL CONSULTATIVE INFORMAL INTIMATE

Other Vocab/Meanings:

GLOSS(ES)

(DH) Dominant Handshape:

(NDH) NonDominant Handshape:

(PO) Palm Orientation:

Movement:

Location (if not neutral):

NMS (if not neutral):

Looks like:

Variation(s):

Initialized Variation(s):

Specify if Regional:

Linguistic Register (if specific): FORMAL CONSULTATIVE INFORMAL INTIMATE

Other Vocab/Meanings:

GLOSS(ES)

(DH) Dominant Handshape:

(NDH) NonDominant Handshape:

(PO) Palm Orientation:

Movement:

Location (if not neutral):

NMS (if not neutral):

Looks like:

Variation(s):

Initialized Variation(s):

Specify if Regional:

Linguistic Register (if specific): FORMAL CONSULTATIVE INFORMAL INTIMATE

Other Vocab/Meanings:

GLOSS(ES)

(DH) Dominant Handshape:

(NDH) NonDominant Handshape:

(PO) Palm Orientation:

Movement:

Location (if not neutral):

NMS (if not neutral):

Looks like:

Variation(s):

Initialized Variation(s):

Specify if Regional:

Linguistic Register (if specific): FORMAL CONSULTATIVE INFORMAL INTIMATE

Other Vocab/Meanings:

GLOSS(ES)

(DH) <u>Dominant Handshape</u>:

(NDH) <u>NonDominant Handshape</u>:

(PO) <u>Palm Orientation</u>:

<u>Movement</u>:

<u>Location</u> (if not neutral):

<u>NMS</u> (if not neutral):

Looks like:

Variation(s):

Initialized Variation(s):

Specify if Regional:

Linguistic Register (if specific): FORMAL   CONSULTATIVE   INFORMAL   INTIMATE

Other Vocab/Meanings:

GLOSS(ES)

(DH) <u>Dominant Handshape</u>:

(NDH) <u>NonDominant Handshape</u>:

(PO) <u>Palm Orientation</u>:

<u>Movement</u>:

<u>Location</u> (if not neutral):

<u>NMS</u> (if not neutral):

Looks like:

Variation(s):

Initialized Variation(s):

Specify if Regional:

Linguistic Register (if specific): FORMAL   CONSULTATIVE   INFORMAL   INTIMATE

Other Vocab/Meanings:

GLOSS(ES)

(DH) <u>Dominant Handshape</u>:

(NDH) <u>NonDominant Handshape</u>:

(PO) <u>Palm Orientation</u>:

<u>Movement</u>:

<u>Location</u> (if not neutral):

<u>NMS</u> (if not neutral):

Looks like:

Variation(s):

Initialized Variation(s):

Specify if Regional:

Linguistic Register (if specific): FORMAL   CONSULTATIVE   INFORMAL   INTIMATE

Other Vocab/Meanings:

GLOSS(ES)

(DH) <u>Dominant Handshape</u>:

(NDH) <u>NonDominant Handshape</u>:

(PO) <u>Palm Orientation</u>:

<u>Movement</u>:

<u>Location</u> (if not neutral):

<u>NMS</u> (if not neutral):

Looks like:

Variation(s):

Initialized Variation(s):

Specify if Regional:

Linguistic Register (if specific): FORMAL   CONSULTATIVE   INFORMAL   INTIMATE

Other Vocab/Meanings:

GLOSS(ES)

(DH) <u>Dominant Handshape</u>:

(NDH) <u>NonDominant Handshape</u>:

(PO) <u>Palm Orientation</u>:

<u>Movement</u>:

<u>Location</u> (if not neutral):

<u>NMS</u> (if not neutral):

Looks like:

Variation(s):

Initialized Variation(s):

Specify if Regional:

Linguistic Register (if specific): FORMAL   CONSULTATIVE   INFORMAL   INTIMATE

Other Vocab/Meanings:

GLOSS(ES)

(DH) <u>Dominant Handshape</u>:

(NDH) <u>NonDominant Handshape</u>:

(PO) <u>Palm Orientation</u>:

<u>Movement</u>:

<u>Location</u> (if not neutral):

<u>NMS</u> (if not neutral):

Looks like:

Variation(s):

Initialized Variation(s):

Specify if Regional:

Linguistic Register (if specific): FORMAL   CONSULTATIVE   INFORMAL   INTIMATE

Other Vocab/Meanings:

GLOSS(ES)

(DH) <u>Dominant Handshape</u>:

(NDH) <u>NonDominant Handshape</u>:

(PO) <u>Palm Orientation</u>:

<u>Movement</u>:

<u>Location</u> (if not neutral):

<u>NMS</u> (if not neutral):

Looks like:

Variation(s):

Initialized Variation(s):

Specify if Regional:

Linguistic Register (if specific): FORMAL CONSULTATIVE INFORMAL INTIMATE

Other Vocab/Meanings:

GLOSS(ES)

(DH) <u>Dominant Handshape</u>:

(NDH) <u>NonDominant Handshape</u>:

(PO) <u>Palm Orientation</u>:

<u>Movement</u>:

<u>Location</u> (if not neutral):

<u>NMS</u> (if not neutral):

Looks like:

Variation(s):

Initialized Variation(s):

Specify if Regional:

Linguistic Register (if specific): FORMAL CONSULTATIVE INFORMAL INTIMATE

Other Vocab/Meanings:

GLOSS(ES)

(DH) <u>Dominant Handshape</u>:

(NDH) <u>NonDominant Handshape</u>:

(PO) <u>Palm Orientation</u>:

<u>Movement</u>:

<u>Location</u> (if not neutral):

<u>NMS</u> (if not neutral):

Looks like:

Variation(s):

Initialized Variation(s):

Specify if Regional:

Linguistic Register (if specific): FORMAL CONSULTATIVE INFORMAL INTIMATE

Other Vocab/Meanings:

GLOSS(ES)

(DH) <u>Dominant Handshape</u>:

(NDH) <u>NonDominant Handshape</u>:

(PO) <u>Palm Orientation</u>:

<u>Movement</u>:

<u>Location</u> (if not neutral):

<u>NMS</u> (if not neutral):

Looks like:

Variation(s):

Initialized Variation(s):

Specify if Regional:

Linguistic Register (if specific): FORMAL CONSULTATIVE INFORMAL INTIMATE

Other Vocab/Meanings:

GLOSS(ES)

(DH) <u>Dominant Handshape</u>:

(NDH) <u>NonDominant Handshape</u>:

(PO) <u>Palm Orientation</u>:

<u>Movement</u>:

<u>Location</u> (if not neutral):

<u>NMS</u> (if not neutral):

Looks like:

Variation(s):

Initialized Variation(s):

Specify if Regional:

Linguistic Register (if specific): FORMAL CONSULTATIVE INFORMAL INTIMATE

Other Vocab/Meanings:

GLOSS(ES)

(DH) <u>Dominant Handshape</u>:

(NDH) <u>NonDominant Handshape</u>:

(PO) <u>Palm Orientation</u>:

<u>Movement</u>:

<u>Location</u> (if not neutral):

<u>NMS</u> (if not neutral):

Looks like:

Variation(s):

Initialized Variation(s):

Specify if Regional:

Linguistic Register (if specific): FORMAL CONSULTATIVE INFORMAL INTIMATE

Other Vocab/Meanings:

GLOSS(ES)

(DH) Dominant Handshape:

(NDH) NonDominant Handshape:

(PO) Palm Orientation:

Movement:

Location (if not neutral):

NMS (if not neutral):

Looks like:

Variation(s):

Initialized Variation(s):

Specify if Regional:

Linguistic Register (if specific): FORMAL   CONSULTATIVE   INFORMAL   INTIMATE

Other Vocab/Meanings:

GLOSS(ES)

(DH) Dominant Handshape:

(NDH) NonDominant Handshape:

(PO) Palm Orientation:

Movement:

Location (if not neutral):

NMS (if not neutral):

Looks like:

Variation(s):

Initialized Variation(s):

Specify if Regional:

Linguistic Register (if specific): FORMAL   CONSULTATIVE   INFORMAL   INTIMATE

Other Vocab/Meanings:

GLOSS(ES)

(DH) Dominant Handshape:

(NDH) NonDominant Handshape:

(PO) Palm Orientation:

Movement:

Location (if not neutral):

NMS (if not neutral):

Looks like:

Variation(s):

Initialized Variation(s):

Specify if Regional:

Linguistic Register (if specific): FORMAL   CONSULTATIVE   INFORMAL   INTIMATE

Other Vocab/Meanings:

GLOSS(ES)

(DH) Dominant Handshape:

(NDH) NonDominant Handshape:

(PO) Palm Orientation:

Movement:

Location (if not neutral):

NMS (if not neutral):

Looks like:

Variation(s):

Initialized Variation(s):

Specify if Regional:

Linguistic Register (if specific): FORMAL   CONSULTATIVE   INFORMAL   INTIMATE

Other Vocab/Meanings:

GLOSS(ES)

(DH) Dominant Handshape:

(NDH) NonDominant Handshape:

(PO) Palm Orientation:

Movement:

Location (if not neutral):

NMS (if not neutral):

Looks like:

Variation(s):

Initialized Variation(s):

Specify if Regional:

Linguistic Register (if specific): FORMAL   CONSULTATIVE   INFORMAL   INTIMATE

Other Vocab/Meanings:

GLOSS(ES)

(DH) Dominant Handshape:

(NDH) NonDominant Handshape:

(PO) Palm Orientation:

Movement:

Location (if not neutral):

NMS (if not neutral):

Looks like:

Variation(s):

Initialized Variation(s):

Specify if Regional:

Linguistic Register (if specific): FORMAL   CONSULTATIVE   INFORMAL   INTIMATE

Other Vocab/Meanings:

GLOSS(ES)

(DH) Dominant Handshape:

(NDH) NonDominant Handshape:

(PO) Palm Orientation:

Movement:

Location (if not neutral):

NMS (if not neutral):

Looks like:

Variation(s):

Initialized Variation(s):

Specify if Regional:

Linguistic Register (if specific): FORMAL CONSULTATIVE INFORMAL INTIMATE

Other Vocab/Meanings:

GLOSS(ES)

(DH) Dominant Handshape:

(NDH) NonDominant Handshape:

(PO) Palm Orientation:

Movement:

Location (if not neutral):

NMS (if not neutral):

Looks like:

Variation(s):

Initialized Variation(s):

Specify if Regional:

Linguistic Register (if specific): FORMAL CONSULTATIVE INFORMAL INTIMATE

Other Vocab/Meanings:

GLOSS(ES)

(DH) Dominant Handshape:

(NDH) NonDominant Handshape:

(PO) Palm Orientation:

Movement:

Location (if not neutral):

NMS (if not neutral):

Looks like:

Variation(s):

Initialized Variation(s):

Specify if Regional:

Linguistic Register (if specific): FORMAL CONSULTATIVE INFORMAL INTIMATE

Other Vocab/Meanings:

GLOSS(ES)

(DH) Dominant Handshape:

(NDH) NonDominant Handshape:

(PO) Palm Orientation:

Movement:

Location (if not neutral):

NMS (if not neutral):

Looks like:

Variation(s):

Initialized Variation(s):

Specify if Regional:

Linguistic Register (if specific): FORMAL CONSULTATIVE INFORMAL INTIMATE

Other Vocab/Meanings:

GLOSS(ES)

(DH) Dominant Handshape:

(NDH) NonDominant Handshape:

(PO) Palm Orientation:

Movement:

Location (if not neutral):

NMS (if not neutral):

Looks like:

Variation(s):

Initialized Variation(s):

Specify if Regional:

Linguistic Register (if specific): FORMAL CONSULTATIVE INFORMAL INTIMATE

Other Vocab/Meanings:

GLOSS(ES)

(DH) Dominant Handshape:

(NDH) NonDominant Handshape:

(PO) Palm Orientation:

Movement:

Location (if not neutral):

NMS (if not neutral):

Looks like:

Variation(s):

Initialized Variation(s):

Specify if Regional:

Linguistic Register (if specific): FORMAL CONSULTATIVE INFORMAL INTIMATE

Other Vocab/Meanings:

GLOSS(ES)

(DH) <u>Dominant Handshape</u>:

(NDH) <u>NonDominant Handshape</u>:

(PO) <u>Palm Orientation</u>:

<u>Movement</u>:

<u>Location</u> (if not neutral):

<u>NMS</u> (if not neutral):

Looks like:

Variation(s):

Initialized Variation(s):

Specify if Regional:

Linguistic Register (if specific): FORMAL   CONSULTATIVE   INFORMAL   INTIMATE

Other Vocab/Meanings:

GLOSS(ES)

(DH) <u>Dominant Handshape</u>:

(NDH) <u>NonDominant Handshape</u>:

(PO) <u>Palm Orientation</u>:

<u>Movement</u>:

<u>Location</u> (if not neutral):

<u>NMS</u> (if not neutral):

Looks like:

Variation(s):

Initialized Variation(s):

Specify if Regional:

Linguistic Register (if specific): FORMAL   CONSULTATIVE   INFORMAL   INTIMATE

Other Vocab/Meanings:

GLOSS(ES)

(DH) <u>Dominant Handshape</u>:

(NDH) <u>NonDominant Handshape</u>:

(PO) <u>Palm Orientation</u>:

<u>Movement</u>:

<u>Location</u> (if not neutral):

<u>NMS</u> (if not neutral):

Looks like:

Variation(s):

Initialized Variation(s):

Specify if Regional:

Linguistic Register (if specific): FORMAL   CONSULTATIVE   INFORMAL   INTIMATE

Other Vocab/Meanings:

GLOSS(ES)

(DH) <u>Dominant Handshape</u>:

(NDH) <u>NonDominant Handshape</u>:

(PO) <u>Palm Orientation</u>:

<u>Movement</u>:

<u>Location</u> (if not neutral):

<u>NMS</u> (if not neutral):

Looks like:

Variation(s):

Initialized Variation(s):

Specify if Regional:

Linguistic Register (if specific): FORMAL   CONSULTATIVE   INFORMAL   INTIMATE

Other Vocab/Meanings:

GLOSS(ES)

(DH) <u>Dominant Handshape</u>:

(NDH) <u>NonDominant Handshape</u>:

(PO) <u>Palm Orientation</u>:

<u>Movement</u>:

<u>Location</u> (if not neutral):

<u>NMS</u> (if not neutral):

Looks like:

Variation(s):

Initialized Variation(s):

Specify if Regional:

Linguistic Register (if specific): FORMAL   CONSULTATIVE   INFORMAL   INTIMATE

Other Vocab/Meanings:

GLOSS(ES)

(DH) <u>Dominant Handshape</u>:

(NDH) <u>NonDominant Handshape</u>:

(PO) <u>Palm Orientation</u>:

<u>Movement</u>:

<u>Location</u> (if not neutral):

<u>NMS</u> (if not neutral):

Looks like:

Variation(s):

Initialized Variation(s):

Specify if Regional:

Linguistic Register (if specific): FORMAL   CONSULTATIVE   INFORMAL   INTIMATE

Other Vocab/Meanings:

GLOSS(ES)

(DH) Dominant Handshape:

(NDH) NonDominant Handshape:

(PO) Palm Orientation:

Movement:

Location (if not neutral):

NMS (if not neutral):

Looks like:

Variation(s):

Initialized Variation(s):

Specify if Regional:

Linguistic Register (if specific): FORMAL CONSULTATIVE INFORMAL INTIMATE

Other Vocab/Meanings:

GLOSS(ES)

(DH) Dominant Handshape:

(NDH) NonDominant Handshape:

(PO) Palm Orientation:

Movement:

Location (if not neutral):

NMS (if not neutral):

Looks like:

Variation(s):

Initialized Variation(s):

Specify if Regional:

Linguistic Register (if specific): FORMAL CONSULTATIVE INFORMAL INTIMATE

Other Vocab/Meanings:

GLOSS(ES)

(DH) Dominant Handshape:

(NDH) NonDominant Handshape:

(PO) Palm Orientation:

Movement:

Location (if not neutral):

NMS (if not neutral):

Looks like:

Variation(s):

Initialized Variation(s):

Specify if Regional:

Linguistic Register (if specific): FORMAL CONSULTATIVE INFORMAL INTIMATE

Other Vocab/Meanings:

GLOSS(ES)

(DH) Dominant Handshape:

(NDH) NonDominant Handshape:

(PO) Palm Orientation:

Movement:

Location (if not neutral):

NMS (if not neutral):

Looks like:

Variation(s):

Initialized Variation(s):

Specify if Regional:

Linguistic Register (if specific): FORMAL CONSULTATIVE INFORMAL INTIMATE

Other Vocab/Meanings:

GLOSS(ES)

(DH) Dominant Handshape:

(NDH) NonDominant Handshape:

(PO) Palm Orientation:

Movement:

Location (if not neutral):

NMS (if not neutral):

Looks like:

Variation(s):

Initialized Variation(s):

Specify if Regional:

Linguistic Register (if specific): FORMAL CONSULTATIVE INFORMAL INTIMATE

Other Vocab/Meanings:

GLOSS(ES)

(DH) Dominant Handshape:

(NDH) NonDominant Handshape:

(PO) Palm Orientation:

Movement:

Location (if not neutral):

NMS (if not neutral):

Looks like:

Variation(s):

Initialized Variation(s):

Specify if Regional:

Linguistic Register (if specific): FORMAL CONSULTATIVE INFORMAL INTIMATE

Other Vocab/Meanings:

GLOSS(ES)

(DH) <u>Dominant Handshape</u>:

(NDH) <u>NonDominant Handshape</u>:

(PO) <u>Palm Orientation</u>:

<u>Movement</u>:

<u>Location</u> (if not neutral):

<u>NMS</u> (if not neutral):

Looks like:

Variation(s):

Initialized Variation(s):

Specify if Regional:

Linguistic Register (if specific): FORMAL CONSULTATIVE INFORMAL INTIMATE

Other Vocab/Meanings:

GLOSS(ES)

(DH) <u>Dominant Handshape</u>:

(NDH) <u>NonDominant Handshape</u>:

(PO) <u>Palm Orientation</u>:

<u>Movement</u>:

<u>Location</u> (if not neutral):

<u>NMS</u> (if not neutral):

Looks like:

Variation(s):

Initialized Variation(s):

Specify if Regional:

Linguistic Register (if specific): FORMAL CONSULTATIVE INFORMAL INTIMATE

Other Vocab/Meanings:

GLOSS(ES)

(DH) <u>Dominant Handshape</u>:

(NDH) <u>NonDominant Handshape</u>:

(PO) <u>Palm Orientation</u>:

<u>Movement</u>:

<u>Location</u> (if not neutral):

<u>NMS</u> (if not neutral):

Looks like:

Variation(s):

Initialized Variation(s):

Specify if Regional:

Linguistic Register (if specific): FORMAL CONSULTATIVE INFORMAL INTIMATE

Other Vocab/Meanings:

GLOSS(ES)

(DH) <u>Dominant Handshape</u>:

(NDH) <u>NonDominant Handshape</u>:

(PO) <u>Palm Orientation</u>:

<u>Movement</u>:

<u>Location</u> (if not neutral):

<u>NMS</u> (if not neutral):

Looks like:

Variation(s):

Initialized Variation(s):

Specify if Regional:

Linguistic Register (if specific): FORMAL CONSULTATIVE INFORMAL INTIMATE

Other Vocab/Meanings:

GLOSS(ES)

(DH) <u>Dominant Handshape</u>:

(NDH) <u>NonDominant Handshape</u>:

(PO) <u>Palm Orientation</u>:

<u>Movement</u>:

<u>Location</u> (if not neutral):

<u>NMS</u> (if not neutral):

Looks like:

Variation(s):

Initialized Variation(s):

Specify if Regional:

Linguistic Register (if specific): FORMAL CONSULTATIVE INFORMAL INTIMATE

Other Vocab/Meanings:

GLOSS(ES)

(DH) <u>Dominant Handshape</u>:

(NDH) <u>NonDominant Handshape</u>:

(PO) <u>Palm Orientation</u>:

<u>Movement</u>:

<u>Location</u> (if not neutral):

<u>NMS</u> (if not neutral):

Looks like:

Variation(s):

Initialized Variation(s):

Specify if Regional:

Linguistic Register (if specific): FORMAL CONSULTATIVE INFORMAL INTIMATE

Other Vocab/Meanings:

GLOSS(ES)

(DH) Dominant Handshape:

(NDH) NonDominant Handshape:

(PO) Palm Orientation:

Movement:

Location (if not neutral):

NMS (if not neutral):

Looks like:

Variation(s):

Initialized Variation(s):

Specify if Regional:

Linguistic Register (if specific): FORMAL CONSULTATIVE INFORMAL INTIMATE

Other Vocab/Meanings:

GLOSS(ES)

(DH) Dominant Handshape:

(NDH) NonDominant Handshape:

(PO) Palm Orientation:

Movement:

Location (if not neutral):

NMS (if not neutral):

Looks like:

Variation(s):

Initialized Variation(s):

Specify if Regional:

Linguistic Register (if specific): FORMAL CONSULTATIVE INFORMAL INTIMATE

Other Vocab/Meanings:

GLOSS(ES)

(DH) Dominant Handshape:

(NDH) NonDominant Handshape:

(PO) Palm Orientation:

Movement:

Location (if not neutral):

NMS (if not neutral):

Looks like:

Variation(s):

Initialized Variation(s):

Specify if Regional:

Linguistic Register (if specific): FORMAL CONSULTATIVE INFORMAL INTIMATE

Other Vocab/Meanings:

GLOSS(ES)

(DH) Dominant Handshape:

(NDH) NonDominant Handshape:

(PO) Palm Orientation:

Movement:

Location (if not neutral):

NMS (if not neutral):

Looks like:

Variation(s):

Initialized Variation(s):

Specify if Regional:

Linguistic Register (if specific): FORMAL CONSULTATIVE INFORMAL INTIMATE

Other Vocab/Meanings:

GLOSS(ES)

(DH) Dominant Handshape:

(NDH) NonDominant Handshape:

(PO) Palm Orientation:

Movement:

Location (if not neutral):

NMS (if not neutral):

Looks like:

Variation(s):

Initialized Variation(s):

Specify if Regional:

Linguistic Register (if specific): FORMAL CONSULTATIVE INFORMAL INTIMATE

Other Vocab/Meanings:

GLOSS(ES)

(DH) Dominant Handshape:

(NDH) NonDominant Handshape:

(PO) Palm Orientation:

Movement:

Location (if not neutral):

NMS (if not neutral):

Looks like:

Variation(s):

Initialized Variation(s):

Specify if Regional:

Linguistic Register (if specific): FORMAL CONSULTATIVE INFORMAL INTIMATE

Other Vocab/Meanings:

GLOSS(ES)

(DH) <u>Dominant Handshape</u>:

(NDH) <u>NonDominant Handshape</u>:

(PO) <u>Palm Orientation</u>:

<u>Movement</u>:

<u>Location</u> (if not neutral):

<u>NMS</u> (if not neutral):

Looks like:

Variation(s):

Initialized Variation(s):

Specify if Regional:

Linguistic Register (if specific): FORMAL   CONSULTATIVE   INFORMAL   INTIMATE

Other Vocab/Meanings:

GLOSS(ES)

(DH) <u>Dominant Handshape</u>:

(NDH) <u>NonDominant Handshape</u>:

(PO) <u>Palm Orientation</u>:

<u>Movement</u>:

<u>Location</u> (if not neutral):

<u>NMS</u> (if not neutral):

Looks like:

Variation(s):

Initialized Variation(s):

Specify if Regional:

Linguistic Register (if specific): FORMAL   CONSULTATIVE   INFORMAL   INTIMATE

Other Vocab/Meanings:

GLOSS(ES)

(DH) <u>Dominant Handshape</u>:

(NDH) <u>NonDominant Handshape</u>:

(PO) <u>Palm Orientation</u>:

<u>Movement</u>:

<u>Location</u> (if not neutral):

<u>NMS</u> (if not neutral):

Looks like:

Variation(s):

Initialized Variation(s):

Specify if Regional:

Linguistic Register (if specific): FORMAL   CONSULTATIVE   INFORMAL   INTIMATE

Other Vocab/Meanings:

GLOSS(ES)

(DH) <u>Dominant Handshape</u>:

(NDH) <u>NonDominant Handshape</u>:

(PO) <u>Palm Orientation</u>:

<u>Movement</u>:

<u>Location</u> (if not neutral):

<u>NMS</u> (if not neutral):

Looks like:

Variation(s):

Initialized Variation(s):

Specify if Regional:

Linguistic Register (if specific): FORMAL   CONSULTATIVE   INFORMAL   INTIMATE

Other Vocab/Meanings:

GLOSS(ES)

(DH) <u>Dominant Handshape</u>:

(NDH) <u>NonDominant Handshape</u>:

(PO) <u>Palm Orientation</u>:

<u>Movement</u>:

<u>Location</u> (if not neutral):

<u>NMS</u> (if not neutral):

Looks like:

Variation(s):

Initialized Variation(s):

Specify if Regional:

Linguistic Register (if specific): FORMAL   CONSULTATIVE   INFORMAL   INTIMATE

Other Vocab/Meanings:

GLOSS(ES)

(DH) <u>Dominant Handshape</u>:

(NDH) <u>NonDominant Handshape</u>:

(PO) <u>Palm Orientation</u>:

<u>Movement</u>:

<u>Location</u> (if not neutral):

<u>NMS</u> (if not neutral):

Looks like:

Variation(s):

Initialized Variation(s):

Specify if Regional:

Linguistic Register (if specific): FORMAL   CONSULTATIVE   INFORMAL   INTIMATE

Other Vocab/Meanings:

GLOSS(ES)

(DH) <u>Dominant Handshape</u>:

(NDH) <u>NonDominant Handshape</u>:

(PO) <u>Palm Orientation</u>:

<u>Movement</u>:

<u>Location</u> (if not neutral):

<u>NMS</u> (if not neutral):

Looks like:

Variation(s):

Initialized Variation(s):

Specify if Regional:

Linguistic Register (if specific): FORMAL CONSULTATIVE INFORMAL INTIMATE

Other Vocab/Meanings:

GLOSS(ES)

(DH) <u>Dominant Handshape</u>:

(NDH) <u>NonDominant Handshape</u>:

(PO) <u>Palm Orientation</u>:

<u>Movement</u>:

<u>Location</u> (if not neutral):

<u>NMS</u> (if not neutral):

Looks like:

Variation(s):

Initialized Variation(s):

Specify if Regional:

Linguistic Register (if specific): FORMAL CONSULTATIVE INFORMAL INTIMATE

Other Vocab/Meanings:

GLOSS(ES)

(DH) <u>Dominant Handshape</u>:

(NDH) <u>NonDominant Handshape</u>:

(PO) <u>Palm Orientation</u>:

<u>Movement</u>:

<u>Location</u> (if not neutral):

<u>NMS</u> (if not neutral):

Looks like:

Variation(s):

Initialized Variation(s):

Specify if Regional:

Linguistic Register (if specific): FORMAL CONSULTATIVE INFORMAL INTIMATE

Other Vocab/Meanings:

GLOSS(ES)

(DH) <u>Dominant Handshape</u>:

(NDH) <u>NonDominant Handshape</u>:

(PO) <u>Palm Orientation</u>:

<u>Movement</u>:

<u>Location</u> (if not neutral):

<u>NMS</u> (if not neutral):

Looks like:

Variation(s):

Initialized Variation(s):

Specify if Regional:

Linguistic Register (if specific): FORMAL CONSULTATIVE INFORMAL INTIMATE

Other Vocab/Meanings:

GLOSS(ES)

(DH) <u>Dominant Handshape</u>:

(NDH) <u>NonDominant Handshape</u>:

(PO) <u>Palm Orientation</u>:

<u>Movement</u>:

<u>Location</u> (if not neutral):

<u>NMS</u> (if not neutral):

Looks like:

Variation(s):

Initialized Variation(s):

Specify if Regional:

Linguistic Register (if specific): FORMAL CONSULTATIVE INFORMAL INTIMATE

Other Vocab/Meanings:

GLOSS(ES)

(DH) <u>Dominant Handshape</u>:

(NDH) <u>NonDominant Handshape</u>:

(PO) <u>Palm Orientation</u>:

<u>Movement</u>:

<u>Location</u> (if not neutral):

<u>NMS</u> (if not neutral):

Looks like:

Variation(s):

Initialized Variation(s):

Specify if Regional:

Linguistic Register (if specific): FORMAL CONSULTATIVE INFORMAL INTIMATE

Other Vocab/Meanings:

GLOSS(ES)

(DH) Dominant Handshape:

(NDH) NonDominant Handshape:

(PO) Palm Orientation:

Movement:

Location (if not neutral):

NMS (if not neutral):

Looks like:

Variation(s):

Initialized Variation(s):

Specify if Regional:

Linguistic Register (if specific): FORMAL   CONSULTATIVE   INFORMAL   INTIMATE

Other Vocab/Meanings:

GLOSS(ES)

(DH) Dominant Handshape:

(NDH) NonDominant Handshape:

(PO) Palm Orientation:

Movement:

Location (if not neutral):

NMS (if not neutral):

Looks like:

Variation(s):

Initialized Variation(s):

Specify if Regional:

Linguistic Register (if specific): FORMAL   CONSULTATIVE   INFORMAL   INTIMATE

Other Vocab/Meanings:

GLOSS(ES)

(DH) Dominant Handshape:

(NDH) NonDominant Handshape:

(PO) Palm Orientation:

Movement:

Location (if not neutral):

NMS (if not neutral):

Looks like:

Variation(s):

Initialized Variation(s):

Specify if Regional:

Linguistic Register (if specific): FORMAL   CONSULTATIVE   INFORMAL   INTIMATE

Other Vocab/Meanings:

GLOSS(ES)

(DH) Dominant Handshape:

(NDH) NonDominant Handshape:

(PO) Palm Orientation:

Movement:

Location (if not neutral):

NMS (if not neutral):

Looks like:

Variation(s):

Initialized Variation(s):

Specify if Regional:

Linguistic Register (if specific): FORMAL   CONSULTATIVE   INFORMAL   INTIMATE

Other Vocab/Meanings:

GLOSS(ES)

(DH) Dominant Handshape:

(NDH) NonDominant Handshape:

(PO) Palm Orientation:

Movement:

Location (if not neutral):

NMS (if not neutral):

Looks like:

Variation(s):

Initialized Variation(s):

Specify if Regional:

Linguistic Register (if specific): FORMAL   CONSULTATIVE   INFORMAL   INTIMATE

Other Vocab/Meanings:

GLOSS(ES)

(DH) Dominant Handshape:

(NDH) NonDominant Handshape:

(PO) Palm Orientation:

Movement:

Location (if not neutral):

NMS (if not neutral):

Looks like:

Variation(s):

Initialized Variation(s):

Specify if Regional:

Linguistic Register (if specific): FORMAL   CONSULTATIVE   INFORMAL   INTIMATE

Other Vocab/Meanings:

GLOSS(ES)

(DH) <u>Dominant Handshape</u>:

(NDH) <u>NonDominant Handshape</u>:

(PO) <u>Palm Orientation</u>:

<u>Movement</u>:

<u>Location</u> (if not neutral):

<u>NMS</u> (if not neutral):

Looks like:

Variation(s):

Initialized Variation(s):

Specify if Regional:

Linguistic Register (if specific): FORMAL   CONSULTATIVE   INFORMAL   INTIMATE

Other Vocab/Meanings:

GLOSS(ES)

(DH) <u>Dominant Handshape</u>:

(NDH) <u>NonDominant Handshape</u>:

(PO) <u>Palm Orientation</u>:

<u>Movement</u>:

<u>Location</u> (if not neutral):

<u>NMS</u> (if not neutral):

Looks like:

Variation(s):

Initialized Variation(s):

Specify if Regional:

Linguistic Register (if specific): FORMAL   CONSULTATIVE   INFORMAL   INTIMATE

Other Vocab/Meanings:

GLOSS(ES)

(DH) <u>Dominant Handshape</u>:

(NDH) <u>NonDominant Handshape</u>:

(PO) <u>Palm Orientation</u>:

<u>Movement</u>:

<u>Location</u> (if not neutral):

<u>NMS</u> (if not neutral):

Looks like:

Variation(s):

Initialized Variation(s):

Specify if Regional:

Linguistic Register (if specific): FORMAL   CONSULTATIVE   INFORMAL   INTIMATE

Other Vocab/Meanings:

GLOSS(ES)

(DH) <u>Dominant Handshape</u>:

(NDH) <u>NonDominant Handshape</u>:

(PO) <u>Palm Orientation</u>:

<u>Movement</u>:

<u>Location</u> (if not neutral):

<u>NMS</u> (if not neutral):

Looks like:

Variation(s):

Initialized Variation(s):

Specify if Regional:

Linguistic Register (if specific): FORMAL   CONSULTATIVE   INFORMAL   INTIMATE

Other Vocab/Meanings:

GLOSS(ES)

(DH) <u>Dominant Handshape</u>:

(NDH) <u>NonDominant Handshape</u>:

(PO) <u>Palm Orientation</u>:

<u>Movement</u>:

<u>Location</u> (if not neutral):

<u>NMS</u> (if not neutral):

Looks like:

Variation(s):

Initialized Variation(s):

Specify if Regional:

Linguistic Register (if specific): FORMAL   CONSULTATIVE   INFORMAL   INTIMATE

Other Vocab/Meanings:

GLOSS(ES)

(DH) <u>Dominant Handshape</u>:

(NDH) <u>NonDominant Handshape</u>:

(PO) <u>Palm Orientation</u>:

<u>Movement</u>:

<u>Location</u> (if not neutral):

<u>NMS</u> (if not neutral):

Looks like:

Variation(s):

Initialized Variation(s):

Specify if Regional:

Linguistic Register (if specific): FORMAL   CONSULTATIVE   INFORMAL   INTIMATE

Other Vocab/Meanings:

GLOSS(ES)

(DH) Dominant Handshape:

(NDH) NonDominant Handshape:

(PO) Palm Orientation:

Movement:

Location (if not neutral):

NMS (if not neutral):

Looks like:

Variation(s):

Initialized Variation(s):

Specify if Regional:

Linguistic Register (if specific): FORMAL   CONSULTATIVE   INFORMAL   INTIMATE

Other Vocab/Meanings:

GLOSS(ES)

(DH) Dominant Handshape:

(NDH) NonDominant Handshape:

(PO) Palm Orientation:

Movement:

Location (if not neutral):

NMS (if not neutral):

Looks like:

Variation(s):

Initialized Variation(s):

Specify if Regional:

Linguistic Register (if specific): FORMAL   CONSULTATIVE   INFORMAL   INTIMATE

Other Vocab/Meanings:

GLOSS(ES)

(DH) Dominant Handshape:

(NDH) NonDominant Handshape:

(PO) Palm Orientation:

Movement:

Location (if not neutral):

NMS (if not neutral):

Looks like:

Variation(s):

Initialized Variation(s):

Specify if Regional:

Linguistic Register (if specific): FORMAL   CONSULTATIVE   INFORMAL   INTIMATE

Other Vocab/Meanings:

GLOSS(ES)

(DH) Dominant Handshape:

(NDH) NonDominant Handshape:

(PO) Palm Orientation:

Movement:

Location (if not neutral):

NMS (if not neutral):

Looks like:

Variation(s):

Initialized Variation(s):

Specify if Regional:

Linguistic Register (if specific): FORMAL   CONSULTATIVE   INFORMAL   INTIMATE

Other Vocab/Meanings:

GLOSS(ES)

(DH) Dominant Handshape:

(NDH) NonDominant Handshape:

(PO) Palm Orientation:

Movement:

Location (if not neutral):

NMS (if not neutral):

Looks like:

Variation(s):

Initialized Variation(s):

Specify if Regional:

Linguistic Register (if specific): FORMAL   CONSULTATIVE   INFORMAL   INTIMATE

Other Vocab/Meanings:

GLOSS(ES)

(DH) Dominant Handshape:

(NDH) NonDominant Handshape:

(PO) Palm Orientation:

Movement:

Location (if not neutral):

NMS (if not neutral):

Looks like:

Variation(s):

Initialized Variation(s):

Specify if Regional:

Linguistic Register (if specific): FORMAL   CONSULTATIVE   INFORMAL   INTIMATE

Other Vocab/Meanings:

GLOSS(ES)

(DH) <u>Dominant Handshape</u>:

(NDH) <u>NonDominant Handshape</u>:

(PO) <u>Palm Orientation</u>:

<u>Movement</u>:

<u>Location</u> (if not neutral):

<u>NMS</u> (if not neutral):

Looks like:

Variation(s):

Initialized Variation(s):

Specify if Regional:

Linguistic Register (if specific): FORMAL   CONSULTATIVE   INFORMAL   INTIMATE

Other Vocab/Meanings:

GLOSS(ES)

(DH) <u>Dominant Handshape</u>:

(NDH) <u>NonDominant Handshape</u>:

(PO) <u>Palm Orientation</u>:

<u>Movement</u>:

<u>Location</u> (if not neutral):

<u>NMS</u> (if not neutral):

Looks like:

Variation(s):

Initialized Variation(s):

Specify if Regional:

Linguistic Register (if specific): FORMAL   CONSULTATIVE   INFORMAL   INTIMATE

Other Vocab/Meanings:

GLOSS(ES)

(DH) <u>Dominant Handshape</u>:

(NDH) <u>NonDominant Handshape</u>:

(PO) <u>Palm Orientation</u>:

<u>Movement</u>:

<u>Location</u> (if not neutral):

<u>NMS</u> (if not neutral):

Looks like:

Variation(s):

Initialized Variation(s):

Specify if Regional:

Linguistic Register (if specific): FORMAL   CONSULTATIVE   INFORMAL   INTIMATE

Other Vocab/Meanings:

GLOSS(ES)

(DH) <u>Dominant Handshape</u>:

(NDH) <u>NonDominant Handshape</u>:

(PO) <u>Palm Orientation</u>:

<u>Movement</u>:

<u>Location</u> (if not neutral):

<u>NMS</u> (if not neutral):

Looks like:

Variation(s):

Initialized Variation(s):

Specify if Regional:

Linguistic Register (if specific): FORMAL   CONSULTATIVE   INFORMAL   INTIMATE

Other Vocab/Meanings:

GLOSS(ES)

(DH) <u>Dominant Handshape</u>:

(NDH) <u>NonDominant Handshape</u>:

(PO) <u>Palm Orientation</u>:

<u>Movement</u>:

<u>Location</u> (if not neutral):

<u>NMS</u> (if not neutral):

Looks like:

Variation(s):

Initialized Variation(s):

Specify if Regional:

Linguistic Register (if specific): FORMAL   CONSULTATIVE   INFORMAL   INTIMATE

Other Vocab/Meanings:

GLOSS(ES)

(DH) <u>Dominant Handshape</u>:

(NDH) <u>NonDominant Handshape</u>:

(PO) <u>Palm Orientation</u>:

<u>Movement</u>:

<u>Location</u> (if not neutral):

<u>NMS</u> (if not neutral):

Looks like:

Variation(s):

Initialized Variation(s):

Specify if Regional:

Linguistic Register (if specific): FORMAL   CONSULTATIVE   INFORMAL   INTIMATE

Other Vocab/Meanings:

GLOSS(ES)

(DH) <u>Dominant Handshape</u>:

(NDH) <u>NonDominant Handshape</u>:

(PO) <u>Palm Orientation</u>:

<u>Movement</u>:

<u>Location</u> (if not neutral):

<u>NMS</u> (if not neutral):

Looks like:

Variation(s):

Initialized Variation(s):

Specify if Regional:

Linguistic Register (if specific): FORMAL CONSULTATIVE INFORMAL INTIMATE

Other Vocab/Meanings:

GLOSS(ES)

(DH) <u>Dominant Handshape</u>:

(NDH) <u>NonDominant Handshape</u>:

(PO) <u>Palm Orientation</u>:

<u>Movement</u>:

<u>Location</u> (if not neutral):

<u>NMS</u> (if not neutral):

Looks like:

Variation(s):

Initialized Variation(s):

Specify if Regional:

Linguistic Register (if specific): FORMAL CONSULTATIVE INFORMAL INTIMATE

Other Vocab/Meanings:

GLOSS(ES)

(DH) <u>Dominant Handshape</u>:

(NDH) <u>NonDominant Handshape</u>:

(PO) <u>Palm Orientation</u>:

<u>Movement</u>:

<u>Location</u> (if not neutral):

<u>NMS</u> (if not neutral):

Looks like:

Variation(s):

Initialized Variation(s):

Specify if Regional:

Linguistic Register (if specific): FORMAL CONSULTATIVE INFORMAL INTIMATE

Other Vocab/Meanings:

GLOSS(ES)

(DH) <u>Dominant Handshape</u>:

(NDH) <u>NonDominant Handshape</u>:

(PO) <u>Palm Orientation</u>:

<u>Movement</u>:

<u>Location</u> (if not neutral):

<u>NMS</u> (if not neutral):

Looks like:

Variation(s):

Initialized Variation(s):

Specify if Regional:

Linguistic Register (if specific): FORMAL CONSULTATIVE INFORMAL INTIMATE

Other Vocab/Meanings:

GLOSS(ES)

(DH) <u>Dominant Handshape</u>:

(NDH) <u>NonDominant Handshape</u>:

(PO) <u>Palm Orientation</u>:

<u>Movement</u>:

<u>Location</u> (if not neutral):

<u>NMS</u> (if not neutral):

Looks like:

Variation(s):

Initialized Variation(s):

Specify if Regional:

Linguistic Register (if specific): FORMAL CONSULTATIVE INFORMAL INTIMATE

Other Vocab/Meanings:

GLOSS(ES)

(DH) <u>Dominant Handshape</u>:

(NDH) <u>NonDominant Handshape</u>:

(PO) <u>Palm Orientation</u>:

<u>Movement</u>:

<u>Location</u> (if not neutral):

<u>NMS</u> (if not neutral):

Looks like:

Variation(s):

Initialized Variation(s):

Specify if Regional:

Linguistic Register (if specific): FORMAL CONSULTATIVE INFORMAL INTIMATE

Other Vocab/Meanings:

GLOSS(ES)

(DH) <u>Dominant Handshape</u>:

(NDH) <u>NonDominant Handshape</u>:

(PO) <u>Palm Orientation</u>:

<u>Movement</u>:

<u>Location</u> (if not neutral):

<u>NMS</u> (if not neutral):

Looks like:

Variation(s):

Initialized Variation(s):

Specify if Regional:

Linguistic Register (if specific): FORMAL   CONSULTATIVE   INFORMAL   INTIMATE

Other Vocab/Meanings:

GLOSS(ES)

(DH) <u>Dominant Handshape</u>:

(NDH) <u>NonDominant Handshape</u>:

(PO) <u>Palm Orientation</u>:

<u>Movement</u>:

<u>Location</u> (if not neutral):

<u>NMS</u> (if not neutral):

Looks like:

Variation(s):

Initialized Variation(s):

Specify if Regional:

Linguistic Register (if specific): FORMAL   CONSULTATIVE   INFORMAL   INTIMATE

Other Vocab/Meanings:

GLOSS(ES)

(DH) <u>Dominant Handshape</u>:

(NDH) <u>NonDominant Handshape</u>:

(PO) <u>Palm Orientation</u>:

<u>Movement</u>:

<u>Location</u> (if not neutral):

<u>NMS</u> (if not neutral):

Looks like:

Variation(s):

Initialized Variation(s):

Specify if Regional:

Linguistic Register (if specific): FORMAL   CONSULTATIVE   INFORMAL   INTIMATE

Other Vocab/Meanings:

GLOSS(ES)

(DH) <u>Dominant Handshape</u>:

(NDH) <u>NonDominant Handshape</u>:

(PO) <u>Palm Orientation</u>:

<u>Movement</u>:

<u>Location</u> (if not neutral):

<u>NMS</u> (if not neutral):

Looks like:

Variation(s):

Initialized Variation(s):

Specify if Regional:

Linguistic Register (if specific): FORMAL   CONSULTATIVE   INFORMAL   INTIMATE

Other Vocab/Meanings:

GLOSS(ES)

(DH) <u>Dominant Handshape</u>:

(NDH) <u>NonDominant Handshape</u>:

(PO) <u>Palm Orientation</u>:

<u>Movement</u>:

<u>Location</u> (if not neutral):

<u>NMS</u> (if not neutral):

Looks like:

Variation(s):

Initialized Variation(s):

Specify if Regional:

Linguistic Register (if specific): FORMAL   CONSULTATIVE   INFORMAL   INTIMATE

Other Vocab/Meanings:

GLOSS(ES)

(DH) <u>Dominant Handshape</u>:

(NDH) <u>NonDominant Handshape</u>:

(PO) <u>Palm Orientation</u>:

<u>Movement</u>:

<u>Location</u> (if not neutral):

<u>NMS</u> (if not neutral):

Looks like:

Variation(s):

Initialized Variation(s):

Specify if Regional:

Linguistic Register (if specific): FORMAL   CONSULTATIVE   INFORMAL   INTIMATE

Other Vocab/Meanings:

GLOSS(ES)

(DH) <u>Dominant Handshape</u>:

(NDH) <u>NonDominant Handshape</u>:

(PO) <u>Palm Orientation</u>:

<u>Movement</u>:

<u>Location</u> (if not neutral):

<u>NMS</u> (if not neutral):

Looks like:

Variation(s):

Initialized Variation(s):

Specify if Regional:

Linguistic Register (if specific): FORMAL CONSULTATIVE INFORMAL INTIMATE

Other Vocab/Meanings:

GLOSS(ES)

(DH) <u>Dominant Handshape</u>:

(NDH) <u>NonDominant Handshape</u>:

(PO) <u>Palm Orientation</u>:

<u>Movement</u>:

<u>Location</u> (if not neutral):

<u>NMS</u> (if not neutral):

Looks like:

Variation(s):

Initialized Variation(s):

Specify if Regional:

Linguistic Register (if specific): FORMAL CONSULTATIVE INFORMAL INTIMATE

Other Vocab/Meanings:

GLOSS(ES)

(DH) <u>Dominant Handshape</u>:

(NDH) <u>NonDominant Handshape</u>:

(PO) <u>Palm Orientation</u>:

<u>Movement</u>:

<u>Location</u> (if not neutral):

<u>NMS</u> (if not neutral):

Looks like:

Variation(s):

Initialized Variation(s):

Specify if Regional:

Linguistic Register (if specific): FORMAL CONSULTATIVE INFORMAL INTIMATE

Other Vocab/Meanings:

GLOSS(ES)

(DH) <u>Dominant Handshape</u>:

(NDH) <u>NonDominant Handshape</u>:

(PO) <u>Palm Orientation</u>:

<u>Movement</u>:

<u>Location</u> (if not neutral):

<u>NMS</u> (if not neutral):

Looks like:

Variation(s):

Initialized Variation(s):

Specify if Regional:

Linguistic Register (if specific): FORMAL CONSULTATIVE INFORMAL INTIMATE

Other Vocab/Meanings:

GLOSS(ES)

(DH) <u>Dominant Handshape</u>:

(NDH) <u>NonDominant Handshape</u>:

(PO) <u>Palm Orientation</u>:

<u>Movement</u>:

<u>Location</u> (if not neutral):

<u>NMS</u> (if not neutral):

Looks like:

Variation(s):

Initialized Variation(s):

Specify if Regional:

Linguistic Register (if specific): FORMAL CONSULTATIVE INFORMAL INTIMATE

Other Vocab/Meanings:

GLOSS(ES)

(DH) <u>Dominant Handshape</u>:

(NDH) <u>NonDominant Handshape</u>:

(PO) <u>Palm Orientation</u>:

<u>Movement</u>:

<u>Location</u> (if not neutral):

<u>NMS</u> (if not neutral):

Looks like:

Variation(s):

Initialized Variation(s):

Specify if Regional:

Linguistic Register (if specific): FORMAL CONSULTATIVE INFORMAL INTIMATE

Other Vocab/Meanings:

GLOSS(ES)

(DH) <u>Dominant Handshape</u>:

(NDH) <u>NonDominant Handshape</u>:

(PO) <u>Palm Orientation</u>:

<u>Movement</u>:

<u>Location</u> (if not neutral):

<u>NMS</u> (if not neutral):

Looks like:

Variation(s):

Initialized Variation(s):

Specify if Regional:

Linguistic Register (if specific): FORMAL CONSULTATIVE INFORMAL INTIMATE

Other Vocab/Meanings:

GLOSS(ES)

(DH) <u>Dominant Handshape</u>:

(NDH) <u>NonDominant Handshape</u>:

(PO) <u>Palm Orientation</u>:

<u>Movement</u>:

<u>Location</u> (if not neutral):

<u>NMS</u> (if not neutral):

Looks like:

Variation(s):

Initialized Variation(s):

Specify if Regional:

Linguistic Register (if specific): FORMAL CONSULTATIVE INFORMAL INTIMATE

Other Vocab/Meanings:

GLOSS(ES)

(DH) <u>Dominant Handshape</u>:

(NDH) <u>NonDominant Handshape</u>:

(PO) <u>Palm Orientation</u>:

<u>Movement</u>:

<u>Location</u> (if not neutral):

<u>NMS</u> (if not neutral):

Looks like:

Variation(s):

Initialized Variation(s):

Specify if Regional:

Linguistic Register (if specific): FORMAL CONSULTATIVE INFORMAL INTIMATE

Other Vocab/Meanings:

GLOSS(ES)

(DH) <u>Dominant Handshape</u>:

(NDH) <u>NonDominant Handshape</u>:

(PO) <u>Palm Orientation</u>:

<u>Movement</u>:

<u>Location</u> (if not neutral):

<u>NMS</u> (if not neutral):

Looks like:

Variation(s):

Initialized Variation(s):

Specify if Regional:

Linguistic Register (if specific): FORMAL CONSULTATIVE INFORMAL INTIMATE

Other Vocab/Meanings:

GLOSS(ES)

(DH) <u>Dominant Handshape</u>:

(NDH) <u>NonDominant Handshape</u>:

(PO) <u>Palm Orientation</u>:

<u>Movement</u>:

<u>Location</u> (if not neutral):

<u>NMS</u> (if not neutral):

Looks like:

Variation(s):

Initialized Variation(s):

Specify if Regional:

Linguistic Register (if specific): FORMAL CONSULTATIVE INFORMAL INTIMATE

Other Vocab/Meanings:

GLOSS(ES)

(DH) <u>Dominant Handshape</u>:

(NDH) <u>NonDominant Handshape</u>:

(PO) <u>Palm Orientation</u>:

<u>Movement</u>:

<u>Location</u> (if not neutral):

<u>NMS</u> (if not neutral):

Looks like:

Variation(s):

Initialized Variation(s):

Specify if Regional:

Linguistic Register (if specific): FORMAL CONSULTATIVE INFORMAL INTIMATE

Other Vocab/Meanings:

GLOSS(ES)

(DH) Dominant Handshape:

(NDH) NonDominant Handshape:

(PO) Palm Orientation:

Movement:

Location (if not neutral):

NMS (if not neutral):

Looks like:

Variation(s):

Initialized Variation(s):

Specify if Regional:

Linguistic Register (if specific): FORMAL CONSULTATIVE INFORMAL INTIMATE

Other Vocab/Meanings:

GLOSS(ES)

(DH) Dominant Handshape:

(NDH) NonDominant Handshape:

(PO) Palm Orientation:

Movement:

Location (if not neutral):

NMS (if not neutral):

Looks like:

Variation(s):

Initialized Variation(s):

Specify if Regional:

Linguistic Register (if specific): FORMAL CONSULTATIVE INFORMAL INTIMATE

Other Vocab/Meanings:

GLOSS(ES)

(DH) Dominant Handshape:

(NDH) NonDominant Handshape:

(PO) Palm Orientation:

Movement:

Location (if not neutral):

NMS (if not neutral):

Looks like:

Variation(s):

Initialized Variation(s):

Specify if Regional:

Linguistic Register (if specific): FORMAL CONSULTATIVE INFORMAL INTIMATE

Other Vocab/Meanings:

GLOSS(ES)

(DH) Dominant Handshape:

(NDH) NonDominant Handshape:

(PO) Palm Orientation:

Movement:

Location (if not neutral):

NMS (if not neutral):

Looks like:

Variation(s):

Initialized Variation(s):

Specify if Regional:

Linguistic Register (if specific): FORMAL CONSULTATIVE INFORMAL INTIMATE

Other Vocab/Meanings:

GLOSS(ES)

(DH) Dominant Handshape:

(NDH) NonDominant Handshape:

(PO) Palm Orientation:

Movement:

Location (if not neutral):

NMS (if not neutral):

Looks like:

Variation(s):

Initialized Variation(s):

Specify if Regional:

Linguistic Register (if specific): FORMAL CONSULTATIVE INFORMAL INTIMATE

Other Vocab/Meanings:

GLOSS(ES)

(DH) Dominant Handshape:

(NDH) NonDominant Handshape:

(PO) Palm Orientation:

Movement:

Location (if not neutral):

NMS (if not neutral):

Looks like:

Variation(s):

Initialized Variation(s):

Specify if Regional:

Linguistic Register (if specific): FORMAL CONSULTATIVE INFORMAL INTIMATE

Other Vocab/Meanings:

GLOSS(ES)

(DH) Dominant Handshape:

(NDH) NonDominant Handshape:

(PO) Palm Orientation:

Movement:

Location (if not neutral):

NMS (if not neutral):

Looks like:

Variation(s):

Initialized Variation(s):

Specify if Regional:

Linguistic Register (if specific): FORMAL CONSULTATIVE INFORMAL INTIMATE

Other Vocab/Meanings:

GLOSS(ES)

(DH) Dominant Handshape:

(NDH) NonDominant Handshape:

(PO) Palm Orientation:

Movement:

Location (if not neutral):

NMS (if not neutral):

Looks like:

Variation(s):

Initialized Variation(s):

Specify if Regional:

Linguistic Register (if specific): FORMAL CONSULTATIVE INFORMAL INTIMATE

Other Vocab/Meanings:

GLOSS(ES)

(DH) Dominant Handshape:

(NDH) NonDominant Handshape:

(PO) Palm Orientation:

Movement:

Location (if not neutral):

NMS (if not neutral):

Looks like:

Variation(s):

Initialized Variation(s):

Specify if Regional:

Linguistic Register (if specific): FORMAL CONSULTATIVE INFORMAL INTIMATE

Other Vocab/Meanings:

GLOSS(ES)

(DH) Dominant Handshape:

(NDH) NonDominant Handshape:

(PO) Palm Orientation:

Movement:

Location (if not neutral):

NMS (if not neutral):

Looks like:

Variation(s):

Initialized Variation(s):

Specify if Regional:

Linguistic Register (if specific): FORMAL CONSULTATIVE INFORMAL INTIMATE

Other Vocab/Meanings:

GLOSS(ES)

(DH) Dominant Handshape:

(NDH) NonDominant Handshape:

(PO) Palm Orientation:

Movement:

Location (if not neutral):

NMS (if not neutral):

Looks like:

Variation(s):

Initialized Variation(s):

Specify if Regional:

Linguistic Register (if specific): FORMAL CONSULTATIVE INFORMAL INTIMATE

Other Vocab/Meanings:

GLOSS(ES)

(DH) Dominant Handshape:

(NDH) NonDominant Handshape:

(PO) Palm Orientation:

Movement:

Location (if not neutral):

NMS (if not neutral):

Looks like:

Variation(s):

Initialized Variation(s):

Specify if Regional:

Linguistic Register (if specific): FORMAL CONSULTATIVE INFORMAL INTIMATE

Other Vocab/Meanings:

GLOSS(ES)

(DH) Dominant Handshape:

(NDH) NonDominant Handshape:

(PO) Palm Orientation:

Movement:

Location (if not neutral):

NMS (if not neutral):

Looks like:

Variation(s):

Initialized Variation(s):

Specify if Regional:

Linguistic Register (if specific): FORMAL CONSULTATIVE INFORMAL INTIMATE

Other Vocab/Meanings:

GLOSS(ES)

(DH) Dominant Handshape:

(NDH) NonDominant Handshape:

(PO) Palm Orientation:

Movement:

Location (if not neutral):

NMS (if not neutral):

Looks like:

Variation(s):

Initialized Variation(s):

Specify if Regional:

Linguistic Register (if specific): FORMAL CONSULTATIVE INFORMAL INTIMATE

Other Vocab/Meanings:

GLOSS(ES)

(DH) Dominant Handshape:

(NDH) NonDominant Handshape:

(PO) Palm Orientation:

Movement:

Location (if not neutral):

NMS (if not neutral):

Looks like:

Variation(s):

Initialized Variation(s):

Specify if Regional:

Linguistic Register (if specific): FORMAL CONSULTATIVE INFORMAL INTIMATE

Other Vocab/Meanings:

GLOSS(ES)

(DH) Dominant Handshape:

(NDH) NonDominant Handshape:

(PO) Palm Orientation:

Movement:

Location (if not neutral):

NMS (if not neutral):

Looks like:

Variation(s):

Initialized Variation(s):

Specify if Regional:

Linguistic Register (if specific): FORMAL CONSULTATIVE INFORMAL INTIMATE

Other Vocab/Meanings:

GLOSS(ES)

(DH) Dominant Handshape:

(NDH) NonDominant Handshape:

(PO) Palm Orientation:

Movement:

Location (if not neutral):

NMS (if not neutral):

Looks like:

Variation(s):

Initialized Variation(s):

Specify if Regional:

Linguistic Register (if specific): FORMAL CONSULTATIVE INFORMAL INTIMATE

Other Vocab/Meanings:

GLOSS(ES)

(DH) Dominant Handshape:

(NDH) NonDominant Handshape:

(PO) Palm Orientation:

Movement:

Location (if not neutral):

NMS (if not neutral):

Looks like:

Variation(s):

Initialized Variation(s):

Specify if Regional:

Linguistic Register (if specific): FORMAL CONSULTATIVE INFORMAL INTIMATE

Other Vocab/Meanings:

GLOSS(ES)

(DH) Dominant Handshape:

(NDH) NonDominant Handshape:

(PO) Palm Orientation:

Movement:

Location (if not neutral):

NMS (if not neutral):

Looks like:

Variation(s):

Initialized Variation(s):

Specify if Regional:

Linguistic Register (if specific): FORMAL CONSULTATIVE INFORMAL INTIMATE

Other Vocab/Meanings:

GLOSS(ES)

(DH) Dominant Handshape:

(NDH) NonDominant Handshape:

(PO) Palm Orientation:

Movement:

Location (if not neutral):

NMS (if not neutral):

Looks like:

Variation(s):

Initialized Variation(s):

Specify if Regional:

Linguistic Register (if specific): FORMAL CONSULTATIVE INFORMAL INTIMATE

Other Vocab/Meanings:

GLOSS(ES)

(DH) Dominant Handshape:

(NDH) NonDominant Handshape:

(PO) Palm Orientation:

Movement:

Location (if not neutral):

NMS (if not neutral):

Looks like:

Variation(s):

Initialized Variation(s):

Specify if Regional:

Linguistic Register (if specific): FORMAL CONSULTATIVE INFORMAL INTIMATE

Other Vocab/Meanings:

GLOSS(ES)

(DH) Dominant Handshape:

(NDH) NonDominant Handshape:

(PO) Palm Orientation:

Movement:

Location (if not neutral):

NMS (if not neutral):

Looks like:

Variation(s):

Initialized Variation(s):

Specify if Regional:

Linguistic Register (if specific): FORMAL CONSULTATIVE INFORMAL INTIMATE

Other Vocab/Meanings:

GLOSS(ES)

(DH) Dominant Handshape:

(NDH) NonDominant Handshape:

(PO) Palm Orientation:

Movement:

Location (if not neutral):

NMS (if not neutral):

Looks like:

Variation(s):

Initialized Variation(s):

Specify if Regional:

Linguistic Register (if specific): FORMAL CONSULTATIVE INFORMAL INTIMATE

Other Vocab/Meanings:

GLOSS(ES)

(DH) Dominant Handshape:

(NDH) NonDominant Handshape:

(PO) Palm Orientation:

Movement:

Location (if not neutral):

NMS (if not neutral):

Looks like:

Variation(s):

Initialized Variation(s):

Specify if Regional:

Linguistic Register (if specific): FORMAL CONSULTATIVE INFORMAL INTIMATE

Other Vocab/Meanings:

GLOSS(ES)

(DH) <u>Dominant Handshape</u>:

(NDH) <u>NonDominant Handshape</u>:

(PO) <u>Palm Orientation</u>:

<u>Movement</u>:

<u>Location</u> (if not neutral):

<u>NMS</u> (if not neutral):

Looks like:

Variation(s):

Initialized Variation(s):

Specify if Regional:

Linguistic Register (if specific): FORMAL   CONSULTATIVE   INFORMAL   INTIMATE

Other Vocab/Meanings:

GLOSS(ES)

(DH) <u>Dominant Handshape</u>:

(NDH) <u>NonDominant Handshape</u>:

(PO) <u>Palm Orientation</u>:

<u>Movement</u>:

<u>Location</u> (if not neutral):

<u>NMS</u> (if not neutral):

Looks like:

Variation(s):

Initialized Variation(s):

Specify if Regional:

Linguistic Register (if specific): FORMAL   CONSULTATIVE   INFORMAL   INTIMATE

Other Vocab/Meanings:

GLOSS(ES)

(DH) <u>Dominant Handshape</u>:

(NDH) <u>NonDominant Handshape</u>:

(PO) <u>Palm Orientation</u>:

<u>Movement</u>:

<u>Location</u> (if not neutral):

<u>NMS</u> (if not neutral):

Looks like:

Variation(s):

Initialized Variation(s):

Specify if Regional:

Linguistic Register (if specific): FORMAL   CONSULTATIVE   INFORMAL   INTIMATE

Other Vocab/Meanings:

GLOSS(ES)

(DH) <u>Dominant Handshape</u>:

(NDH) <u>NonDominant Handshape</u>:

(PO) <u>Palm Orientation</u>:

<u>Movement</u>:

<u>Location</u> (if not neutral):

<u>NMS</u> (if not neutral):

Looks like:

Variation(s):

Initialized Variation(s):

Specify if Regional:

Linguistic Register (if specific): FORMAL   CONSULTATIVE   INFORMAL   INTIMATE

Other Vocab/Meanings:

GLOSS(ES)

(DH) <u>Dominant Handshape</u>:

(NDH) <u>NonDominant Handshape</u>:

(PO) <u>Palm Orientation</u>:

<u>Movement</u>:

<u>Location</u> (if not neutral):

<u>NMS</u> (if not neutral):

Looks like:

Variation(s):

Initialized Variation(s):

Specify if Regional:

Linguistic Register (if specific): FORMAL   CONSULTATIVE   INFORMAL   INTIMATE

Other Vocab/Meanings:

GLOSS(ES)

(DH) <u>Dominant Handshape</u>:

(NDH) <u>NonDominant Handshape</u>:

(PO) <u>Palm Orientation</u>:

<u>Movement</u>:

<u>Location</u> (if not neutral):

<u>NMS</u> (if not neutral):

Looks like:

Variation(s):

Initialized Variation(s):

Specify if Regional:

Linguistic Register (if specific): FORMAL   CONSULTATIVE   INFORMAL   INTIMATE

Other Vocab/Meanings:

GLOSS(ES)

(DH) Dominant Handshape:

(NDH) NonDominant Handshape:

(PO) Palm Orientation:

Movement:

Location (if not neutral):

NMS (if not neutral):

Looks like:

Variation(s):

Initialized Variation(s):

Specify if Regional:

Linguistic Register (if specific): FORMAL CONSULTATIVE INFORMAL INTIMATE

Other Vocab/Meanings:

GLOSS(ES)

(DH) Dominant Handshape:

(NDH) NonDominant Handshape:

(PO) Palm Orientation:

Movement:

Location (if not neutral):

NMS (if not neutral):

Looks like:

Variation(s):

Initialized Variation(s):

Specify if Regional:

Linguistic Register (if specific): FORMAL CONSULTATIVE INFORMAL INTIMATE

Other Vocab/Meanings:

GLOSS(ES)

(DH) Dominant Handshape:

(NDH) NonDominant Handshape:

(PO) Palm Orientation:

Movement:

Location (if not neutral):

NMS (if not neutral):

Looks like:

Variation(s):

Initialized Variation(s):

Specify if Regional:

Linguistic Register (if specific): FORMAL CONSULTATIVE INFORMAL INTIMATE

Other Vocab/Meanings:

GLOSS(ES)

(DH) Dominant Handshape:

(NDH) NonDominant Handshape:

(PO) Palm Orientation:

Movement:

Location (if not neutral):

NMS (if not neutral):

Looks like:

Variation(s):

Initialized Variation(s):

Specify if Regional:

Linguistic Register (if specific): FORMAL CONSULTATIVE INFORMAL INTIMATE

Other Vocab/Meanings:

GLOSS(ES)

(DH) Dominant Handshape:

(NDH) NonDominant Handshape:

(PO) Palm Orientation:

Movement:

Location (if not neutral):

NMS (if not neutral):

Looks like:

Variation(s):

Initialized Variation(s):

Specify if Regional:

Linguistic Register (if specific): FORMAL CONSULTATIVE INFORMAL INTIMATE

Other Vocab/Meanings:

GLOSS(ES)

(DH) Dominant Handshape:

(NDH) NonDominant Handshape:

(PO) Palm Orientation:

Movement:

Location (if not neutral):

NMS (if not neutral):

Looks like:

Variation(s):

Initialized Variation(s):

Specify if Regional:

Linguistic Register (if specific): FORMAL CONSULTATIVE INFORMAL INTIMATE

Other Vocab/Meanings:

GLOSS(ES)

(DH) Dominant Handshape:

(NDH) NonDominant Handshape:

(PO) Palm Orientation:

Movement:

Location (if not neutral):

NMS (if not neutral):

Looks like:

Variation(s):

Initialized Variation(s):

Specify if Regional:

Linguistic Register (if specific): FORMAL CONSULTATIVE INFORMAL INTIMATE

Other Vocab/Meanings:

GLOSS(ES)

(DH) Dominant Handshape:

(NDH) NonDominant Handshape:

(PO) Palm Orientation:

Movement:

Location (if not neutral):

NMS (if not neutral):

Looks like:

Variation(s):

Initialized Variation(s):

Specify if Regional:

Linguistic Register (if specific): FORMAL CONSULTATIVE INFORMAL INTIMATE

Other Vocab/Meanings:

GLOSS(ES)

(DH) Dominant Handshape:

(NDH) NonDominant Handshape:

(PO) Palm Orientation:

Movement:

Location (if not neutral):

NMS (if not neutral):

Looks like:

Variation(s):

Initialized Variation(s):

Specify if Regional:

Linguistic Register (if specific): FORMAL CONSULTATIVE INFORMAL INTIMATE

Other Vocab/Meanings:

GLOSS(ES)

(DH) Dominant Handshape:

(NDH) NonDominant Handshape:

(PO) Palm Orientation:

Movement:

Location (if not neutral):

NMS (if not neutral):

Looks like:

Variation(s):

Initialized Variation(s):

Specify if Regional:

Linguistic Register (if specific): FORMAL CONSULTATIVE INFORMAL INTIMATE

Other Vocab/Meanings:

GLOSS(ES)

(DH) Dominant Handshape:

(NDH) NonDominant Handshape:

(PO) Palm Orientation:

Movement:

Location (if not neutral):

NMS (if not neutral):

Looks like:

Variation(s):

Initialized Variation(s):

Specify if Regional:

Linguistic Register (if specific): FORMAL CONSULTATIVE INFORMAL INTIMATE

Other Vocab/Meanings:

GLOSS(ES)

(DH) Dominant Handshape:

(NDH) NonDominant Handshape:

(PO) Palm Orientation:

Movement:

Location (if not neutral):

NMS (if not neutral):

Looks like:

Variation(s):

Initialized Variation(s):

Specify if Regional:

Linguistic Register (if specific): FORMAL CONSULTATIVE INFORMAL INTIMATE

Other Vocab/Meanings:

GLOSS(ES)

(DH) Dominant Handshape:

(NDH) NonDominant Handshape:

(PO) Palm Orientation:

Movement:

Location (if not neutral):

NMS (if not neutral):

Looks like:

Variation(s):

Initialized Variation(s):

Specify if Regional:

Linguistic Register (if specific): FORMAL   CONSULTATIVE   INFORMAL   INTIMATE

Other Vocab/Meanings:

GLOSS(ES)

(DH) Dominant Handshape:

(NDH) NonDominant Handshape:

(PO) Palm Orientation:

Movement:

Location (if not neutral):

NMS (if not neutral):

Looks like:

Variation(s):

Initialized Variation(s):

Specify if Regional:

Linguistic Register (if specific): FORMAL   CONSULTATIVE   INFORMAL   INTIMATE

Other Vocab/Meanings:

GLOSS(ES)

(DH) Dominant Handshape:

(NDH) NonDominant Handshape:

(PO) Palm Orientation:

Movement:

Location (if not neutral):

NMS (if not neutral):

Looks like:

Variation(s):

Initialized Variation(s):

Specify if Regional:

Linguistic Register (if specific): FORMAL   CONSULTATIVE   INFORMAL   INTIMATE

Other Vocab/Meanings:

GLOSS(ES)

(DH) Dominant Handshape:

(NDH) NonDominant Handshape:

(PO) Palm Orientation:

Movement:

Location (if not neutral):

NMS (if not neutral):

Looks like:

Variation(s):

Initialized Variation(s):

Specify if Regional:

Linguistic Register (if specific): FORMAL   CONSULTATIVE   INFORMAL   INTIMATE

Other Vocab/Meanings:

GLOSS(ES)

(DH) Dominant Handshape:

(NDH) NonDominant Handshape:

(PO) Palm Orientation:

Movement:

Location (if not neutral):

NMS (if not neutral):

Looks like:

Variation(s):

Initialized Variation(s):

Specify if Regional:

Linguistic Register (if specific): FORMAL   CONSULTATIVE   INFORMAL   INTIMATE

Other Vocab/Meanings:

GLOSS(ES)

(DH) Dominant Handshape:

(NDH) NonDominant Handshape:

(PO) Palm Orientation:

Movement:

Location (if not neutral):

NMS (if not neutral):

Looks like:

Variation(s):

Initialized Variation(s):

Specify if Regional:

Linguistic Register (if specific): FORMAL   CONSULTATIVE   INFORMAL   INTIMATE

Other Vocab/Meanings:

GLOSS(ES)

(DH) <u>Dominant Handshape:</u>

(NDH) <u>NonDominant Handshape:</u>

(PO) <u>Palm Orientation:</u>

<u>Movement:</u>

<u>Location</u> (if not neutral):

<u>NMS</u> (if not neutral):

Looks like:

Variation(s):

Initialized Variation(s):

Specify if Regional:

Linguistic Register (if specific): FORMAL CONSULTATIVE INFORMAL INTIMATE

Other Vocab/Meanings:

GLOSS(ES)

(DH) <u>Dominant Handshape:</u>

(NDH) <u>NonDominant Handshape:</u>

(PO) <u>Palm Orientation:</u>

<u>Movement:</u>

<u>Location</u> (if not neutral):

<u>NMS</u> (if not neutral):

Looks like:

Variation(s):

Initialized Variation(s):

Specify if Regional:

Linguistic Register (if specific): FORMAL CONSULTATIVE INFORMAL INTIMATE

Other Vocab/Meanings:

GLOSS(ES)

(DH) <u>Dominant Handshape:</u>

(NDH) <u>NonDominant Handshape:</u>

(PO) <u>Palm Orientation:</u>

<u>Movement:</u>

<u>Location</u> (if not neutral):

<u>NMS</u> (if not neutral):

Looks like:

Variation(s):

Initialized Variation(s):

Specify if Regional:

Linguistic Register (if specific): FORMAL CONSULTATIVE INFORMAL INTIMATE

Other Vocab/Meanings:

GLOSS(ES)

(DH) <u>Dominant Handshape:</u>

(NDH) <u>NonDominant Handshape:</u>

(PO) <u>Palm Orientation:</u>

<u>Movement:</u>

<u>Location</u> (if not neutral):

<u>NMS</u> (if not neutral):

Looks like:

Variation(s):

Initialized Variation(s):

Specify if Regional:

Linguistic Register (if specific): FORMAL CONSULTATIVE INFORMAL INTIMATE

Other Vocab/Meanings:

GLOSS(ES)

(DH) <u>Dominant Handshape:</u>

(NDH) <u>NonDominant Handshape:</u>

(PO) <u>Palm Orientation:</u>

<u>Movement:</u>

<u>Location</u> (if not neutral):

<u>NMS</u> (if not neutral):

Looks like:

Variation(s):

Initialized Variation(s):

Specify if Regional:

Linguistic Register (if specific): FORMAL CONSULTATIVE INFORMAL INTIMATE

Other Vocab/Meanings:

GLOSS(ES)

(DH) <u>Dominant Handshape:</u>

(NDH) <u>NonDominant Handshape:</u>

(PO) <u>Palm Orientation:</u>

<u>Movement:</u>

<u>Location</u> (if not neutral):

<u>NMS</u> (if not neutral):

Looks like:

Variation(s):

Initialized Variation(s):

Specify if Regional:

Linguistic Register (if specific): FORMAL CONSULTATIVE INFORMAL INTIMATE

Other Vocab/Meanings:

GLOSS(ES)

(DH) Dominant Handshape:

(NDH) NonDominant Handshape:

(PO) Palm Orientation:

Movement:

Location (if not neutral):

NMS (if not neutral):

Looks like:

Variation(s):

Initialized Variation(s):

Specify if Regional:

Linguistic Register (if specific): FORMAL   CONSULTATIVE   INFORMAL   INTIMATE

Other Vocab/Meanings:

GLOSS(ES)

(DH) Dominant Handshape:

(NDH) NonDominant Handshape:

(PO) Palm Orientation:

Movement:

Location (if not neutral):

NMS (if not neutral):

Looks like:

Variation(s):

Initialized Variation(s):

Specify if Regional:

Linguistic Register (if specific): FORMAL   CONSULTATIVE   INFORMAL   INTIMATE

Other Vocab/Meanings:

GLOSS(ES)

(DH) Dominant Handshape:

(NDH) NonDominant Handshape:

(PO) Palm Orientation:

Movement:

Location (if not neutral):

NMS (if not neutral):

Looks like:

Variation(s):

Initialized Variation(s):

Specify if Regional:

Linguistic Register (if specific): FORMAL   CONSULTATIVE   INFORMAL   INTIMATE

Other Vocab/Meanings:

GLOSS(ES)

(DH) Dominant Handshape:

(NDH) NonDominant Handshape:

(PO) Palm Orientation:

Movement:

Location (if not neutral):

NMS (if not neutral):

Looks like:

Variation(s):

Initialized Variation(s):

Specify if Regional:

Linguistic Register (if specific): FORMAL   CONSULTATIVE   INFORMAL   INTIMATE

Other Vocab/Meanings:

GLOSS(ES)

(DH) Dominant Handshape:

(NDH) NonDominant Handshape:

(PO) Palm Orientation:

Movement:

Location (if not neutral):

NMS (if not neutral):

Looks like:

Variation(s):

Initialized Variation(s):

Specify if Regional:

Linguistic Register (if specific): FORMAL   CONSULTATIVE   INFORMAL   INTIMATE

Other Vocab/Meanings:

GLOSS(ES)

(DH) Dominant Handshape:

(NDH) NonDominant Handshape:

(PO) Palm Orientation:

Movement:

Location (if not neutral):

NMS (if not neutral):

Looks like:

Variation(s):

Initialized Variation(s):

Specify if Regional:

Linguistic Register (if specific): FORMAL   CONSULTATIVE   INFORMAL   INTIMATE

Other Vocab/Meanings:

GLOSS(ES)

(DH) Dominant Handshape:

(NDH) NonDominant Handshape:

(PO) Palm Orientation:

Movement:

Location (if not neutral):

NMS (if not neutral):

Looks like:

Variation(s):

Initialized Variation(s):

Specify if Regional:

Linguistic Register (if specific): FORMAL CONSULTATIVE INFORMAL INTIMATE

Other Vocab/Meanings:

GLOSS(ES)

(DH) Dominant Handshape:

(NDH) NonDominant Handshape:

(PO) Palm Orientation:

Movement:

Location (if not neutral):

NMS (if not neutral):

Looks like:

Variation(s):

Initialized Variation(s):

Specify if Regional:

Linguistic Register (if specific): FORMAL CONSULTATIVE INFORMAL INTIMATE

Other Vocab/Meanings:

GLOSS(ES)

(DH) Dominant Handshape:

(NDH) NonDominant Handshape:

(PO) Palm Orientation:

Movement:

Location (if not neutral):

NMS (if not neutral):

Looks like:

Variation(s):

Initialized Variation(s):

Specify if Regional:

Linguistic Register (if specific): FORMAL CONSULTATIVE INFORMAL INTIMATE

Other Vocab/Meanings:

GLOSS(ES)

(DH) Dominant Handshape:

(NDH) NonDominant Handshape:

(PO) Palm Orientation:

Movement:

Location (if not neutral):

NMS (if not neutral):

Looks like:

Variation(s):

Initialized Variation(s):

Specify if Regional:

Linguistic Register (if specific): FORMAL CONSULTATIVE INFORMAL INTIMATE

Other Vocab/Meanings:

GLOSS(ES)

(DH) Dominant Handshape:

(NDH) NonDominant Handshape:

(PO) Palm Orientation:

Movement:

Location (if not neutral):

NMS (if not neutral):

Looks like:

Variation(s):

Initialized Variation(s):

Specify if Regional:

Linguistic Register (if specific): FORMAL CONSULTATIVE INFORMAL INTIMATE

Other Vocab/Meanings:

GLOSS(ES)

(DH) Dominant Handshape:

(NDH) NonDominant Handshape:

(PO) Palm Orientation:

Movement:

Location (if not neutral):

NMS (if not neutral):

Looks like:

Variation(s):

Initialized Variation(s):

Specify if Regional:

Linguistic Register (if specific): FORMAL CONSULTATIVE INFORMAL INTIMATE

Other Vocab/Meanings:

GLOSS(ES)

(DH) Dominant Handshape:

(NDH) NonDominant Handshape:

(PO) Palm Orientation:

Movement:

Location (if not neutral):

NMS (if not neutral):

Looks like:

Variation(s):

Initialized Variation(s):

Specify if Regional:

Linguistic Register (if specific): FORMAL CONSULTATIVE INFORMAL INTIMATE

Other Vocab/Meanings:

GLOSS(ES)

(DH) Dominant Handshape:

(NDH) NonDominant Handshape:

(PO) Palm Orientation:

Movement:

Location (if not neutral):

NMS (if not neutral):

Looks like:

Variation(s):

Initialized Variation(s):

Specify if Regional:

Linguistic Register (if specific): FORMAL CONSULTATIVE INFORMAL INTIMATE

Other Vocab/Meanings:

GLOSS(ES)

(DH) Dominant Handshape:

(NDH) NonDominant Handshape:

(PO) Palm Orientation:

Movement:

Location (if not neutral):

NMS (if not neutral):

Looks like:

Variation(s):

Initialized Variation(s):

Specify if Regional:

Linguistic Register (if specific): FORMAL CONSULTATIVE INFORMAL INTIMATE

Other Vocab/Meanings:

GLOSS(ES)

(DH) Dominant Handshape:

(NDH) NonDominant Handshape:

(PO) Palm Orientation:

Movement:

Location (if not neutral):

NMS (if not neutral):

Looks like:

Variation(s):

Initialized Variation(s):

Specify if Regional:

Linguistic Register (if specific): FORMAL CONSULTATIVE INFORMAL INTIMATE

Other Vocab/Meanings:

GLOSS(ES)

(DH) Dominant Handshape:

(NDH) NonDominant Handshape:

(PO) Palm Orientation:

Movement:

Location (if not neutral):

NMS (if not neutral):

Looks like:

Variation(s):

Initialized Variation(s):

Specify if Regional:

Linguistic Register (if specific): FORMAL CONSULTATIVE INFORMAL INTIMATE

Other Vocab/Meanings:

GLOSS(ES)

(DH) Dominant Handshape:

(NDH) NonDominant Handshape:

(PO) Palm Orientation:

Movement:

Location (if not neutral):

NMS (if not neutral):

Looks like:

Variation(s):

Initialized Variation(s):

Specify if Regional:

Linguistic Register (if specific): FORMAL CONSULTATIVE INFORMAL INTIMATE

Other Vocab/Meanings:

GLOSS(ES)

(DH) <u>Dominant Handshape</u>:

(NDH) <u>NonDominant Handshape</u>:

(PO) <u>Palm Orientation</u>:

<u>Movement</u>:

<u>Location</u> (if not neutral):

<u>NMS</u> (if not neutral):

Looks like:

Variation(s):

Initialized Variation(s):

Specify if Regional:

Linguistic Register (if specific): FORMAL   CONSULTATIVE   INFORMAL   INTIMATE

Other Vocab/Meanings:

GLOSS(ES)

(DH) <u>Dominant Handshape</u>:

(NDH) <u>NonDominant Handshape</u>:

(PO) <u>Palm Orientation</u>:

<u>Movement</u>:

<u>Location</u> (if not neutral):

<u>NMS</u> (if not neutral):

Looks like:

Variation(s):

Initialized Variation(s):

Specify if Regional:

Linguistic Register (if specific): FORMAL   CONSULTATIVE   INFORMAL   INTIMATE

Other Vocab/Meanings:

GLOSS(ES)

(DH) <u>Dominant Handshape</u>:

(NDH) <u>NonDominant Handshape</u>:

(PO) <u>Palm Orientation</u>:

<u>Movement</u>:

<u>Location</u> (if not neutral):

<u>NMS</u> (if not neutral):

Looks like:

Variation(s):

Initialized Variation(s):

Specify if Regional:

Linguistic Register (if specific): FORMAL   CONSULTATIVE   INFORMAL   INTIMATE

Other Vocab/Meanings:

GLOSS(ES)

(DH) <u>Dominant Handshape</u>:

(NDH) <u>NonDominant Handshape</u>:

(PO) <u>Palm Orientation</u>:

<u>Movement</u>:

<u>Location</u> (if not neutral):

<u>NMS</u> (if not neutral):

Looks like:

Variation(s):

Initialized Variation(s):

Specify if Regional:

Linguistic Register (if specific): FORMAL   CONSULTATIVE   INFORMAL   INTIMATE

Other Vocab/Meanings:

GLOSS(ES)

(DH) <u>Dominant Handshape</u>:

(NDH) <u>NonDominant Handshape</u>:

(PO) <u>Palm Orientation</u>:

<u>Movement</u>:

<u>Location</u> (if not neutral):

<u>NMS</u> (if not neutral):

Looks like:

Variation(s):

Initialized Variation(s):

Specify if Regional:

Linguistic Register (if specific): FORMAL   CONSULTATIVE   INFORMAL   INTIMATE

Other Vocab/Meanings:

GLOSS(ES)

(DH) <u>Dominant Handshape</u>:

(NDH) <u>NonDominant Handshape</u>:

(PO) <u>Palm Orientation</u>:

<u>Movement</u>:

<u>Location</u> (if not neutral):

<u>NMS</u> (if not neutral):

Looks like:

Variation(s):

Initialized Variation(s):

Specify if Regional:

Linguistic Register (if specific): FORMAL   CONSULTATIVE   INFORMAL   INTIMATE

Other Vocab/Meanings:

GLOSS(ES)

(DH) <u>Dominant Handshape</u>:

(NDH) <u>NonDominant Handshape</u>:

(PO) <u>Palm Orientation</u>:

<u>Movement</u>:

<u>Location</u> (if not neutral):

<u>NMS</u> (if not neutral):

Looks like:

Variation(s):

Initialized Variation(s):

Specify if Regional:

<u>Linguistic Register</u> (if specific): FORMAL CONSULTATIVE INFORMAL INTIMATE

Other Vocab/Meanings:

GLOSS(ES)

(DH) <u>Dominant Handshape</u>:

(NDH) <u>NonDominant Handshape</u>:

(PO) <u>Palm Orientation</u>:

<u>Movement</u>:

<u>Location</u> (if not neutral):

<u>NMS</u> (if not neutral):

Looks like:

Variation(s):

Initialized Variation(s):

Specify if Regional:

<u>Linguistic Register</u> (if specific): FORMAL CONSULTATIVE INFORMAL INTIMATE

Other Vocab/Meanings:

GLOSS(ES)

(DH) <u>Dominant Handshape</u>:

(NDH) <u>NonDominant Handshape</u>:

(PO) <u>Palm Orientation</u>:

<u>Movement</u>:

<u>Location</u> (if not neutral):

<u>NMS</u> (if not neutral):

Looks like:

Variation(s):

Initialized Variation(s):

Specify if Regional:

<u>Linguistic Register</u> (if specific): FORMAL CONSULTATIVE INFORMAL INTIMATE

Other Vocab/Meanings:

GLOSS(ES)

(DH) <u>Dominant Handshape</u>:

(NDH) <u>NonDominant Handshape</u>:

(PO) <u>Palm Orientation</u>:

<u>Movement</u>:

<u>Location</u> (if not neutral):

<u>NMS</u> (if not neutral):

Looks like:

Variation(s):

Initialized Variation(s):

Specify if Regional:

<u>Linguistic Register</u> (if specific): FORMAL CONSULTATIVE INFORMAL INTIMATE

Other Vocab/Meanings:

GLOSS(ES)

(DH) <u>Dominant Handshape</u>:

(NDH) <u>NonDominant Handshape</u>:

(PO) <u>Palm Orientation</u>:

<u>Movement</u>:

<u>Location</u> (if not neutral):

<u>NMS</u> (if not neutral):

Looks like:

Variation(s):

Initialized Variation(s):

Specify if Regional:

<u>Linguistic Register</u> (if specific): FORMAL CONSULTATIVE INFORMAL INTIMATE

Other Vocab/Meanings:

GLOSS(ES)

(DH) <u>Dominant Handshape</u>:

(NDH) <u>NonDominant Handshape</u>:

(PO) <u>Palm Orientation</u>:

<u>Movement</u>:

<u>Location</u> (if not neutral):

<u>NMS</u> (if not neutral):

Looks like:

Variation(s):

Initialized Variation(s):

Specify if Regional:

<u>Linguistic Register</u> (if specific): FORMAL CONSULTATIVE INFORMAL INTIMATE

Other Vocab/Meanings:

GLOSS(ES)

(DH) <u>Dominant Handshape</u>:

(NDH) <u>NonDominant Handshape</u>:

(PO) <u>Palm Orientation</u>:

<u>Movement</u>:

<u>Location</u> (if not neutral):

<u>NMS</u> (if not neutral):

Looks like:

Variation(s):

Initialized Variation(s):

Specify if Regional:

Linguistic Register (if specific): FORMAL CONSULTATIVE INFORMAL INTIMATE

Other Vocab/Meanings:

GLOSS(ES)

(DH) <u>Dominant Handshape</u>:

(NDH) <u>NonDominant Handshape</u>:

(PO) <u>Palm Orientation</u>:

<u>Movement</u>:

<u>Location</u> (if not neutral):

<u>NMS</u> (if not neutral):

Looks like:

Variation(s):

Initialized Variation(s):

Specify if Regional:

Linguistic Register (if specific): FORMAL CONSULTATIVE INFORMAL INTIMATE

Other Vocab/Meanings:

GLOSS(ES)

(DH) <u>Dominant Handshape</u>:

(NDH) <u>NonDominant Handshape</u>:

(PO) <u>Palm Orientation</u>:

<u>Movement</u>:

<u>Location</u> (if not neutral):

<u>NMS</u> (if not neutral):

Looks like:

Variation(s):

Initialized Variation(s):

Specify if Regional:

Linguistic Register (if specific): FORMAL CONSULTATIVE INFORMAL INTIMATE

Other Vocab/Meanings:

GLOSS(ES)

(DH) <u>Dominant Handshape</u>:

(NDH) <u>NonDominant Handshape</u>:

(PO) <u>Palm Orientation</u>:

<u>Movement</u>:

<u>Location</u> (if not neutral):

<u>NMS</u> (if not neutral):

Looks like:

Variation(s):

Initialized Variation(s):

Specify if Regional:

Linguistic Register (if specific): FORMAL CONSULTATIVE INFORMAL INTIMATE

Other Vocab/Meanings:

GLOSS(ES)

(DH) <u>Dominant Handshape</u>:

(NDH) <u>NonDominant Handshape</u>:

(PO) <u>Palm Orientation</u>:

<u>Movement</u>:

<u>Location</u> (if not neutral):

<u>NMS</u> (if not neutral):

Looks like:

Variation(s):

Initialized Variation(s):

Specify if Regional:

Linguistic Register (if specific): FORMAL CONSULTATIVE INFORMAL INTIMATE

Other Vocab/Meanings:

GLOSS(ES)

(DH) <u>Dominant Handshape</u>:

(NDH) <u>NonDominant Handshape</u>:

(PO) <u>Palm Orientation</u>:

<u>Movement</u>:

<u>Location</u> (if not neutral):

<u>NMS</u> (if not neutral):

Looks like:

Variation(s):

Initialized Variation(s):

Specify if Regional:

Linguistic Register (if specific): FORMAL CONSULTATIVE INFORMAL INTIMATE

Other Vocab/Meanings:

GLOSS(ES)

(DH) <u>Dominant Handshape</u>:

(NDH) <u>NonDominant Handshape</u>:

(PO) <u>Palm Orientation</u>:

<u>Movement</u>:

<u>Location</u> (if not neutral):

<u>NMS</u> (if not neutral):

Looks like:

Variation(s):

Initialized Variation(s):

Specify if Regional:

Linguistic Register (if specific): FORMAL CONSULTATIVE INFORMAL INTIMATE

Other Vocab/Meanings:

GLOSS(ES)

(DH) <u>Dominant Handshape</u>:

(NDH) <u>NonDominant Handshape</u>:

(PO) <u>Palm Orientation</u>:

<u>Movement</u>:

<u>Location</u> (if not neutral):

<u>NMS</u> (if not neutral):

Looks like:

Variation(s):

Initialized Variation(s):

Specify if Regional:

Linguistic Register (if specific): FORMAL CONSULTATIVE INFORMAL INTIMATE

Other Vocab/Meanings:

GLOSS(ES)

(DH) <u>Dominant Handshape</u>:

(NDH) <u>NonDominant Handshape</u>:

(PO) <u>Palm Orientation</u>:

<u>Movement</u>:

<u>Location</u> (if not neutral):

<u>NMS</u> (if not neutral):

Looks like:

Variation(s):

Initialized Variation(s):

Specify if Regional:

Linguistic Register (if specific): FORMAL CONSULTATIVE INFORMAL INTIMATE

Other Vocab/Meanings:

GLOSS(ES)

(DH) <u>Dominant Handshape</u>:

(NDH) <u>NonDominant Handshape</u>:

(PO) <u>Palm Orientation</u>:

<u>Movement</u>:

<u>Location</u> (if not neutral):

<u>NMS</u> (if not neutral):

Looks like:

Variation(s):

Initialized Variation(s):

Specify if Regional:

Linguistic Register (if specific): FORMAL CONSULTATIVE INFORMAL INTIMATE

Other Vocab/Meanings:

GLOSS(ES)

(DH) <u>Dominant Handshape</u>:

(NDH) <u>NonDominant Handshape</u>:

(PO) <u>Palm Orientation</u>:

<u>Movement</u>:

<u>Location</u> (if not neutral):

<u>NMS</u> (if not neutral):

Looks like:

Variation(s):

Initialized Variation(s):

Specify if Regional:

Linguistic Register (if specific): FORMAL CONSULTATIVE INFORMAL INTIMATE

Other Vocab/Meanings:

GLOSS(ES)

(DH) <u>Dominant Handshape</u>:

(NDH) <u>NonDominant Handshape</u>:

(PO) <u>Palm Orientation</u>:

<u>Movement</u>:

<u>Location</u> (if not neutral):

<u>NMS</u> (if not neutral):

Looks like:

Variation(s):

Initialized Variation(s):

Specify if Regional:

Linguistic Register (if specific): FORMAL CONSULTATIVE INFORMAL INTIMATE

Other Vocab/Meanings:

GLOSS(ES)

(DH) <u>Dominant Handshape</u>:

(NDH) <u>NonDominant Handshape</u>:

(PO) <u>Palm Orientation</u>:

<u>Movement</u>:

<u>Location</u> (if not neutral):

<u>NMS</u> (if not neutral):

Looks like:

Variation(s):

Initialized Variation(s):

Specify if Regional:

Linguistic Register (if specific): FORMAL CONSULTATIVE INFORMAL INTIMATE

Other Vocab/Meanings:

GLOSS(ES)

(DH) <u>Dominant Handshape</u>:

(NDH) <u>NonDominant Handshape</u>:

(PO) <u>Palm Orientation</u>:

<u>Movement</u>:

<u>Location</u> (if not neutral):

<u>NMS</u> (if not neutral):

Looks like:

Variation(s):

Initialized Variation(s):

Specify if Regional:

Linguistic Register (if specific): FORMAL CONSULTATIVE INFORMAL INTIMATE

Other Vocab/Meanings:

GLOSS(ES)

(DH) <u>Dominant Handshape</u>:

(NDH) <u>NonDominant Handshape</u>:

(PO) <u>Palm Orientation</u>:

<u>Movement</u>:

<u>Location</u> (if not neutral):

<u>NMS</u> (if not neutral):

Looks like:

Variation(s):

Initialized Variation(s):

Specify if Regional:

Linguistic Register (if specific): FORMAL CONSULTATIVE INFORMAL INTIMATE

Other Vocab/Meanings:

GLOSS(ES)

(DH) <u>Dominant Handshape</u>:

(NDH) <u>NonDominant Handshape</u>:

(PO) <u>Palm Orientation</u>:

<u>Movement</u>:

<u>Location</u> (if not neutral):

<u>NMS</u> (if not neutral):

Looks like:

Variation(s):

Initialized Variation(s):

Specify if Regional:

Linguistic Register (if specific): FORMAL CONSULTATIVE INFORMAL INTIMATE

Other Vocab/Meanings:

GLOSS(ES)

(DH) <u>Dominant Handshape</u>:

(NDH) <u>NonDominant Handshape</u>:

(PO) <u>Palm Orientation</u>:

<u>Movement</u>:

<u>Location</u> (if not neutral):

<u>NMS</u> (if not neutral):

Looks like:

Variation(s):

Initialized Variation(s):

Specify if Regional:

Linguistic Register (if specific): FORMAL CONSULTATIVE INFORMAL INTIMATE

Other Vocab/Meanings:

GLOSS(ES)

(DH) <u>Dominant Handshape</u>:

(NDH) <u>NonDominant Handshape</u>:

(PO) <u>Palm Orientation</u>:

<u>Movement</u>:

<u>Location</u> (if not neutral):

<u>NMS</u> (if not neutral):

Looks like:

Variation(s):

Initialized Variation(s):

Specify if Regional:

Linguistic Register (if specific): FORMAL CONSULTATIVE INFORMAL INTIMATE

Other Vocab/Meanings:

GLOSS(ES)

(DH) <u>Dominant Handshape</u>:

(NDH) <u>NonDominant Handshape</u>:

(PO) <u>Palm Orientation</u>:

<u>Movement</u>:

<u>Location</u> (if not neutral):

<u>NMS</u> (if not neutral):

Looks like:

Variation(s):

Initialized Variation(s):

Specify if Regional:

Linguistic Register (if specific): FORMAL CONSULTATIVE INFORMAL INTIMATE

Other Vocab/Meanings:

GLOSS(ES)

(DH) <u>Dominant Handshape</u>:

(NDH) <u>NonDominant Handshape</u>:

(PO) <u>Palm Orientation</u>:

<u>Movement</u>:

<u>Location</u> (if not neutral):

<u>NMS</u> (if not neutral):

Looks like:

Variation(s):

Initialized Variation(s):

Specify if Regional:

Linguistic Register (if specific): FORMAL CONSULTATIVE INFORMAL INTIMATE

Other Vocab/Meanings:

GLOSS(ES)

(DH) <u>Dominant Handshape</u>:

(NDH) <u>NonDominant Handshape</u>:

(PO) <u>Palm Orientation</u>:

<u>Movement</u>:

<u>Location</u> (if not neutral):

<u>NMS</u> (if not neutral):

Looks like:

Variation(s):

Initialized Variation(s):

Specify if Regional:

Linguistic Register (if specific): FORMAL CONSULTATIVE INFORMAL INTIMATE

Other Vocab/Meanings:

GLOSS(ES)

(DH) <u>Dominant Handshape</u>:

(NDH) <u>NonDominant Handshape</u>:

(PO) <u>Palm Orientation</u>:

<u>Movement</u>:

<u>Location</u> (if not neutral):

<u>NMS</u> (if not neutral):

Looks like:

Variation(s):

Initialized Variation(s):

Specify if Regional:

Linguistic Register (if specific): FORMAL CONSULTATIVE INFORMAL INTIMATE

Other Vocab/Meanings:

GLOSS(ES)

(DH) <u>Dominant Handshape</u>:

(NDH) <u>NonDominant Handshape</u>:

(PO) <u>Palm Orientation</u>:

<u>Movement</u>:

<u>Location</u> (if not neutral):

<u>NMS</u> (if not neutral):

Looks like:

Variation(s):

Initialized Variation(s):

Specify if Regional:

Linguistic Register (if specific): FORMAL CONSULTATIVE INFORMAL INTIMATE

Other Vocab/Meanings:

GLOSS(ES)

(DH) <u>Dominant Handshape</u>:

(NDH) <u>NonDominant Handshape</u>:

(PO) <u>Palm Orientation</u>:

<u>Movement</u>:

<u>Location</u> (if not neutral):

<u>NMS</u> (if not neutral):

Looks like:

Variation(s):

Initialized Variation(s):

Specify if Regional:

Linguistic Register (if specific): FORMAL CONSULTATIVE INFORMAL INTIMATE

Other Vocab/Meanings:

GLOSS(ES)

(DH) <u>Dominant Handshape</u>:

(NDH) <u>NonDominant Handshape</u>:

(PO) <u>Palm Orientation</u>:

<u>Movement</u>:

<u>Location</u> (if not neutral):

<u>NMS</u> (if not neutral):

Looks like:

Variation(s):

Initialized Variation(s):

Specify if Regional:

Linguistic Register (if specific): FORMAL CONSULTATIVE INFORMAL INTIMATE

Other Vocab/Meanings:

GLOSS(ES)

(DH) <u>Dominant Handshape</u>:

(NDH) <u>NonDominant Handshape</u>:

(PO) <u>Palm Orientation</u>:

<u>Movement</u>:

<u>Location</u> (if not neutral):

<u>NMS</u> (if not neutral):

Looks like:

Variation(s):

Initialized Variation(s):

Specify if Regional:

Linguistic Register (if specific): FORMAL CONSULTATIVE INFORMAL INTIMATE

Other Vocab/Meanings:

GLOSS(ES)

(DH) <u>Dominant Handshape</u>:

(NDH) <u>NonDominant Handshape</u>:

(PO) <u>Palm Orientation</u>:

<u>Movement</u>:

<u>Location</u> (if not neutral):

<u>NMS</u> (if not neutral):

Looks like:

Variation(s):

Initialized Variation(s):

Specify if Regional:

Linguistic Register (if specific): FORMAL CONSULTATIVE INFORMAL INTIMATE

Other Vocab/Meanings:

GLOSS(ES)

(DH) <u>Dominant Handshape</u>:

(NDH) <u>NonDominant Handshape</u>:

(PO) <u>Palm Orientation</u>:

<u>Movement</u>:

<u>Location</u> (if not neutral):

<u>NMS</u> (if not neutral):

Looks like:

Variation(s):

Initialized Variation(s):

Specify if Regional:

Linguistic Register (if specific): FORMAL CONSULTATIVE INFORMAL INTIMATE

Other Vocab/Meanings:

GLOSS(ES)

(DH) <u>Dominant Handshape</u>:

(NDH) <u>NonDominant Handshape</u>:

(PO) <u>Palm Orientation</u>:

<u>Movement</u>:

<u>Location</u> (if not neutral):

<u>NMS</u> (if not neutral):

Looks like:

Variation(s):

Initialized Variation(s):

Specify if Regional:

Linguistic Register (if specific): FORMAL CONSULTATIVE INFORMAL INTIMATE

Other Vocab/Meanings:

GLOSS(ES)

(DH) <u>Dominant Handshape</u>:

(NDH) <u>NonDominant Handshape</u>:

(PO) <u>Palm Orientation</u>:

<u>Movement</u>:

<u>Location</u> (if not neutral):

<u>NMS</u> (if not neutral):

Looks like:

Variation(s):

Initialized Variation(s):

Specify if Regional:

Linguistic Register (if specific): FORMAL CONSULTATIVE INFORMAL INTIMATE

Other Vocab/Meanings:

GLOSS(ES)

(DH) <u>Dominant Handshape</u>:

(NDH) <u>NonDominant Handshape</u>:

(PO) <u>Palm Orientation</u>:

<u>Movement</u>:

<u>Location</u> (if not neutral):

<u>NMS</u> (if not neutral):

Looks like:

Variation(s):

Initialized Variation(s):

Specify if Regional:

Linguistic Register (if specific): FORMAL CONSULTATIVE INFORMAL INTIMATE

Other Vocab/Meanings:

GLOSS(ES)

(DH) <u>Dominant Handshape</u>:

(NDH) <u>NonDominant Handshape</u>:

(PO) <u>Palm Orientation</u>:

<u>Movement</u>:

<u>Location</u> (if not neutral):

<u>NMS</u> (if not neutral):

Looks like:

Variation(s):

Initialized Variation(s):

Specify if Regional:

Linguistic Register (if specific): FORMAL CONSULTATIVE INFORMAL INTIMATE

Other Vocab/Meanings:

GLOSS(ES)

(DH) <u>Dominant Handshape</u>:

(NDH) <u>NonDominant Handshape</u>:

(PO) <u>Palm Orientation</u>:

<u>Movement</u>:

<u>Location</u> (if not neutral):

<u>NMS</u> (if not neutral):

Looks like:

Variation(s):

Initialized Variation(s):

Specify if Regional:

Linguistic Register (if specific): FORMAL CONSULTATIVE INFORMAL INTIMATE

Other Vocab/Meanings:

GLOSS(ES)

(DH) <u>Dominant Handshape</u>:

(NDH) <u>NonDominant Handshape</u>:

(PO) <u>Palm Orientation</u>:

<u>Movement</u>:

<u>Location</u> (if not neutral):

<u>NMS</u> (if not neutral):

Looks like:

Variation(s):

Initialized Variation(s):

Specify if Regional:

Linguistic Register (if specific): FORMAL CONSULTATIVE INFORMAL INTIMATE

Other Vocab/Meanings:

GLOSS(ES)

(DH) <u>Dominant Handshape</u>:

(NDH) <u>NonDominant Handshape</u>:

(PO) <u>Palm Orientation</u>:

<u>Movement</u>:

<u>Location</u> (if not neutral):

<u>NMS</u> (if not neutral):

Looks like:

Variation(s):

Initialized Variation(s):

Specify if Regional:

Linguistic Register (if specific): FORMAL CONSULTATIVE INFORMAL INTIMATE

Other Vocab/Meanings:

GLOSS(ES)

(DH) <u>Dominant Handshape</u>:

(NDH) <u>NonDominant Handshape</u>:

(PO) <u>Palm Orientation</u>:

<u>Movement</u>:

<u>Location</u> (if not neutral):

<u>NMS</u> (if not neutral):

Looks like:

Variation(s):

Initialized Variation(s):

Specify if Regional:

Linguistic Register (if specific): FORMAL CONSULTATIVE INFORMAL INTIMATE

Other Vocab/Meanings:

GLOSS(ES)

(DH) Dominant Handshape:

(NDH) NonDominant Handshape:

(PO) Palm Orientation:

Movement:

Location (if not neutral):

NMS (if not neutral):

Looks like:

Variation(s):

Initialized Variation(s):

Specify if Regional:

Linguistic Register (if specific): FORMAL CONSULTATIVE INFORMAL INTIMATE

Other Vocab/Meanings:

GLOSS(ES)

(DH) Dominant Handshape:

(NDH) NonDominant Handshape:

(PO) Palm Orientation:

Movement:

Location (if not neutral):

NMS (if not neutral):

Looks like:

Variation(s):

Initialized Variation(s):

Specify if Regional:

Linguistic Register (if specific): FORMAL CONSULTATIVE INFORMAL INTIMATE

Other Vocab/Meanings:

GLOSS(ES)

(DH) Dominant Handshape:

(NDH) NonDominant Handshape:

(PO) Palm Orientation:

Movement:

Location (if not neutral):

NMS (if not neutral):

Looks like:

Variation(s):

Initialized Variation(s):

Specify if Regional:

Linguistic Register (if specific): FORMAL CONSULTATIVE INFORMAL INTIMATE

Other Vocab/Meanings:

GLOSS(ES)

(DH) Dominant Handshape:

(NDH) NonDominant Handshape:

(PO) Palm Orientation:

Movement:

Location (if not neutral):

NMS (if not neutral):

Looks like:

Variation(s):

Initialized Variation(s):

Specify if Regional:

Linguistic Register (if specific): FORMAL CONSULTATIVE INFORMAL INTIMATE

Other Vocab/Meanings:

GLOSS(ES)

(DH) Dominant Handshape:

(NDH) NonDominant Handshape:

(PO) Palm Orientation:

Movement:

Location (if not neutral):

NMS (if not neutral):

Looks like:

Variation(s):

Initialized Variation(s):

Specify if Regional:

Linguistic Register (if specific): FORMAL CONSULTATIVE INFORMAL INTIMATE

Other Vocab/Meanings:

GLOSS(ES)

(DH) Dominant Handshape:

(NDH) NonDominant Handshape:

(PO) Palm Orientation:

Movement:

Location (if not neutral):

NMS (if not neutral):

Looks like:

Variation(s):

Initialized Variation(s):

Specify if Regional:

Linguistic Register (if specific): FORMAL CONSULTATIVE INFORMAL INTIMATE

Other Vocab/Meanings:

GLOSS(ES)

(DH) Dominant Handshape:

(NDH) NonDominant Handshape:

(PO) Palm Orientation:

Movement:

Location (if not neutral):

NMS (if not neutral):

Looks like:

Variation(s):

Initialized Variation(s):

Specify if Regional:

Linguistic Register (if specific): FORMAL CONSULTATIVE INFORMAL INTIMATE

Other Vocab/Meanings:

GLOSS(ES)

(DH) Dominant Handshape:

(NDH) NonDominant Handshape:

(PO) Palm Orientation:

Movement:

Location (if not neutral):

NMS (if not neutral):

Looks like:

Variation(s):

Initialized Variation(s):

Specify if Regional:

Linguistic Register (if specific): FORMAL CONSULTATIVE INFORMAL INTIMATE

Other Vocab/Meanings:

GLOSS(ES)

(DH) Dominant Handshape:

(NDH) NonDominant Handshape:

(PO) Palm Orientation:

Movement:

Location (if not neutral):

NMS (if not neutral):

Looks like:

Variation(s):

Initialized Variation(s):

Specify if Regional:

Linguistic Register (if specific): FORMAL CONSULTATIVE INFORMAL INTIMATE

Other Vocab/Meanings:

GLOSS(ES)

(DH) Dominant Handshape:

(NDH) NonDominant Handshape:

(PO) Palm Orientation:

Movement:

Location (if not neutral):

NMS (if not neutral):

Looks like:

Variation(s):

Initialized Variation(s):

Specify if Regional:

Linguistic Register (if specific): FORMAL CONSULTATIVE INFORMAL INTIMATE

Other Vocab/Meanings:

GLOSS(ES)

(DH) Dominant Handshape:

(NDH) NonDominant Handshape:

(PO) Palm Orientation:

Movement:

Location (if not neutral):

NMS (if not neutral):

Looks like:

Variation(s):

Initialized Variation(s):

Specify if Regional:

Linguistic Register (if specific): FORMAL CONSULTATIVE INFORMAL INTIMATE

Other Vocab/Meanings:

GLOSS(ES)

(DH) Dominant Handshape:

(NDH) NonDominant Handshape:

(PO) Palm Orientation:

Movement:

Location (if not neutral):

NMS (if not neutral):

Looks like:

Variation(s):

Initialized Variation(s):

Specify if Regional:

Linguistic Register (if specific): FORMAL CONSULTATIVE INFORMAL INTIMATE

Other Vocab/Meanings:

GLOSS(ES)

(DH) Dominant Handshape:

(NDH) NonDominant Handshape:

(PO) Palm Orientation:

Movement:

Location (if not neutral):

NMS (if not neutral):

Looks like:

Variation(s):

Initialized Variation(s):

Specify if Regional:

Linguistic Register (if specific): FORMAL CONSULTATIVE INFORMAL INTIMATE

Other Vocab/Meanings:

GLOSS(ES)

(DH) Dominant Handshape:

(NDH) NonDominant Handshape:

(PO) Palm Orientation:

Movement:

Location (if not neutral):

NMS (if not neutral):

Looks like:

Variation(s):

Initialized Variation(s):

Specify if Regional:

Linguistic Register (if specific): FORMAL CONSULTATIVE INFORMAL INTIMATE

Other Vocab/Meanings:

GLOSS(ES)

(DH) Dominant Handshape:

(NDH) NonDominant Handshape:

(PO) Palm Orientation:

Movement:

Location (if not neutral):

NMS (if not neutral):

Looks like:

Variation(s):

Initialized Variation(s):

Specify if Regional:

Linguistic Register (if specific): FORMAL CONSULTATIVE INFORMAL INTIMATE

Other Vocab/Meanings:

GLOSS(ES)

(DH) Dominant Handshape:

(NDH) NonDominant Handshape:

(PO) Palm Orientation:

Movement:

Location (if not neutral):

NMS (if not neutral):

Looks like:

Variation(s):

Initialized Variation(s):

Specify if Regional:

Linguistic Register (if specific): FORMAL CONSULTATIVE INFORMAL INTIMATE

Other Vocab/Meanings:

GLOSS(ES)

(DH) Dominant Handshape:

(NDH) NonDominant Handshape:

(PO) Palm Orientation:

Movement:

Location (if not neutral):

NMS (if not neutral):

Looks like:

Variation(s):

Initialized Variation(s):

Specify if Regional:

Linguistic Register (if specific): FORMAL CONSULTATIVE INFORMAL INTIMATE

Other Vocab/Meanings:

GLOSS(ES)

(DH) Dominant Handshape:

(NDH) NonDominant Handshape:

(PO) Palm Orientation:

Movement:

Location (if not neutral):

NMS (if not neutral):

Looks like:

Variation(s):

Initialized Variation(s):

Specify if Regional:

Linguistic Register (if specific): FORMAL CONSULTATIVE INFORMAL INTIMATE

Other Vocab/Meanings:

GLOSS(ES)

(DH) <u>Dominant Handshape</u>:

(NDH) <u>NonDominant Handshape</u>:

(PO) <u>Palm Orientation</u>:

<u>Movement</u>:

<u>Location</u> (if not neutral):

<u>NMS</u> (if not neutral):

Looks like:

Variation(s):

Initialized Variation(s):

Specify if Regional:

Linguistic Register (if specific): FORMAL CONSULTATIVE INFORMAL INTIMATE

Other Vocab/Meanings:

GLOSS(ES)

(DH) <u>Dominant Handshape</u>:

(NDH) <u>NonDominant Handshape</u>:

(PO) <u>Palm Orientation</u>:

<u>Movement</u>:

<u>Location</u> (if not neutral):

<u>NMS</u> (if not neutral):

Looks like:

Variation(s):

Initialized Variation(s):

Specify if Regional:

Linguistic Register (if specific): FORMAL CONSULTATIVE INFORMAL INTIMATE

Other Vocab/Meanings:

GLOSS(ES)

(DH) <u>Dominant Handshape</u>:

(NDH) <u>NonDominant Handshape</u>:

(PO) <u>Palm Orientation</u>:

<u>Movement</u>:

<u>Location</u> (if not neutral):

<u>NMS</u> (if not neutral):

Looks like:

Variation(s):

Initialized Variation(s):

Specify if Regional:

Linguistic Register (if specific): FORMAL CONSULTATIVE INFORMAL INTIMATE

Other Vocab/Meanings:

GLOSS(ES)

(DH) <u>Dominant Handshape</u>:

(NDH) <u>NonDominant Handshape</u>:

(PO) <u>Palm Orientation</u>:

<u>Movement</u>:

<u>Location</u> (if not neutral):

<u>NMS</u> (if not neutral):

Looks like:

Variation(s):

Initialized Variation(s):

Specify if Regional:

Linguistic Register (if specific): FORMAL CONSULTATIVE INFORMAL INTIMATE

Other Vocab/Meanings:

GLOSS(ES)

(DH) <u>Dominant Handshape</u>:

(NDH) <u>NonDominant Handshape</u>:

(PO) <u>Palm Orientation</u>:

<u>Movement</u>:

<u>Location</u> (if not neutral):

<u>NMS</u> (if not neutral):

Looks like:

Variation(s):

Initialized Variation(s):

Specify if Regional:

Linguistic Register (if specific): FORMAL CONSULTATIVE INFORMAL INTIMATE

Other Vocab/Meanings:

GLOSS(ES)

(DH) <u>Dominant Handshape</u>:

(NDH) <u>NonDominant Handshape</u>:

(PO) <u>Palm Orientation</u>:

<u>Movement</u>:

<u>Location</u> (if not neutral):

<u>NMS</u> (if not neutral):

Looks like:

Variation(s):

Initialized Variation(s):

Specify if Regional:

Linguistic Register (if specific): FORMAL CONSULTATIVE INFORMAL INTIMATE

Other Vocab/Meanings:

GLOSS(ES)

(DH) Dominant Handshape:

(NDH) NonDominant Handshape:

(PO) Palm Orientation:

Movement:

Location (if not neutral):

NMS (if not neutral):

Looks like:

Variation(s):

Initialized Variation(s):

Specify if Regional:

Linguistic Register (if specific): FORMAL CONSULTATIVE INFORMAL INTIMATE

Other Vocab/Meanings:

GLOSS(ES)

(DH) Dominant Handshape:

(NDH) NonDominant Handshape:

(PO) Palm Orientation:

Movement:

Location (if not neutral):

NMS (if not neutral):

Looks like:

Variation(s):

Initialized Variation(s):

Specify if Regional:

Linguistic Register (if specific): FORMAL CONSULTATIVE INFORMAL INTIMATE

Other Vocab/Meanings:

GLOSS(ES)

(DH) Dominant Handshape:

(NDH) NonDominant Handshape:

(PO) Palm Orientation:

Movement:

Location (if not neutral):

NMS (if not neutral):

Looks like:

Variation(s):

Initialized Variation(s):

Specify if Regional:

Linguistic Register (if specific): FORMAL CONSULTATIVE INFORMAL INTIMATE

Other Vocab/Meanings:

GLOSS(ES)

(DH) Dominant Handshape:

(NDH) NonDominant Handshape:

(PO) Palm Orientation:

Movement:

Location (if not neutral):

NMS (if not neutral):

Looks like:

Variation(s):

Initialized Variation(s):

Specify if Regional:

Linguistic Register (if specific): FORMAL CONSULTATIVE INFORMAL INTIMATE

Other Vocab/Meanings:

GLOSS(ES)

(DH) Dominant Handshape:

(NDH) NonDominant Handshape:

(PO) Palm Orientation:

Movement:

Location (if not neutral):

NMS (if not neutral):

Looks like:

Variation(s):

Initialized Variation(s):

Specify if Regional:

Linguistic Register (if specific): FORMAL CONSULTATIVE INFORMAL INTIMATE

Other Vocab/Meanings:

GLOSS(ES)

(DH) Dominant Handshape:

(NDH) NonDominant Handshape:

(PO) Palm Orientation:

Movement:

Location (if not neutral):

NMS (if not neutral):

Looks like:

Variation(s):

Initialized Variation(s):

Specify if Regional:

Linguistic Register (if specific): FORMAL CONSULTATIVE INFORMAL INTIMATE

Other Vocab/Meanings:

GLOSS(ES)

(DH) Dominant Handshape:

(NDH) NonDominant Handshape:

(PO) Palm Orientation:

Movement:

Location (if not neutral):

NMS (if not neutral):

Looks like:

Variation(s):

Initialized Variation(s):

Specify if Regional:

Linguistic Register (if specific): FORMAL   CONSULTATIVE   INFORMAL   INTIMATE

Other Vocab/Meanings:

GLOSS(ES)

(DH) Dominant Handshape:

(NDH) NonDominant Handshape:

(PO) Palm Orientation:

Movement:

Location (if not neutral):

NMS (if not neutral):

Looks like:

Variation(s):

Initialized Variation(s):

Specify if Regional:

Linguistic Register (if specific): FORMAL   CONSULTATIVE   INFORMAL   INTIMATE

Other Vocab/Meanings:

GLOSS(ES)

(DH) Dominant Handshape:

(NDH) NonDominant Handshape:

(PO) Palm Orientation:

Movement:

Location (if not neutral):

NMS (if not neutral):

Looks like:

Variation(s):

Initialized Variation(s):

Specify if Regional:

Linguistic Register (if specific): FORMAL   CONSULTATIVE   INFORMAL   INTIMATE

Other Vocab/Meanings:

GLOSS(ES)

(DH) Dominant Handshape:

(NDH) NonDominant Handshape:

(PO) Palm Orientation:

Movement:

Location (if not neutral):

NMS (if not neutral):

Looks like:

Variation(s):

Initialized Variation(s):

Specify if Regional:

Linguistic Register (if specific): FORMAL   CONSULTATIVE   INFORMAL   INTIMATE

Other Vocab/Meanings:

GLOSS(ES)

(DH) Dominant Handshape:

(NDH) NonDominant Handshape:

(PO) Palm Orientation:

Movement:

Location (if not neutral):

NMS (if not neutral):

Looks like:

Variation(s):

Initialized Variation(s):

Specify if Regional:

Linguistic Register (if specific): FORMAL   CONSULTATIVE   INFORMAL   INTIMATE

Other Vocab/Meanings:

GLOSS(ES)

(DH) Dominant Handshape:

(NDH) NonDominant Handshape:

(PO) Palm Orientation:

Movement:

Location (if not neutral):

NMS (if not neutral):

Looks like:

Variation(s):

Initialized Variation(s):

Specify if Regional:

Linguistic Register (if specific): FORMAL   CONSULTATIVE   INFORMAL   INTIMATE

Other Vocab/Meanings:

GLOSS(ES)

(DH) Dominant Handshape:

(NDH) NonDominant Handshape:

(PO) Palm Orientation:

Movement:

Location (if not neutral):

NMS (if not neutral):

Looks like:

Variation(s):

Initialized Variation(s):

Specify if Regional:

Linguistic Register (if specific): FORMAL   CONSULTATIVE   INFORMAL   INTIMATE

Other Vocab/Meanings:

GLOSS(ES)

(DH) Dominant Handshape:

(NDH) NonDominant Handshape:

(PO) Palm Orientation:

Movement:

Location (if not neutral):

NMS (if not neutral):

Looks like:

Variation(s):

Initialized Variation(s):

Specify if Regional:

Linguistic Register (if specific): FORMAL   CONSULTATIVE   INFORMAL   INTIMATE

Other Vocab/Meanings:

GLOSS(ES)

(DH) Dominant Handshape:

(NDH) NonDominant Handshape:

(PO) Palm Orientation:

Movement:

Location (if not neutral):

NMS (if not neutral):

Looks like:

Variation(s):

Initialized Variation(s):

Specify if Regional:

Linguistic Register (if specific): FORMAL   CONSULTATIVE   INFORMAL   INTIMATE

Other Vocab/Meanings:

GLOSS(ES)

(DH) Dominant Handshape:

(NDH) NonDominant Handshape:

(PO) Palm Orientation:

Movement:

Location (if not neutral):

NMS (if not neutral):

Looks like:

Variation(s):

Initialized Variation(s):

Specify if Regional:

Linguistic Register (if specific): FORMAL   CONSULTATIVE   INFORMAL   INTIMATE

Other Vocab/Meanings:

GLOSS(ES)

(DH) Dominant Handshape:

(NDH) NonDominant Handshape:

(PO) Palm Orientation:

Movement:

Location (if not neutral):

NMS (if not neutral):

Looks like:

Variation(s):

Initialized Variation(s):

Specify if Regional:

Linguistic Register (if specific): FORMAL   CONSULTATIVE   INFORMAL   INTIMATE

Other Vocab/Meanings:

GLOSS(ES)

(DH) Dominant Handshape:

(NDH) NonDominant Handshape:

(PO) Palm Orientation:

Movement:

Location (if not neutral):

NMS (if not neutral):

Looks like:

Variation(s):

Initialized Variation(s):

Specify if Regional:

Linguistic Register (if specific): FORMAL   CONSULTATIVE   INFORMAL   INTIMATE

Other Vocab/Meanings:

GLOSS(ES)

(DH) Dominant Handshape:

(NDH) NonDominant Handshape:

(PO) Palm Orientation:

Movement:

Location (if not neutral):

NMS (if not neutral):

Looks like:

Variation(s):

Initialized Variation(s):

Specify if Regional:

Linguistic Register (if specific): FORMAL CONSULTATIVE INFORMAL INTIMATE

Other Vocab/Meanings:

GLOSS(ES)

(DH) Dominant Handshape:

(NDH) NonDominant Handshape:

(PO) Palm Orientation:

Movement:

Location (if not neutral):

NMS (if not neutral):

Looks like:

Variation(s):

Initialized Variation(s):

Specify if Regional:

Linguistic Register (if specific): FORMAL CONSULTATIVE INFORMAL INTIMATE

Other Vocab/Meanings:

GLOSS(ES)

(DH) Dominant Handshape:

(NDH) NonDominant Handshape:

(PO) Palm Orientation:

Movement:

Location (if not neutral):

NMS (if not neutral):

Looks like:

Variation(s):

Initialized Variation(s):

Specify if Regional:

Linguistic Register (if specific): FORMAL CONSULTATIVE INFORMAL INTIMATE

Other Vocab/Meanings:

GLOSS(ES)

(DH) Dominant Handshape:

(NDH) NonDominant Handshape:

(PO) Palm Orientation:

Movement:

Location (if not neutral):

NMS (if not neutral):

Looks like:

Variation(s):

Initialized Variation(s):

Specify if Regional:

Linguistic Register (if specific): FORMAL CONSULTATIVE INFORMAL INTIMATE

Other Vocab/Meanings:

GLOSS(ES)

(DH) Dominant Handshape:

(NDH) NonDominant Handshape:

(PO) Palm Orientation:

Movement:

Location (if not neutral):

NMS (if not neutral):

Looks like:

Variation(s):

Initialized Variation(s):

Specify if Regional:

Linguistic Register (if specific): FORMAL CONSULTATIVE INFORMAL INTIMATE

Other Vocab/Meanings:

GLOSS(ES)

(DH) Dominant Handshape:

(NDH) NonDominant Handshape:

(PO) Palm Orientation:

Movement:

Location (if not neutral):

NMS (if not neutral):

Looks like:

Variation(s):

Initialized Variation(s):

Specify if Regional:

Linguistic Register (if specific): FORMAL CONSULTATIVE INFORMAL INTIMATE

Other Vocab/Meanings:

GLOSS(ES)

(DH) Dominant Handshape:

(NDH) NonDominant Handshape:

(PO) Palm Orientation:

Movement:

Location (if not neutral):

NMS (if not neutral):

Looks like:

Variation(s):

Initialized Variation(s):

Specify if Regional:

Linguistic Register (if specific): FORMAL CONSULTATIVE INFORMAL INTIMATE

Other Vocab/Meanings:

GLOSS(ES)

(DH) Dominant Handshape:

(NDH) NonDominant Handshape:

(PO) Palm Orientation:

Movement:

Location (if not neutral):

NMS (if not neutral):

Looks like:

Variation(s):

Initialized Variation(s):

Specify if Regional:

Linguistic Register (if specific): FORMAL CONSULTATIVE INFORMAL INTIMATE

Other Vocab/Meanings:

GLOSS(ES)

(DH) Dominant Handshape:

(NDH) NonDominant Handshape:

(PO) Palm Orientation:

Movement:

Location (if not neutral):

NMS (if not neutral):

Looks like:

Variation(s):

Initialized Variation(s):

Specify if Regional:

Linguistic Register (if specific): FORMAL CONSULTATIVE INFORMAL INTIMATE

Other Vocab/Meanings:

GLOSS(ES)

(DH) Dominant Handshape:

(NDH) NonDominant Handshape:

(PO) Palm Orientation:

Movement:

Location (if not neutral):

NMS (if not neutral):

Looks like:

Variation(s):

Initialized Variation(s):

Specify if Regional:

Linguistic Register (if specific): FORMAL CONSULTATIVE INFORMAL INTIMATE

Other Vocab/Meanings:

GLOSS(ES)

(DH) Dominant Handshape:

(NDH) NonDominant Handshape:

(PO) Palm Orientation:

Movement:

Location (if not neutral):

NMS (if not neutral):

Looks like:

Variation(s):

Initialized Variation(s):

Specify if Regional:

Linguistic Register (if specific): FORMAL CONSULTATIVE INFORMAL INTIMATE

Other Vocab/Meanings:

GLOSS(ES)

(DH) Dominant Handshape:

(NDH) NonDominant Handshape:

(PO) Palm Orientation:

Movement:

Location (if not neutral):

NMS (if not neutral):

Looks like:

Variation(s):

Initialized Variation(s):

Specify if Regional:

Linguistic Register (if specific): FORMAL CONSULTATIVE INFORMAL INTIMATE

Other Vocab/Meanings:

GLOSS(ES)

(DH) <u>Dominant Handshape</u>:

(NDH) <u>NonDominant Handshape</u>:

(PO) <u>Palm Orientation</u>:

<u>Movement</u>:

<u>Location</u> (if not neutral):

<u>NMS</u> (if not neutral):

Looks like:

Variation(s):

Initialized Variation(s):

Specify if Regional:

Linguistic Register (if specific): FORMAL CONSULTATIVE INFORMAL INTIMATE

Other Vocab/Meanings:

GLOSS(ES)

(DH) <u>Dominant Handshape</u>:

(NDH) <u>NonDominant Handshape</u>:

(PO) <u>Palm Orientation</u>:

<u>Movement</u>:

<u>Location</u> (if not neutral):

<u>NMS</u> (if not neutral):

Looks like:

Variation(s):

Initialized Variation(s):

Specify if Regional:

Linguistic Register (if specific): FORMAL CONSULTATIVE INFORMAL INTIMATE

Other Vocab/Meanings:

GLOSS(ES)

(DH) <u>Dominant Handshape</u>:

(NDH) <u>NonDominant Handshape</u>:

(PO) <u>Palm Orientation</u>:

<u>Movement</u>:

<u>Location</u> (if not neutral):

<u>NMS</u> (if not neutral):

Looks like:

Variation(s):

Initialized Variation(s):

Specify if Regional:

Linguistic Register (if specific): FORMAL CONSULTATIVE INFORMAL INTIMATE

Other Vocab/Meanings:

GLOSS(ES)

(DH) <u>Dominant Handshape</u>:

(NDH) <u>NonDominant Handshape</u>:

(PO) <u>Palm Orientation</u>:

<u>Movement</u>:

<u>Location</u> (if not neutral):

<u>NMS</u> (if not neutral):

Looks like:

Variation(s):

Initialized Variation(s):

Specify if Regional:

Linguistic Register (if specific): FORMAL CONSULTATIVE INFORMAL INTIMATE

Other Vocab/Meanings:

GLOSS(ES)

(DH) <u>Dominant Handshape</u>:

(NDH) <u>NonDominant Handshape</u>:

(PO) <u>Palm Orientation</u>:

<u>Movement</u>:

<u>Location</u> (if not neutral):

<u>NMS</u> (if not neutral):

Looks like:

Variation(s):

Initialized Variation(s):

Specify if Regional:

Linguistic Register (if specific): FORMAL CONSULTATIVE INFORMAL INTIMATE

Other Vocab/Meanings:

GLOSS(ES)

(DH) <u>Dominant Handshape</u>:

(NDH) <u>NonDominant Handshape</u>:

(PO) <u>Palm Orientation</u>:

<u>Movement</u>:

<u>Location</u> (if not neutral):

<u>NMS</u> (if not neutral):

Looks like:

Variation(s):

Initialized Variation(s):

Specify if Regional:

Linguistic Register (if specific): FORMAL CONSULTATIVE INFORMAL INTIMATE

Other Vocab/Meanings:

GLOSS(ES)

(DH) <u>Dominant Handshape</u>:

(NDH) <u>NonDominant Handshape</u>:

(PO) <u>Palm Orientation</u>:

<u>Movement</u>:

<u>Location</u> (if not neutral):

<u>NMS</u> (if not neutral):

Looks like:

Variation(s):

Initialized Variation(s):

Specify if Regional:

Linguistic Register (if specific): FORMAL   CONSULTATIVE   INFORMAL   INTIMATE

Other Vocab/Meanings:

GLOSS(ES)

(DH) <u>Dominant Handshape</u>:

(NDH) <u>NonDominant Handshape</u>:

(PO) <u>Palm Orientation</u>:

<u>Movement</u>:

<u>Location</u> (if not neutral):

<u>NMS</u> (if not neutral):

Looks like:

Variation(s):

Initialized Variation(s):

Specify if Regional:

Linguistic Register (if specific): FORMAL   CONSULTATIVE   INFORMAL   INTIMATE

Other Vocab/Meanings:

GLOSS(ES)

(DH) <u>Dominant Handshape</u>:

(NDH) <u>NonDominant Handshape</u>:

(PO) <u>Palm Orientation</u>:

<u>Movement</u>:

<u>Location</u> (if not neutral):

<u>NMS</u> (if not neutral):

Looks like:

Variation(s):

Initialized Variation(s):

Specify if Regional:

Linguistic Register (if specific): FORMAL   CONSULTATIVE   INFORMAL   INTIMATE

Other Vocab/Meanings:

GLOSS(ES)

(DH) <u>Dominant Handshape</u>:

(NDH) <u>NonDominant Handshape</u>:

(PO) <u>Palm Orientation</u>:

<u>Movement</u>:

<u>Location</u> (if not neutral):

<u>NMS</u> (if not neutral):

Looks like:

Variation(s):

Initialized Variation(s):

Specify if Regional:

Linguistic Register (if specific): FORMAL   CONSULTATIVE   INFORMAL   INTIMATE

Other Vocab/Meanings:

GLOSS(ES)

(DH) <u>Dominant Handshape</u>:

(NDH) <u>NonDominant Handshape</u>:

(PO) <u>Palm Orientation</u>:

<u>Movement</u>:

<u>Location</u> (if not neutral):

<u>NMS</u> (if not neutral):

Looks like:

Variation(s):

Initialized Variation(s):

Specify if Regional:

Linguistic Register (if specific): FORMAL   CONSULTATIVE   INFORMAL   INTIMATE

Other Vocab/Meanings:

GLOSS(ES)

(DH) <u>Dominant Handshape</u>:

(NDH) <u>NonDominant Handshape</u>:

(PO) <u>Palm Orientation</u>:

<u>Movement</u>:

<u>Location</u> (if not neutral):

<u>NMS</u> (if not neutral):

Looks like:

Variation(s):

Initialized Variation(s):

Specify if Regional:

Linguistic Register (if specific): FORMAL   CONSULTATIVE   INFORMAL   INTIMATE

Other Vocab/Meanings:

GLOSS(ES)

(DH) Dominant Handshape:

(NDH) NonDominant Handshape:

   (PO) Palm Orientation:

      Movement:

     Location (if not neutral):

      NMS (if not neutral):

  Looks like:

  Variation(s):

Initialized Variation(s):

  Specify if Regional:

  Linguistic Register (if specific): FORMAL CONSULTATIVE INFORMAL INTIMATE

Other Vocab/Meanings:

GLOSS(ES)

(DH) Dominant Handshape:

(NDH) NonDominant Handshape:

   (PO) Palm Orientation:

      Movement:

     Location (if not neutral):

      NMS (if not neutral):

  Looks like:

  Variation(s):

Initialized Variation(s):

  Specify if Regional:

  Linguistic Register (if specific): FORMAL CONSULTATIVE INFORMAL INTIMATE

Other Vocab/Meanings:

GLOSS(ES)

(DH) Dominant Handshape:

(NDH) NonDominant Handshape:

   (PO) Palm Orientation:

      Movement:

     Location (if not neutral):

      NMS (if not neutral):

  Looks like:

  Variation(s):

Initialized Variation(s):

  Specify if Regional:

  Linguistic Register (if specific): FORMAL CONSULTATIVE INFORMAL INTIMATE

Other Vocab/Meanings:

GLOSS(ES)

(DH) Dominant Handshape:

(NDH) NonDominant Handshape:

   (PO) Palm Orientation:

      Movement:

     Location (if not neutral):

      NMS (if not neutral):

  Looks like:

  Variation(s):

Initialized Variation(s):

  Specify if Regional:

  Linguistic Register (if specific): FORMAL CONSULTATIVE INFORMAL INTIMATE

Other Vocab/Meanings:

GLOSS(ES)

(DH) Dominant Handshape:

(NDH) NonDominant Handshape:

   (PO) Palm Orientation:

      Movement:

     Location (if not neutral):

      NMS (if not neutral):

  Looks like:

  Variation(s):

Initialized Variation(s):

  Specify if Regional:

  Linguistic Register (if specific): FORMAL CONSULTATIVE INFORMAL INTIMATE

Other Vocab/Meanings:

GLOSS(ES)

(DH) Dominant Handshape:

(NDH) NonDominant Handshape:

   (PO) Palm Orientation:

      Movement:

     Location (if not neutral):

      NMS (if not neutral):

  Looks like:

  Variation(s):

Initialized Variation(s):

  Specify if Regional:

  Linguistic Register (if specific): FORMAL CONSULTATIVE INFORMAL INTIMATE

Other Vocab/Meanings:

GLOSS(ES)

(DH) <u>Dominant Handshape</u>:

(NDH) <u>NonDominant Handshape</u>:

(PO) <u>Palm Orientation</u>:

<u>Movement</u>:

<u>Location</u> (if not neutral):

<u>NMS</u> (if not neutral):

Looks like:

Variation(s):

Initialized Variation(s):

Specify if Regional:

Linguistic Register (if specific): FORMAL CONSULTATIVE INFORMAL INTIMATE

Other Vocab/Meanings:

GLOSS(ES)

(DH) <u>Dominant Handshape</u>:

(NDH) <u>NonDominant Handshape</u>:

(PO) <u>Palm Orientation</u>:

<u>Movement</u>:

<u>Location</u> (if not neutral):

<u>NMS</u> (if not neutral):

Looks like:

Variation(s):

Initialized Variation(s):

Specify if Regional:

Linguistic Register (if specific): FORMAL CONSULTATIVE INFORMAL INTIMATE

Other Vocab/Meanings:

GLOSS(ES)

(DH) <u>Dominant Handshape</u>:

(NDH) <u>NonDominant Handshape</u>:

(PO) <u>Palm Orientation</u>:

<u>Movement</u>:

<u>Location</u> (if not neutral):

<u>NMS</u> (if not neutral):

Looks like:

Variation(s):

Initialized Variation(s):

Specify if Regional:

Linguistic Register (if specific): FORMAL CONSULTATIVE INFORMAL INTIMATE

Other Vocab/Meanings:

GLOSS(ES)

(DH) <u>Dominant Handshape</u>:

(NDH) <u>NonDominant Handshape</u>:

(PO) <u>Palm Orientation</u>:

<u>Movement</u>:

<u>Location</u> (if not neutral):

<u>NMS</u> (if not neutral):

Looks like:

Variation(s):

Initialized Variation(s):

Specify if Regional:

Linguistic Register (if specific): FORMAL CONSULTATIVE INFORMAL INTIMATE

Other Vocab/Meanings:

GLOSS(ES)

(DH) <u>Dominant Handshape</u>:

(NDH) <u>NonDominant Handshape</u>:

(PO) <u>Palm Orientation</u>:

<u>Movement</u>:

<u>Location</u> (if not neutral):

<u>NMS</u> (if not neutral):

Looks like:

Variation(s):

Initialized Variation(s):

Specify if Regional:

Linguistic Register (if specific): FORMAL CONSULTATIVE INFORMAL INTIMATE

Other Vocab/Meanings:

GLOSS(ES)

(DH) <u>Dominant Handshape</u>:

(NDH) <u>NonDominant Handshape</u>:

(PO) <u>Palm Orientation</u>:

<u>Movement</u>:

<u>Location</u> (if not neutral):

<u>NMS</u> (if not neutral):

Looks like:

Variation(s):

Initialized Variation(s):

Specify if Regional:

Linguistic Register (if specific): FORMAL CONSULTATIVE INFORMAL INTIMATE

Other Vocab/Meanings:

GLOSS(ES)

(DH) Dominant Handshape:

(NDH) NonDominant Handshape:

(PO) Palm Orientation:

Movement:

Location (if not neutral):

NMS (if not neutral):

Looks like:

Variation(s):

Initialized Variation(s):

Specify if Regional:

Linguistic Register (if specific): FORMAL   CONSULTATIVE   INFORMAL   INTIMATE

Other Vocab/Meanings:

GLOSS(ES)

(DH) Dominant Handshape:

(NDH) NonDominant Handshape:

(PO) Palm Orientation:

Movement:

Location (if not neutral):

NMS (if not neutral):

Looks like:

Variation(s):

Initialized Variation(s):

Specify if Regional:

Linguistic Register (if specific): FORMAL   CONSULTATIVE   INFORMAL   INTIMATE

Other Vocab/Meanings:

GLOSS(ES)

(DH) Dominant Handshape:

(NDH) NonDominant Handshape:

(PO) Palm Orientation:

Movement:

Location (if not neutral):

NMS (if not neutral):

Looks like:

Variation(s):

Initialized Variation(s):

Specify if Regional:

Linguistic Register (if specific): FORMAL   CONSULTATIVE   INFORMAL   INTIMATE

Other Vocab/Meanings:

GLOSS(ES)

(DH) Dominant Handshape:

(NDH) NonDominant Handshape:

(PO) Palm Orientation:

Movement:

Location (if not neutral):

NMS (if not neutral):

Looks like:

Variation(s):

Initialized Variation(s):

Specify if Regional:

Linguistic Register (if specific): FORMAL   CONSULTATIVE   INFORMAL   INTIMATE

Other Vocab/Meanings:

GLOSS(ES)

(DH) Dominant Handshape:

(NDH) NonDominant Handshape:

(PO) Palm Orientation:

Movement:

Location (if not neutral):

NMS (if not neutral):

Looks like:

Variation(s):

Initialized Variation(s):

Specify if Regional:

Linguistic Register (if specific): FORMAL   CONSULTATIVE   INFORMAL   INTIMATE

Other Vocab/Meanings:

GLOSS(ES)

(DH) Dominant Handshape:

(NDH) NonDominant Handshape:

(PO) Palm Orientation:

Movement:

Location (if not neutral):

NMS (if not neutral):

Looks like:

Variation(s):

Initialized Variation(s):

Specify if Regional:

Linguistic Register (if specific): FORMAL   CONSULTATIVE   INFORMAL   INTIMATE

Other Vocab/Meanings:

GLOSS(ES)

(DH) <u>Dominant Handshape</u>:

(NDH) <u>NonDominant Handshape</u>:

(PO) <u>Palm Orientation</u>:

<u>Movement</u>:

<u>Location</u> (if not neutral):

<u>NMS</u> (if not neutral):

Looks like:

Variation(s):

Initialized Variation(s):

Specify if Regional:

Linguistic Register (if specific): FORMAL   CONSULTATIVE   INFORMAL   INTIMATE

Other Vocab/Meanings:

GLOSS(ES)

(DH) <u>Dominant Handshape</u>:

(NDH) <u>NonDominant Handshape</u>:

(PO) <u>Palm Orientation</u>:

<u>Movement</u>:

<u>Location</u> (if not neutral):

<u>NMS</u> (if not neutral):

Looks like:

Variation(s):

Initialized Variation(s):

Specify if Regional:

Linguistic Register (if specific): FORMAL   CONSULTATIVE   INFORMAL   INTIMATE

Other Vocab/Meanings:

GLOSS(ES)

(DH) <u>Dominant Handshape</u>:

(NDH) <u>NonDominant Handshape</u>:

(PO) <u>Palm Orientation</u>:

<u>Movement</u>:

<u>Location</u> (if not neutral):

<u>NMS</u> (if not neutral):

Looks like:

Variation(s):

Initialized Variation(s):

Specify if Regional:

Linguistic Register (if specific): FORMAL   CONSULTATIVE   INFORMAL   INTIMATE

Other Vocab/Meanings:

GLOSS(ES)

(DH) <u>Dominant Handshape</u>:

(NDH) <u>NonDominant Handshape</u>:

(PO) <u>Palm Orientation</u>:

<u>Movement</u>:

<u>Location</u> (if not neutral):

<u>NMS</u> (if not neutral):

Looks like:

Variation(s):

Initialized Variation(s):

Specify if Regional:

Linguistic Register (if specific): FORMAL   CONSULTATIVE   INFORMAL   INTIMATE

Other Vocab/Meanings:

GLOSS(ES)

(DH) <u>Dominant Handshape</u>:

(NDH) <u>NonDominant Handshape</u>:

(PO) <u>Palm Orientation</u>:

<u>Movement</u>:

<u>Location</u> (if not neutral):

<u>NMS</u> (if not neutral):

Looks like:

Variation(s):

Initialized Variation(s):

Specify if Regional:

Linguistic Register (if specific): FORMAL   CONSULTATIVE   INFORMAL   INTIMATE

Other Vocab/Meanings:

GLOSS(ES)

(DH) <u>Dominant Handshape</u>:

(NDH) <u>NonDominant Handshape</u>:

(PO) <u>Palm Orientation</u>:

<u>Movement</u>:

<u>Location</u> (if not neutral):

<u>NMS</u> (if not neutral):

Looks like:

Variation(s):

Initialized Variation(s):

Specify if Regional:

Linguistic Register (if specific): FORMAL   CONSULTATIVE   INFORMAL   INTIMATE

Other Vocab/Meanings:

GLOSS(ES)

(DH) <u>Dominant Handshape</u>:

(NDH) <u>NonDominant Handshape</u>:

(PO) <u>Palm Orientation</u>:

<u>Movement</u>:

<u>Location</u> (if not neutral):

<u>NMS</u> (if not neutral):

Looks like:

Variation(s):

Initialized Variation(s):

Specify if Regional:

Linguistic Register (if specific): FORMAL CONSULTATIVE INFORMAL INTIMATE

Other Vocab/Meanings:

GLOSS(ES)

(DH) <u>Dominant Handshape</u>:

(NDH) <u>NonDominant Handshape</u>:

(PO) <u>Palm Orientation</u>:

<u>Movement</u>:

<u>Location</u> (if not neutral):

<u>NMS</u> (if not neutral):

Looks like:

Variation(s):

Initialized Variation(s):

Specify if Regional:

Linguistic Register (if specific): FORMAL CONSULTATIVE INFORMAL INTIMATE

Other Vocab/Meanings:

GLOSS(ES)

(DH) <u>Dominant Handshape</u>:

(NDH) <u>NonDominant Handshape</u>:

(PO) <u>Palm Orientation</u>:

<u>Movement</u>:

<u>Location</u> (if not neutral):

<u>NMS</u> (if not neutral):

Looks like:

Variation(s):

Initialized Variation(s):

Specify if Regional:

Linguistic Register (if specific): FORMAL CONSULTATIVE INFORMAL INTIMATE

Other Vocab/Meanings:

GLOSS(ES)

(DH) <u>Dominant Handshape</u>:

(NDH) <u>NonDominant Handshape</u>:

(PO) <u>Palm Orientation</u>:

<u>Movement</u>:

<u>Location</u> (if not neutral):

<u>NMS</u> (if not neutral):

Looks like:

Variation(s):

Initialized Variation(s):

Specify if Regional:

Linguistic Register (if specific): FORMAL CONSULTATIVE INFORMAL INTIMATE

Other Vocab/Meanings:

GLOSS(ES)

(DH) <u>Dominant Handshape</u>:

(NDH) <u>NonDominant Handshape</u>:

(PO) <u>Palm Orientation</u>:

<u>Movement</u>:

<u>Location</u> (if not neutral):

<u>NMS</u> (if not neutral):

Looks like:

Variation(s):

Initialized Variation(s):

Specify if Regional:

Linguistic Register (if specific): FORMAL CONSULTATIVE INFORMAL INTIMATE

Other Vocab/Meanings:

GLOSS(ES)

(DH) <u>Dominant Handshape</u>:

(NDH) <u>NonDominant Handshape</u>:

(PO) <u>Palm Orientation</u>:

<u>Movement</u>:

<u>Location</u> (if not neutral):

<u>NMS</u> (if not neutral):

Looks like:

Variation(s):

Initialized Variation(s):

Specify if Regional:

Linguistic Register (if specific): FORMAL CONSULTATIVE INFORMAL INTIMATE

Other Vocab/Meanings:

GLOSS(ES)

(DH) Dominant Handshape:

(NDH) NonDominant Handshape:

(PO) Palm Orientation:

Movement:

Location (if not neutral):

NMS (if not neutral):

Looks like:

Variation(s):

Initialized Variation(s):

Specify if Regional:

Linguistic Register (if specific): FORMAL CONSULTATIVE INFORMAL INTIMATE

Other Vocab/Meanings:

GLOSS(ES)

(DH) Dominant Handshape:

(NDH) NonDominant Handshape:

(PO) Palm Orientation:

Movement:

Location (if not neutral):

NMS (if not neutral):

Looks like:

Variation(s):

Initialized Variation(s):

Specify if Regional:

Linguistic Register (if specific): FORMAL CONSULTATIVE INFORMAL INTIMATE

Other Vocab/Meanings:

GLOSS(ES)

(DH) Dominant Handshape:

(NDH) NonDominant Handshape:

(PO) Palm Orientation:

Movement:

Location (if not neutral):

NMS (if not neutral):

Looks like:

Variation(s):

Initialized Variation(s):

Specify if Regional:

Linguistic Register (if specific): FORMAL CONSULTATIVE INFORMAL INTIMATE

Other Vocab/Meanings:

GLOSS(ES)

(DH) Dominant Handshape:

(NDH) NonDominant Handshape:

(PO) Palm Orientation:

Movement:

Location (if not neutral):

NMS (if not neutral):

Looks like:

Variation(s):

Initialized Variation(s):

Specify if Regional:

Linguistic Register (if specific): FORMAL CONSULTATIVE INFORMAL INTIMATE

Other Vocab/Meanings:

GLOSS(ES)

(DH) Dominant Handshape:

(NDH) NonDominant Handshape:

(PO) Palm Orientation:

Movement:

Location (if not neutral):

NMS (if not neutral):

Looks like:

Variation(s):

Initialized Variation(s):

Specify if Regional:

Linguistic Register (if specific): FORMAL CONSULTATIVE INFORMAL INTIMATE

Other Vocab/Meanings:

GLOSS(ES)

(DH) Dominant Handshape:

(NDH) NonDominant Handshape:

(PO) Palm Orientation:

Movement:

Location (if not neutral):

NMS (if not neutral):

Looks like:

Variation(s):

Initialized Variation(s):

Specify if Regional:

Linguistic Register (if specific): FORMAL CONSULTATIVE INFORMAL INTIMATE

Other Vocab/Meanings:

GLOSS(ES)

(DH) Dominant Handshape:

(NDH) NonDominant Handshape:

(PO) Palm Orientation:

Movement:

Location (if not neutral):

NMS (if not neutral):

Looks like:

Variation(s):

Initialized Variation(s):

Specify if Regional:

Linguistic Register (if specific): FORMAL   CONSULTATIVE   INFORMAL   INTIMATE

Other Vocab/Meanings:

GLOSS(ES)

(DH) Dominant Handshape:

(NDH) NonDominant Handshape:

(PO) Palm Orientation:

Movement:

Location (if not neutral):

NMS (if not neutral):

Looks like:

Variation(s):

Initialized Variation(s):

Specify if Regional:

Linguistic Register (if specific): FORMAL   CONSULTATIVE   INFORMAL   INTIMATE

Other Vocab/Meanings:

GLOSS(ES)

(DH) Dominant Handshape:

(NDH) NonDominant Handshape:

(PO) Palm Orientation:

Movement:

Location (if not neutral):

NMS (if not neutral):

Looks like:

Variation(s):

Initialized Variation(s):

Specify if Regional:

Linguistic Register (if specific): FORMAL   CONSULTATIVE   INFORMAL   INTIMATE

Other Vocab/Meanings:

GLOSS(ES)

(DH) Dominant Handshape:

(NDH) NonDominant Handshape:

(PO) Palm Orientation:

Movement:

Location (if not neutral):

NMS (if not neutral):

Looks like:

Variation(s):

Initialized Variation(s):

Specify if Regional:

Linguistic Register (if specific): FORMAL   CONSULTATIVE   INFORMAL   INTIMATE

Other Vocab/Meanings:

GLOSS(ES)

(DH) Dominant Handshape:

(NDH) NonDominant Handshape:

(PO) Palm Orientation:

Movement:

Location (if not neutral):

NMS (if not neutral):

Looks like:

Variation(s):

Initialized Variation(s):

Specify if Regional:

Linguistic Register (if specific): FORMAL   CONSULTATIVE   INFORMAL   INTIMATE

Other Vocab/Meanings:

GLOSS(ES)

(DH) Dominant Handshape:

(NDH) NonDominant Handshape:

(PO) Palm Orientation:

Movement:

Location (if not neutral):

NMS (if not neutral):

Looks like:

Variation(s):

Initialized Variation(s):

Specify if Regional:

Linguistic Register (if specific): FORMAL   CONSULTATIVE   INFORMAL   INTIMATE

Other Vocab/Meanings:

GLOSS(ES)

(DH) <u>Dominant Handshape</u>:

(NDH) <u>NonDominant Handshape</u>:

(PO) <u>Palm Orientation</u>:

<u>Movement</u>:

<u>Location</u> (if not neutral):

<u>NMS</u> (if not neutral):

Looks like:

Variation(s):

Initialized Variation(s):

Specify if Regional:

Linguistic Register (if specific): FORMAL   CONSULTATIVE   INFORMAL   INTIMATE

Other Vocab/Meanings:

GLOSS(ES)

(DH) <u>Dominant Handshape</u>:

(NDH) <u>NonDominant Handshape</u>:

(PO) <u>Palm Orientation</u>:

<u>Movement</u>:

<u>Location</u> (if not neutral):

<u>NMS</u> (if not neutral):

Looks like:

Variation(s):

Initialized Variation(s):

Specify if Regional:

Linguistic Register (if specific): FORMAL   CONSULTATIVE   INFORMAL   INTIMATE

Other Vocab/Meanings:

GLOSS(ES)

(DH) <u>Dominant Handshape</u>:

(NDH) <u>NonDominant Handshape</u>:

(PO) <u>Palm Orientation</u>:

<u>Movement</u>:

<u>Location</u> (if not neutral):

<u>NMS</u> (if not neutral):

Looks like:

Variation(s):

Initialized Variation(s):

Specify if Regional:

Linguistic Register (if specific): FORMAL   CONSULTATIVE   INFORMAL   INTIMATE

Other Vocab/Meanings:

GLOSS(ES)

(DH) <u>Dominant Handshape</u>:

(NDH) <u>NonDominant Handshape</u>:

(PO) <u>Palm Orientation</u>:

<u>Movement</u>:

<u>Location</u> (if not neutral):

<u>NMS</u> (if not neutral):

Looks like:

Variation(s):

Initialized Variation(s):

Specify if Regional:

Linguistic Register (if specific): FORMAL   CONSULTATIVE   INFORMAL   INTIMATE

Other Vocab/Meanings:

GLOSS(ES)

(DH) <u>Dominant Handshape</u>:

(NDH) <u>NonDominant Handshape</u>:

(PO) <u>Palm Orientation</u>:

<u>Movement</u>:

<u>Location</u> (if not neutral):

<u>NMS</u> (if not neutral):

Looks like:

Variation(s):

Initialized Variation(s):

Specify if Regional:

Linguistic Register (if specific): FORMAL   CONSULTATIVE   INFORMAL   INTIMATE

Other Vocab/Meanings:

GLOSS(ES)

(DH) <u>Dominant Handshape</u>:

(NDH) <u>NonDominant Handshape</u>:

(PO) <u>Palm Orientation</u>:

<u>Movement</u>:

<u>Location</u> (if not neutral):

<u>NMS</u> (if not neutral):

Looks like:

Variation(s):

Initialized Variation(s):

Specify if Regional:

Linguistic Register (if specific): FORMAL   CONSULTATIVE   INFORMAL   INTIMATE

Other Vocab/Meanings:

GLOSS(ES)

(DH) <u>Dominant Handshape</u>:

(NDH) <u>NonDominant Handshape</u>:

(PO) <u>Palm Orientation</u>:

<u>Movement</u>:

<u>Location</u> (if not neutral):

<u>NMS</u> (if not neutral):

Looks like:

Variation(s):

Initialized Variation(s):

Specify if Regional:

Linguistic Register (if specific): FORMAL   CONSULTATIVE   INFORMAL   INTIMATE

Other Vocab/Meanings:

GLOSS(ES)

(DH) <u>Dominant Handshape</u>:

(NDH) <u>NonDominant Handshape</u>:

(PO) <u>Palm Orientation</u>:

<u>Movement</u>:

<u>Location</u> (if not neutral):

<u>NMS</u> (if not neutral):

Looks like:

Variation(s):

Initialized Variation(s):

Specify if Regional:

Linguistic Register (if specific): FORMAL   CONSULTATIVE   INFORMAL   INTIMATE

Other Vocab/Meanings:

GLOSS(ES)

(DH) <u>Dominant Handshape</u>:

(NDH) <u>NonDominant Handshape</u>:

(PO) <u>Palm Orientation</u>:

<u>Movement</u>:

<u>Location</u> (if not neutral):

<u>NMS</u> (if not neutral):

Looks like:

Variation(s):

Initialized Variation(s):

Specify if Regional:

Linguistic Register (if specific): FORMAL   CONSULTATIVE   INFORMAL   INTIMATE

Other Vocab/Meanings:

GLOSS(ES)

(DH) <u>Dominant Handshape</u>:

(NDH) <u>NonDominant Handshape</u>:

(PO) <u>Palm Orientation</u>:

<u>Movement</u>:

<u>Location</u> (if not neutral):

<u>NMS</u> (if not neutral):

Looks like:

Variation(s):

Initialized Variation(s):

Specify if Regional:

Linguistic Register (if specific): FORMAL   CONSULTATIVE   INFORMAL   INTIMATE

Other Vocab/Meanings:

GLOSS(ES)

(DH) <u>Dominant Handshape</u>:

(NDH) <u>NonDominant Handshape</u>:

(PO) <u>Palm Orientation</u>:

<u>Movement</u>:

<u>Location</u> (if not neutral):

<u>NMS</u> (if not neutral):

Looks like:

Variation(s):

Initialized Variation(s):

Specify if Regional:

Linguistic Register (if specific): FORMAL   CONSULTATIVE   INFORMAL   INTIMATE

Other Vocab/Meanings:

GLOSS(ES)

(DH) <u>Dominant Handshape</u>:

(NDH) <u>NonDominant Handshape</u>:

(PO) <u>Palm Orientation</u>:

<u>Movement</u>:

<u>Location</u> (if not neutral):

<u>NMS</u> (if not neutral):

Looks like:

Variation(s):

Initialized Variation(s):

Specify if Regional:

Linguistic Register (if specific): FORMAL   CONSULTATIVE   INFORMAL   INTIMATE

Other Vocab/Meanings:

GLOSS(ES)

(DH) <u>Dominant Handshape</u>:

(NDH) <u>NonDominant Handshape</u>:

(PO) <u>Palm Orientation</u>:

<u>Movement</u>:

<u>Location</u> (if not neutral):

<u>NMS</u> (if not neutral):

Looks like:

Variation(s):

Initialized Variation(s):

Specify if Regional:

Linguistic Register (if specific): FORMAL   CONSULTATIVE   INFORMAL   INTIMATE

Other Vocab/Meanings:

GLOSS(ES)

(DH) <u>Dominant Handshape</u>:

(NDH) <u>NonDominant Handshape</u>:

(PO) <u>Palm Orientation</u>:

<u>Movement</u>:

<u>Location</u> (if not neutral):

<u>NMS</u> (if not neutral):

Looks like:

Variation(s):

Initialized Variation(s):

Specify if Regional:

Linguistic Register (if specific): FORMAL   CONSULTATIVE   INFORMAL   INTIMATE

Other Vocab/Meanings:

GLOSS(ES)

(DH) <u>Dominant Handshape</u>:

(NDH) <u>NonDominant Handshape</u>:

(PO) <u>Palm Orientation</u>:

<u>Movement</u>:

<u>Location</u> (if not neutral):

<u>NMS</u> (if not neutral):

Looks like:

Variation(s):

Initialized Variation(s):

Specify if Regional:

Linguistic Register (if specific): FORMAL   CONSULTATIVE   INFORMAL   INTIMATE

Other Vocab/Meanings:

GLOSS(ES)

(DH) <u>Dominant Handshape</u>:

(NDH) <u>NonDominant Handshape</u>:

(PO) <u>Palm Orientation</u>:

<u>Movement</u>:

<u>Location</u> (if not neutral):

<u>NMS</u> (if not neutral):

Looks like:

Variation(s):

Initialized Variation(s):

Specify if Regional:

Linguistic Register (if specific): FORMAL   CONSULTATIVE   INFORMAL   INTIMATE

Other Vocab/Meanings:

GLOSS(ES)

(DH) <u>Dominant Handshape</u>:

(NDH) <u>NonDominant Handshape</u>:

(PO) <u>Palm Orientation</u>:

<u>Movement</u>:

<u>Location</u> (if not neutral):

<u>NMS</u> (if not neutral):

Looks like:

Variation(s):

Initialized Variation(s):

Specify if Regional:

Linguistic Register (if specific): FORMAL   CONSULTATIVE   INFORMAL   INTIMATE

Other Vocab/Meanings:

GLOSS(ES)

(DH) <u>Dominant Handshape</u>:

(NDH) <u>NonDominant Handshape</u>:

(PO) <u>Palm Orientation</u>:

<u>Movement</u>:

<u>Location</u> (if not neutral):

<u>NMS</u> (if not neutral):

Looks like:

Variation(s):

Initialized Variation(s):

Specify if Regional:

Linguistic Register (if specific): FORMAL   CONSULTATIVE   INFORMAL   INTIMATE

Other Vocab/Meanings:

GLOSS(ES)

(DH) Dominant Handshape:

(NDH) NonDominant Handshape:

(PO) Palm Orientation:

Movement:

Location (if not neutral):

NMS (if not neutral):

Looks like:

Variation(s):

Initialized Variation(s):

Specify if Regional:

Linguistic Register (if specific): FORMAL   CONSULTATIVE   INFORMAL   INTIMATE

Other Vocab/Meanings:

GLOSS(ES)

(DH) Dominant Handshape:

(NDH) NonDominant Handshape:

(PO) Palm Orientation:

Movement:

Location (if not neutral):

NMS (if not neutral):

Looks like:

Variation(s):

Initialized Variation(s):

Specify if Regional:

Linguistic Register (if specific): FORMAL   CONSULTATIVE   INFORMAL   INTIMATE

Other Vocab/Meanings:

GLOSS(ES)

(DH) Dominant Handshape:

(NDH) NonDominant Handshape:

(PO) Palm Orientation:

Movement:

Location (if not neutral):

NMS (if not neutral):

Looks like:

Variation(s):

Initialized Variation(s):

Specify if Regional:

Linguistic Register (if specific): FORMAL   CONSULTATIVE   INFORMAL   INTIMATE

Other Vocab/Meanings:

GLOSS(ES)

(DH) Dominant Handshape:

(NDH) NonDominant Handshape:

(PO) Palm Orientation:

Movement:

Location (if not neutral):

NMS (if not neutral):

Looks like:

Variation(s):

Initialized Variation(s):

Specify if Regional:

Linguistic Register (if specific): FORMAL   CONSULTATIVE   INFORMAL   INTIMATE

Other Vocab/Meanings:

GLOSS(ES)

(DH) Dominant Handshape:

(NDH) NonDominant Handshape:

(PO) Palm Orientation:

Movement:

Location (if not neutral):

NMS (if not neutral):

Looks like:

Variation(s):

Initialized Variation(s):

Specify if Regional:

Linguistic Register (if specific): FORMAL   CONSULTATIVE   INFORMAL   INTIMATE

Other Vocab/Meanings:

GLOSS(ES)

(DH) Dominant Handshape:

(NDH) NonDominant Handshape:

(PO) Palm Orientation:

Movement:

Location (if not neutral):

NMS (if not neutral):

Looks like:

Variation(s):

Initialized Variation(s):

Specify if Regional:

Linguistic Register (if specific): FORMAL   CONSULTATIVE   INFORMAL   INTIMATE

Other Vocab/Meanings:

GLOSS(ES)

(DH) Dominant Handshape:

(NDH) NonDominant Handshape:

(PO) Palm Orientation:

Movement:

Location (if not neutral):

NMS (if not neutral):

Looks like:

Variation(s):

Initialized Variation(s):

Specify if Regional:

Linguistic Register (if specific): FORMAL CONSULTATIVE INFORMAL INTIMATE

Other Vocab/Meanings:

GLOSS(ES)

(DH) Dominant Handshape:

(NDH) NonDominant Handshape:

(PO) Palm Orientation:

Movement:

Location (if not neutral):

NMS (if not neutral):

Looks like:

Variation(s):

Initialized Variation(s):

Specify if Regional:

Linguistic Register (if specific): FORMAL CONSULTATIVE INFORMAL INTIMATE

Other Vocab/Meanings:

GLOSS(ES)

(DH) Dominant Handshape:

(NDH) NonDominant Handshape:

(PO) Palm Orientation:

Movement:

Location (if not neutral):

NMS (if not neutral):

Looks like:

Variation(s):

Initialized Variation(s):

Specify if Regional:

Linguistic Register (if specific): FORMAL CONSULTATIVE INFORMAL INTIMATE

Other Vocab/Meanings:

GLOSS(ES)

(DH) Dominant Handshape:

(NDH) NonDominant Handshape:

(PO) Palm Orientation:

Movement:

Location (if not neutral):

NMS (if not neutral):

Looks like:

Variation(s):

Initialized Variation(s):

Specify if Regional:

Linguistic Register (if specific): FORMAL CONSULTATIVE INFORMAL INTIMATE

Other Vocab/Meanings:

GLOSS(ES)

(DH) Dominant Handshape:

(NDH) NonDominant Handshape:

(PO) Palm Orientation:

Movement:

Location (if not neutral):

NMS (if not neutral):

Looks like:

Variation(s):

Initialized Variation(s):

Specify if Regional:

Linguistic Register (if specific): FORMAL CONSULTATIVE INFORMAL INTIMATE

Other Vocab/Meanings:

GLOSS(ES)

(DH) Dominant Handshape:

(NDH) NonDominant Handshape:

(PO) Palm Orientation:

Movement:

Location (if not neutral):

NMS (if not neutral):

Looks like:

Variation(s):

Initialized Variation(s):

Specify if Regional:

Linguistic Register (if specific): FORMAL CONSULTATIVE INFORMAL INTIMATE

Other Vocab/Meanings:

GLOSS(ES)

(DH) <u>Dominant Handshape</u>:

(NDH) <u>NonDominant Handshape</u>:

(PO) <u>Palm Orientation</u>:

<u>Movement</u>:

<u>Location</u> (if not neutral):

<u>NMS</u> (if not neutral):

Looks like:

Variation(s):

Initialized Variation(s):

Specify if Regional:

Linguistic Register (if specific): FORMAL CONSULTATIVE INFORMAL INTIMATE

Other Vocab/Meanings:

GLOSS(ES)

(DH) <u>Dominant Handshape</u>:

(NDH) <u>NonDominant Handshape</u>:

(PO) <u>Palm Orientation</u>:

<u>Movement</u>:

<u>Location</u> (if not neutral):

<u>NMS</u> (if not neutral):

Looks like:

Variation(s):

Initialized Variation(s):

Specify if Regional:

Linguistic Register (if specific): FORMAL CONSULTATIVE INFORMAL INTIMATE

Other Vocab/Meanings:

GLOSS(ES)

(DH) <u>Dominant Handshape</u>:

(NDH) <u>NonDominant Handshape</u>:

(PO) <u>Palm Orientation</u>:

<u>Movement</u>:

<u>Location</u> (if not neutral):

<u>NMS</u> (if not neutral):

Looks like:

Variation(s):

Initialized Variation(s):

Specify if Regional:

Linguistic Register (if specific): FORMAL CONSULTATIVE INFORMAL INTIMATE

Other Vocab/Meanings:

GLOSS(ES)

(DH) <u>Dominant Handshape</u>:

(NDH) <u>NonDominant Handshape</u>:

(PO) <u>Palm Orientation</u>:

<u>Movement</u>:

<u>Location</u> (if not neutral):

<u>NMS</u> (if not neutral):

Looks like:

Variation(s):

Initialized Variation(s):

Specify if Regional:

Linguistic Register (if specific): FORMAL CONSULTATIVE INFORMAL INTIMATE

Other Vocab/Meanings:

GLOSS(ES)

(DH) <u>Dominant Handshape</u>:

(NDH) <u>NonDominant Handshape</u>:

(PO) <u>Palm Orientation</u>:

<u>Movement</u>:

<u>Location</u> (if not neutral):

<u>NMS</u> (if not neutral):

Looks like:

Variation(s):

Initialized Variation(s):

Specify if Regional:

Linguistic Register (if specific): FORMAL CONSULTATIVE INFORMAL INTIMATE

Other Vocab/Meanings:

GLOSS(ES)

(DH) <u>Dominant Handshape</u>:

(NDH) <u>NonDominant Handshape</u>:

(PO) <u>Palm Orientation</u>:

<u>Movement</u>:

<u>Location</u> (if not neutral):

<u>NMS</u> (if not neutral):

Looks like:

Variation(s):

Initialized Variation(s):

Specify if Regional:

Linguistic Register (if specific): FORMAL CONSULTATIVE INFORMAL INTIMATE

Other Vocab/Meanings:

GLOSS(ES)

(DH) <u>Dominant Handshape</u>:

(NDH) <u>NonDominant Handshape</u>:

(PO) <u>Palm Orientation</u>:

<u>Movement</u>:

<u>Location</u> (if not neutral):

<u>NMS</u> (if not neutral):

Looks like:

Variation(s):

Initialized Variation(s):

Specify if Regional:

Linguistic Register (if specific): FORMAL CONSULTATIVE INFORMAL INTIMATE

Other Vocab/Meanings:

GLOSS(ES)

(DH) <u>Dominant Handshape</u>:

(NDH) <u>NonDominant Handshape</u>:

(PO) <u>Palm Orientation</u>:

<u>Movement</u>:

<u>Location</u> (if not neutral):

<u>NMS</u> (if not neutral):

Looks like:

Variation(s):

Initialized Variation(s):

Specify if Regional:

Linguistic Register (if specific): FORMAL CONSULTATIVE INFORMAL INTIMATE

Other Vocab/Meanings:

GLOSS(ES)

(DH) <u>Dominant Handshape</u>:

(NDH) <u>NonDominant Handshape</u>:

(PO) <u>Palm Orientation</u>:

<u>Movement</u>:

<u>Location</u> (if not neutral):

<u>NMS</u> (if not neutral):

Looks like:

Variation(s):

Initialized Variation(s):

Specify if Regional:

Linguistic Register (if specific): FORMAL CONSULTATIVE INFORMAL INTIMATE

Other Vocab/Meanings:

GLOSS(ES)

(DH) <u>Dominant Handshape</u>:

(NDH) <u>NonDominant Handshape</u>:

(PO) <u>Palm Orientation</u>:

<u>Movement</u>:

<u>Location</u> (if not neutral):

<u>NMS</u> (if not neutral):

Looks like:

Variation(s):

Initialized Variation(s):

Specify if Regional:

Linguistic Register (if specific): FORMAL CONSULTATIVE INFORMAL INTIMATE

Other Vocab/Meanings:

GLOSS(ES)

(DH) <u>Dominant Handshape</u>:

(NDH) <u>NonDominant Handshape</u>:

(PO) <u>Palm Orientation</u>:

<u>Movement</u>:

<u>Location</u> (if not neutral):

<u>NMS</u> (if not neutral):

Looks like:

Variation(s):

Initialized Variation(s):

Specify if Regional:

Linguistic Register (if specific): FORMAL CONSULTATIVE INFORMAL INTIMATE

Other Vocab/Meanings:

GLOSS(ES)

(DH) <u>Dominant Handshape</u>:

(NDH) <u>NonDominant Handshape</u>:

(PO) <u>Palm Orientation</u>:

<u>Movement</u>:

<u>Location</u> (if not neutral):

<u>NMS</u> (if not neutral):

Looks like:

Variation(s):

Initialized Variation(s):

Specify if Regional:

Linguistic Register (if specific): FORMAL CONSULTATIVE INFORMAL INTIMATE

Other Vocab/Meanings:

GLOSS(ES)

(DH) <u>Dominant Handshape</u>:

(NDH) <u>NonDominant Handshape</u>:

(PO) <u>Palm Orientation</u>:

<u>Movement</u>:

<u>Location</u> (if not neutral):

<u>NMS</u> (if not neutral):

Looks like:

Variation(s):

Initialized Variation(s):

Specify if Regional:

Linguistic Register (if specific): FORMAL   CONSULTATIVE   INFORMAL   INTIMATE

Other Vocab/Meanings:

GLOSS(ES)

(DH) <u>Dominant Handshape</u>:

(NDH) <u>NonDominant Handshape</u>:

(PO) <u>Palm Orientation</u>:

<u>Movement</u>:

<u>Location</u> (if not neutral):

<u>NMS</u> (if not neutral):

Looks like:

Variation(s):

Initialized Variation(s):

Specify if Regional:

Linguistic Register (if specific): FORMAL   CONSULTATIVE   INFORMAL   INTIMATE

Other Vocab/Meanings:

GLOSS(ES)

(DH) <u>Dominant Handshape</u>:

(NDH) <u>NonDominant Handshape</u>:

(PO) <u>Palm Orientation</u>:

<u>Movement</u>:

<u>Location</u> (if not neutral):

<u>NMS</u> (if not neutral):

Looks like:

Variation(s):

Initialized Variation(s):

Specify if Regional:

Linguistic Register (if specific): FORMAL   CONSULTATIVE   INFORMAL   INTIMATE

Other Vocab/Meanings:

GLOSS(ES)

(DH) <u>Dominant Handshape</u>:

(NDH) <u>NonDominant Handshape</u>:

(PO) <u>Palm Orientation</u>:

<u>Movement</u>:

<u>Location</u> (if not neutral):

<u>NMS</u> (if not neutral):

Looks like:

Variation(s):

Initialized Variation(s):

Specify if Regional:

Linguistic Register (if specific): FORMAL   CONSULTATIVE   INFORMAL   INTIMATE

Other Vocab/Meanings:

GLOSS(ES)

(DH) <u>Dominant Handshape</u>:

(NDH) <u>NonDominant Handshape</u>:

(PO) <u>Palm Orientation</u>:

<u>Movement</u>:

<u>Location</u> (if not neutral):

<u>NMS</u> (if not neutral):

Looks like:

Variation(s):

Initialized Variation(s):

Specify if Regional:

Linguistic Register (if specific): FORMAL   CONSULTATIVE   INFORMAL   INTIMATE

Other Vocab/Meanings:

GLOSS(ES)

(DH) <u>Dominant Handshape</u>:

(NDH) <u>NonDominant Handshape</u>:

(PO) <u>Palm Orientation</u>:

<u>Movement</u>:

<u>Location</u> (if not neutral):

<u>NMS</u> (if not neutral):

Looks like:

Variation(s):

Initialized Variation(s):

Specify if Regional:

Linguistic Register (if specific): FORMAL   CONSULTATIVE   INFORMAL   INTIMATE

Other Vocab/Meanings:

GLOSS(ES)

(DH) <u>Dominant Handshape</u>:

(NDH) <u>NonDominant Handshape</u>:

(PO) <u>Palm Orientation</u>:

<u>Movement</u>:

<u>Location</u> (if not neutral):

<u>NMS</u> (if not neutral):

Looks like:

Variation(s):

Initialized Variation(s):

Specify if Regional:

Linguistic Register (if specific): FORMAL   CONSULTATIVE   INFORMAL   INTIMATE

Other Vocab/Meanings:

GLOSS(ES)

(DH) <u>Dominant Handshape</u>:

(NDH) <u>NonDominant Handshape</u>:

(PO) <u>Palm Orientation</u>:

<u>Movement</u>:

<u>Location</u> (if not neutral):

<u>NMS</u> (if not neutral):

Looks like:

Variation(s):

Initialized Variation(s):

Specify if Regional:

Linguistic Register (if specific): FORMAL   CONSULTATIVE   INFORMAL   INTIMATE

Other Vocab/Meanings:

GLOSS(ES)

(DH) <u>Dominant Handshape</u>:

(NDH) <u>NonDominant Handshape</u>:

(PO) <u>Palm Orientation</u>:

<u>Movement</u>:

<u>Location</u> (if not neutral):

<u>NMS</u> (if not neutral):

Looks like:

Variation(s):

Initialized Variation(s):

Specify if Regional:

Linguistic Register (if specific): FORMAL   CONSULTATIVE   INFORMAL   INTIMATE

Other Vocab/Meanings:

GLOSS(ES)

(DH) <u>Dominant Handshape</u>:

(NDH) <u>NonDominant Handshape</u>:

(PO) <u>Palm Orientation</u>:

<u>Movement</u>:

<u>Location</u> (if not neutral):

<u>NMS</u> (if not neutral):

Looks like:

Variation(s):

Initialized Variation(s):

Specify if Regional:

Linguistic Register (if specific): FORMAL   CONSULTATIVE   INFORMAL   INTIMATE

Other Vocab/Meanings:

GLOSS(ES)

(DH) <u>Dominant Handshape</u>:

(NDH) <u>NonDominant Handshape</u>:

(PO) <u>Palm Orientation</u>:

<u>Movement</u>:

<u>Location</u> (if not neutral):

<u>NMS</u> (if not neutral):

Looks like:

Variation(s):

Initialized Variation(s):

Specify if Regional:

Linguistic Register (if specific): FORMAL   CONSULTATIVE   INFORMAL   INTIMATE

Other Vocab/Meanings:

GLOSS(ES)

(DH) <u>Dominant Handshape</u>:

(NDH) <u>NonDominant Handshape</u>:

(PO) <u>Palm Orientation</u>:

<u>Movement</u>:

<u>Location</u> (if not neutral):

<u>NMS</u> (if not neutral):

Looks like:

Variation(s):

Initialized Variation(s):

Specify if Regional:

Linguistic Register (if specific): FORMAL   CONSULTATIVE   INFORMAL   INTIMATE

Other Vocab/Meanings:

GLOSS(ES)

(DH) Dominant Handshape:

(NDH) NonDominant Handshape:

(PO) Palm Orientation:

Movement:

Location (if not neutral):

NMS (if not neutral):

Looks like:

Variation(s):

Initialized Variation(s):

Specify if Regional:

Linguistic Register (if specific): FORMAL CONSULTATIVE INFORMAL INTIMATE

Other Vocab/Meanings:

GLOSS(ES)

(DH) Dominant Handshape:

(NDH) NonDominant Handshape:

(PO) Palm Orientation:

Movement:

Location (if not neutral):

NMS (if not neutral):

Looks like:

Variation(s):

Initialized Variation(s):

Specify if Regional:

Linguistic Register (if specific): FORMAL CONSULTATIVE INFORMAL INTIMATE

Other Vocab/Meanings:

GLOSS(ES)

(DH) Dominant Handshape:

(NDH) NonDominant Handshape:

(PO) Palm Orientation:

Movement:

Location (if not neutral):

NMS (if not neutral):

Looks like:

Variation(s):

Initialized Variation(s):

Specify if Regional:

Linguistic Register (if specific): FORMAL CONSULTATIVE INFORMAL INTIMATE

Other Vocab/Meanings:

GLOSS(ES)

(DH) Dominant Handshape:

(NDH) NonDominant Handshape:

(PO) Palm Orientation:

Movement:

Location (if not neutral):

NMS (if not neutral):

Looks like:

Variation(s):

Initialized Variation(s):

Specify if Regional:

Linguistic Register (if specific): FORMAL CONSULTATIVE INFORMAL INTIMATE

Other Vocab/Meanings:

GLOSS(ES)

(DH) Dominant Handshape:

(NDH) NonDominant Handshape:

(PO) Palm Orientation:

Movement:

Location (if not neutral):

NMS (if not neutral):

Looks like:

Variation(s):

Initialized Variation(s):

Specify if Regional:

Linguistic Register (if specific): FORMAL CONSULTATIVE INFORMAL INTIMATE

Other Vocab/Meanings:

GLOSS(ES)

(DH) Dominant Handshape:

(NDH) NonDominant Handshape:

(PO) Palm Orientation:

Movement:

Location (if not neutral):

NMS (if not neutral):

Looks like:

Variation(s):

Initialized Variation(s):

Specify if Regional:

Linguistic Register (if specific): FORMAL CONSULTATIVE INFORMAL INTIMATE

Other Vocab/Meanings:

GLOSS(ES)

(DH) <u>Dominant Handshape</u>:

(NDH) <u>NonDominant Handshape</u>:

(PO) <u>Palm Orientation</u>:

<u>Movement</u>:

<u>Location</u> (if not neutral):

<u>NMS</u> (if not neutral):

Looks like:

Variation(s):

Initialized Variation(s):

Specify if Regional:

Linguistic Register (if specific): FORMAL   CONSULTATIVE   INFORMAL   INTIMATE

Other Vocab/Meanings:

GLOSS(ES)

(DH) <u>Dominant Handshape</u>:

(NDH) <u>NonDominant Handshape</u>:

(PO) <u>Palm Orientation</u>:

<u>Movement</u>:

<u>Location</u> (if not neutral):

<u>NMS</u> (if not neutral):

Looks like:

Variation(s):

Initialized Variation(s):

Specify if Regional:

Linguistic Register (if specific): FORMAL   CONSULTATIVE   INFORMAL   INTIMATE

Other Vocab/Meanings:

GLOSS(ES)

(DH) <u>Dominant Handshape</u>:

(NDH) <u>NonDominant Handshape</u>:

(PO) <u>Palm Orientation</u>:

<u>Movement</u>:

<u>Location</u> (if not neutral):

<u>NMS</u> (if not neutral):

Looks like:

Variation(s):

Initialized Variation(s):

Specify if Regional:

Linguistic Register (if specific): FORMAL   CONSULTATIVE   INFORMAL   INTIMATE

Other Vocab/Meanings:

GLOSS(ES)

(DH) <u>Dominant Handshape</u>:

(NDH) <u>NonDominant Handshape</u>:

(PO) <u>Palm Orientation</u>:

<u>Movement</u>:

<u>Location</u> (if not neutral):

<u>NMS</u> (if not neutral):

Looks like:

Variation(s):

Initialized Variation(s):

Specify if Regional:

Linguistic Register (if specific): FORMAL   CONSULTATIVE   INFORMAL   INTIMATE

Other Vocab/Meanings:

GLOSS(ES)

(DH) <u>Dominant Handshape</u>:

(NDH) <u>NonDominant Handshape</u>:

(PO) <u>Palm Orientation</u>:

<u>Movement</u>:

<u>Location</u> (if not neutral):

<u>NMS</u> (if not neutral):

Looks like:

Variation(s):

Initialized Variation(s):

Specify if Regional:

Linguistic Register (if specific): FORMAL   CONSULTATIVE   INFORMAL   INTIMATE

Other Vocab/Meanings:

GLOSS(ES)

(DH) <u>Dominant Handshape</u>:

(NDH) <u>NonDominant Handshape</u>:

(PO) <u>Palm Orientation</u>:

<u>Movement</u>:

<u>Location</u> (if not neutral):

<u>NMS</u> (if not neutral):

Looks like:

Variation(s):

Initialized Variation(s):

Specify if Regional:

Linguistic Register (if specific): FORMAL   CONSULTATIVE   INFORMAL   INTIMATE

Other Vocab/Meanings:

GLOSS(ES)

(DH) Dominant Handshape:

(NDH) NonDominant Handshape:

(PO) Palm Orientation:

Movement:

Location (if not neutral):

NMS (if not neutral):

Looks like:

Variation(s):

Initialized Variation(s):

Specify if Regional:

Linguistic Register (if specific): FORMAL CONSULTATIVE INFORMAL INTIMATE

Other Vocab/Meanings:

GLOSS(ES)

(DH) Dominant Handshape:

(NDH) NonDominant Handshape:

(PO) Palm Orientation:

Movement:

Location (if not neutral):

NMS (if not neutral):

Looks like:

Variation(s):

Initialized Variation(s):

Specify if Regional:

Linguistic Register (if specific): FORMAL CONSULTATIVE INFORMAL INTIMATE

Other Vocab/Meanings:

GLOSS(ES)

(DH) Dominant Handshape:

(NDH) NonDominant Handshape:

(PO) Palm Orientation:

Movement:

Location (if not neutral):

NMS (if not neutral):

Looks like:

Variation(s):

Initialized Variation(s):

Specify if Regional:

Linguistic Register (if specific): FORMAL CONSULTATIVE INFORMAL INTIMATE

Other Vocab/Meanings:

GLOSS(ES)

(DH) Dominant Handshape:

(NDH) NonDominant Handshape:

(PO) Palm Orientation:

Movement:

Location (if not neutral):

NMS (if not neutral):

Looks like:

Variation(s):

Initialized Variation(s):

Specify if Regional:

Linguistic Register (if specific): FORMAL CONSULTATIVE INFORMAL INTIMATE

Other Vocab/Meanings:

GLOSS(ES)

(DH) Dominant Handshape:

(NDH) NonDominant Handshape:

(PO) Palm Orientation:

Movement:

Location (if not neutral):

NMS (if not neutral):

Looks like:

Variation(s):

Initialized Variation(s):

Specify if Regional:

Linguistic Register (if specific): FORMAL CONSULTATIVE INFORMAL INTIMATE

Other Vocab/Meanings:

GLOSS(ES)

(DH) Dominant Handshape:

(NDH) NonDominant Handshape:

(PO) Palm Orientation:

Movement:

Location (if not neutral):

NMS (if not neutral):

Looks like:

Variation(s):

Initialized Variation(s):

Specify if Regional:

Linguistic Register (if specific): FORMAL CONSULTATIVE INFORMAL INTIMATE

Other Vocab/Meanings:

Handshape Game

The idea for this game came from an ASL 201 student named Kayla Wearne at North Idaho College. It quickly became the most popular game in ASL classes and even made its way into the Deaf community.

This game is a great way to help develop your inner ASL thesaurus.
It's also a great way to remember "rhyming" signs for creative sign performances.

DIRECTIONS: Sit in a circle with 6-10 people in each group.

A random handshape is chosen. That handshape must be used by each person in the group to demonstrate a sign or obvious classifier. Players take turns consecutively in a clockwise motion and continue making the loop until there is only one left.

EXAMPLE: Index (IX) finger is the handshape, the first person may choose the sign DIFFERENT, then the next person may chose sign FOR-FOR. Asymmetrical signs are perfectly acceptable. So in the example, the sign DISCUSS is acceptable even though the NDH is not an IX.

It is not necessary for the signs to have any connection or cohesion other than that handshape itself.

If there is not a group consensuses, the teacher or most proficient signer judges whether or not the sign/classifer is acceptable when it is in doubt.

Continuing with the example: a player signs DECIDE but is unsure if it counts because it ends with the F handshape, but teacher accepts the sign because the IX hand is clearly used in the construction of the sign. The teacher does not accept DORMATORY because the handshape is a D, not an IX.

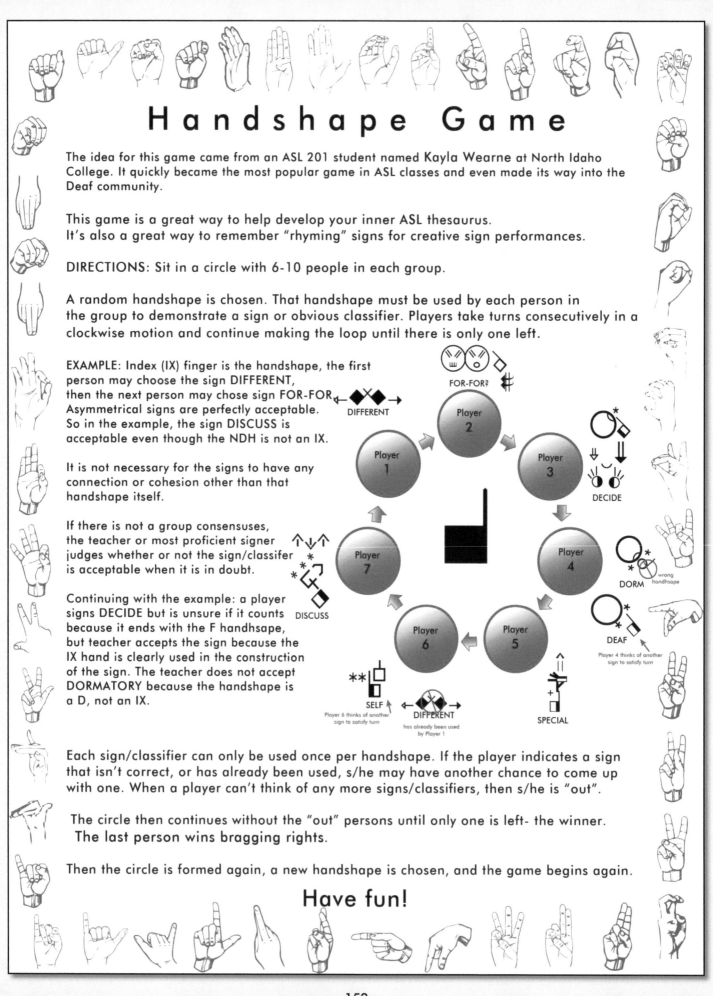

Each sign/classifier can only be used once per handshape. If the player indicates a sign that isn't correct, or has already been used, s/he may have another chance to come up with one. When a player can't think of any more signs/classifiers, then s/he is "out".

The circle then continues without the "out" persons until only one is left- the winner.
The last person wins bragging rights.

Then the circle is formed again, a new handshape is chosen, and the game begins again.

Have fun!

Handshape Thesaurus

Handshape: bent-V	Handshape:	Handshape:
GLOSS	GLOSS	GLOSS
1 BLIND	1	1
2 CL: "fangs"	2	2
3 CL: "infant / toddler"	3	3
4 CL: "small animal"	4	4
5 COCHLEAR IMPLANT	5	5
6 DIFFICULT	6	6
7 DOUBT	7	7
8 IDAHO	8	8
9 POTATO	9	9
10 PROBLEM	10	10
11 STRICT	11	11
12 TRANSFER	12	12
13 TRAVEL	13	13
14 VAMPIRE	14	14
15	15	15
16	16	16
17	17	17
18	18	18
19	19	19
20	20	20
21	21	21
22	22	22
23	23	23
24	24	24
25	25	25
26	26	26
27	27	27
28	28	28
29	29	29
30	30	30
31	31	31
32	32	32
33	33	33
34	34	34
35	35	35
36	36	36
37	37	37
38	38	38
39	39	39
40	40	40

Handshape Thesaurus

Handshape:	Handshape:	Handshape:
GLOSS	GLOSS	GLOSS
1	1	1
2	2	2
3	3	3
4	4	4
5	5	5
6	6	6
7	7	7
8	8	8
9	9	9
10	10	10
11	11	11
12	12	12
13	13	13
14	14	14
15	15	15
16	16	16
17	17	17
18	18	18
19	19	19
20	20	20
21	21	21
22	22	22
23	23	23
24	24	24
25	25	25
26	26	26
27	27	27
28	28	28
29	29	29
30	30	30
31	31	31
32	32	32
33	33	33
34	34	34
35	35	35
36	36	36
37	37	37
38	38	38
39	39	39
40	40	40

Handshape Thesaurus

Handshape: _____

<u>GLOSS</u>

1 _____
2 _____
3 _____
4 _____
5 _____
6 _____
7 _____
8 _____
9 _____
10 _____
11 _____
12 _____
13 _____
14 _____
15 _____
16 _____
17 _____
18 _____
19 _____
20 _____
21 _____
22 _____
23 _____
24 _____
25 _____
26 _____
27 _____
28 _____
29 _____
30 _____
31 _____
32 _____
33 _____
34 _____
35 _____
36 _____
37 _____
38 _____
39 _____
40 _____

Handshape: _____

<u>GLOSS</u>

1 _____
2 _____
3 _____
4 _____
5 _____
6 _____
7 _____
8 _____
9 _____
10 _____
11 _____
12 _____
13 _____
14 _____
15 _____
16 _____
17 _____
18 _____
19 _____
20 _____
21 _____
22 _____
23 _____
24 _____
25 _____
26 _____
27 _____
28 _____
29 _____
30 _____
31 _____
32 _____
33 _____
34 _____
35 _____
36 _____
37 _____
38 _____
39 _____
40 _____

Handshape: _____

<u>GLOSS</u>

1 _____
2 _____
3 _____
4 _____
5 _____
6 _____
7 _____
8 _____
9 _____
10 _____
11 _____
12 _____
13 _____
14 _____
15 _____
16 _____
17 _____
18 _____
19 _____
20 _____
21 _____
22 _____
23 _____
24 _____
25 _____
26 _____
27 _____
28 _____
29 _____
30 _____
31 _____
32 _____
33 _____
34 _____
35 _____
36 _____
37 _____
38 _____
39 _____
40 _____

Handshape Thesaurus

Handshape: _____

GLOSS

1 _____
2 _____
3 _____
4 _____
5 _____
6 _____
7 _____
8 _____
9 _____
10 _____
11 _____
12 _____
13 _____
14 _____
15 _____
16 _____
17 _____
18 _____
19 _____
20 _____
21 _____
22 _____
23 _____
24 _____
25 _____
26 _____
27 _____
28 _____
29 _____
30 _____
31 _____
32 _____
33 _____
34 _____
35 _____
36 _____
37 _____
38 _____
39 _____
40 _____

Handshape: _____

GLOSS

1 _____
2 _____
3 _____
4 _____
5 _____
6 _____
7 _____
8 _____
9 _____
10 _____
11 _____
12 _____
13 _____
14 _____
15 _____
16 _____
17 _____
18 _____
19 _____
20 _____
21 _____
22 _____
23 _____
24 _____
25 _____
26 _____
27 _____
28 _____
29 _____
30 _____
31 _____
32 _____
33 _____
34 _____
35 _____
36 _____
37 _____
38 _____
39 _____
40 _____

Handshape: _____

GLOSS

1 _____
2 _____
3 _____
4 _____
5 _____
6 _____
7 _____
8 _____
9 _____
10 _____
11 _____
12 _____
13 _____
14 _____
15 _____
16 _____
17 _____
18 _____
19 _____
20 _____
21 _____
22 _____
23 _____
24 _____
25 _____
26 _____
27 _____
28 _____
29 _____
30 _____
31 _____
32 _____
33 _____
34 _____
35 _____
36 _____
37 _____
38 _____
39 _____
40 _____

Handshape Thesaurus

Handshape: _____

<u>GLOSS</u>

1 _____
2 _____
3 _____
4 _____
5 _____
6 _____
7 _____
8 _____
9 _____
10 _____
11 _____
12 _____
13 _____
14 _____
15 _____
16 _____
17 _____
18 _____
19 _____
20 _____
21 _____
22 _____
23 _____
24 _____
25 _____
26 _____
27 _____
28 _____
29 _____
30 _____
31 _____
32 _____
33 _____
34 _____
35 _____
36 _____
37 _____
38 _____
39 _____
40 _____

Handshape: _____

<u>GLOSS</u>

1 _____
2 _____
3 _____
4 _____
5 _____
6 _____
7 _____
8 _____
9 _____
10 _____
11 _____
12 _____
13 _____
14 _____
15 _____
16 _____
17 _____
18 _____
19 _____
20 _____
21 _____
22 _____
23 _____
24 _____
25 _____
26 _____
27 _____
28 _____
29 _____
30 _____
31 _____
32 _____
33 _____
34 _____
35 _____
36 _____
37 _____
38 _____
39 _____
40 _____

Handshape: _____

<u>GLOSS</u>

1 _____
2 _____
3 _____
4 _____
5 _____
6 _____
7 _____
8 _____
9 _____
10 _____
11 _____
12 _____
13 _____
14 _____
15 _____
16 _____
17 _____
18 _____
19 _____
20 _____
21 _____
22 _____
23 _____
24 _____
25 _____
26 _____
27 _____
28 _____
29 _____
30 _____
31 _____
32 _____
33 _____
34 _____
35 _____
36 _____
37 _____
38 _____
39 _____
40 _____

Handshape Thesaurus

Handshape:	Handshape:	Handshape:
GLOSS	GLOSS	GLOSS
1	1	1
2	2	2
3	3	3
4	4	4
5	5	5
6	6	6
7	7	7
8	8	8
9	9	9
10	10	10
11	11	11
12	12	12
13	13	13
14	14	14
15	15	15
16	16	16
17	17	17
18	18	18
19	19	19
20	20	20
21	21	21
22	22	22
23	23	23
24	24	24
25	25	25
26	26	26
27	27	27
28	28	28
29	29	29
30	30	30
31	31	31
32	32	32
33	33	33
34	34	34
35	35	35
36	36	36
37	37	37
38	38	38
39	39	39
40	40	40

Handshape Thesaurus

Handshape: _____

<u>GLOSS</u>

1 _____
2 _____
3 _____
4 _____
5 _____
6 _____
7 _____
8 _____
9 _____
10 _____
11 _____
12 _____
13 _____
14 _____
15 _____
16 _____
17 _____
18 _____
19 _____
20 _____
21 _____
22 _____
23 _____
24 _____
25 _____
26 _____
27 _____
28 _____
29 _____
30 _____
31 _____
32 _____
33 _____
34 _____
35 _____
36 _____
37 _____
38 _____
39 _____
40 _____

Handshape: _____

<u>GLOSS</u>

1 _____
2 _____
3 _____
4 _____
5 _____
6 _____
7 _____
8 _____
9 _____
10 _____
11 _____
12 _____
13 _____
14 _____
15 _____
16 _____
17 _____
18 _____
19 _____
20 _____
21 _____
22 _____
23 _____
24 _____
25 _____
26 _____
27 _____
28 _____
29 _____
30 _____
31 _____
32 _____
33 _____
34 _____
35 _____
36 _____
37 _____
38 _____
39 _____
40 _____

Handshape: _____

<u>GLOSS</u>

1 _____
2 _____
3 _____
4 _____
5 _____
6 _____
7 _____
8 _____
9 _____
10 _____
11 _____
12 _____
13 _____
14 _____
15 _____
16 _____
17 _____
18 _____
19 _____
20 _____
21 _____
22 _____
23 _____
24 _____
25 _____
26 _____
27 _____
28 _____
29 _____
30 _____
31 _____
32 _____
33 _____
34 _____
35 _____
36 _____
37 _____
38 _____
39 _____
40 _____

Handshape Thesaurus

Handshape:

<u>GLOSS</u>

1
2
3
4
5
6
7
8
9
10
11
12
13
14
15
16
17
18
19
20
21
22
23
24
25
26
27
28
29
30
31
32
33
34
35
36
37
38
39
40

Handshape:

<u>GLOSS</u>

1
2
3
4
5
6
7
8
9
10
11
12
13
14
15
16
17
18
19
20
21
22
23
24
25
26
27
28
29
30
31
32
33
34
35
36
37
38
39
40

Handshape:

<u>GLOSS</u>

1
2
3
4
5
6
7
8
9
10
11
12
13
14
15
16
17
18
19
20
21
22
23
24
25
26
27
28
29
30
31
32
33
34
35
36
37
38
39
40

Handshape Thesaurus

Handshape:		Handshape:		Handshape:
GLOSS		GLOSS		GLOSS
1		1		1
2		2		2
3		3		3
4		4		4
5		5		5
6		6		6
7		7		7
8		8		8
9		9		9
10		10		10
11		11		11
12		12		12
13		13		13
14		14		14
15		15		15
16		16		16
17		17		17
18		18		18
19		19		19
20		20		20
21		21		21
22		22		22
23		23		23
24		24		24
25		25		25
26		26		26
27		27		27
28		28		28
29		29		29
30		30		30
31		31		31
32		32		32
33		33		33
34		34		34
35		35		35
36		36		36
37		37		37
38		38		38
39		39		39
40		40		40

Handshape Thesaurus

Handshape: _____

<u>GLOSS</u>

1. _____
2. _____
3. _____
4. _____
5. _____
6. _____
7. _____
8. _____
9. _____
10. _____
11. _____
12. _____
13. _____
14. _____
15. _____
16. _____
17. _____
18. _____
19. _____
20. _____
21. _____
22. _____
23. _____
24. _____
25. _____
26. _____
27. _____
28. _____
29. _____
30. _____
31. _____
32. _____
33. _____
34. _____
35. _____
36. _____
37. _____
38. _____
39. _____
40. _____

Handshape: _____

<u>GLOSS</u>

1. _____
2. _____
3. _____
4. _____
5. _____
6. _____
7. _____
8. _____
9. _____
10. _____
11. _____
12. _____
13. _____
14. _____
15. _____
16. _____
17. _____
18. _____
19. _____
20. _____
21. _____
22. _____
23. _____
24. _____
25. _____
26. _____
27. _____
28. _____
29. _____
30. _____
31. _____
32. _____
33. _____
34. _____
35. _____
36. _____
37. _____
38. _____
39. _____
40. _____

Handshape: _____

<u>GLOSS</u>

1. _____
2. _____
3. _____
4. _____
5. _____
6. _____
7. _____
8. _____
9. _____
10. _____
11. _____
12. _____
13. _____
14. _____
15. _____
16. _____
17. _____
18. _____
19. _____
20. _____
21. _____
22. _____
23. _____
24. _____
25. _____
26. _____
27. _____
28. _____
29. _____
30. _____
31. _____
32. _____
33. _____
34. _____
35. _____
36. _____
37. _____
38. _____
39. _____
40. _____

INDEX

To help you stay organized and prevent repetitions, take the time to index your vocabulary/glosses as you add them.

A	page

B	page

Cc	page
CHARACTER (under PERSONAL)	Intro 16

Cc	page
C continued	

D♩	page	D♩	page	E﹃	page	F	page
		D continued		EXCEPT/EXCEPTION	Intro 16		

G | page

H | page

HIMSELF/HERSELF (YOURSELF/ITSELF/MYSELF) Intro 16

I | page

ITSELF (SELF) (HIMSELF/YOURSELF/MYSELF) Intro 16

J | page

K	page

L	page
LOYAL /LOYALTY (under PERSONAL)	Intro 16

M	page
MYSELF (SELF) (HIMSELF/ITSELF/YOURSELF)	Intro 16

M	page
M continued	

N	page		N	page		O	page		P	page
NOTE TAKING (under TRANSCRIPTION)	Intro 4		N continued						P on next page	
									Q	page
									QUALITY/QUALIFY (under PERSONAL)	Intro 16

P page	
PERSONAL /PERSONALITY	Intro 16

Q page	
Q on previous page	

P page	
P continued	

R page	

R page	
R continued	

🤛 S∎	page
SIGNWRITING	Intro 4
SPECIAL (SPECIALIST/SPECIALIZE)	Intro 16
SELF (SPECIFIC) (HIMSELF/YOURSELF/ITSELF/MYSELF)	Intro 16

🤛 S∎	page
S continued	

🤛 T∎	page
TRANSCRIPTION	Intro 4

🤛 T∎	page
T continued	

U UNIQUE	page Intro 16	V	page	W	page	W continued	page

X	page		Y	page		Z	page		#Number Signs#	page
			YOURSELF (SELF) (HIMSELF/ITSELF/MYSELF)	Intro 16						

REFERENCE CHARTS

Language Continuums

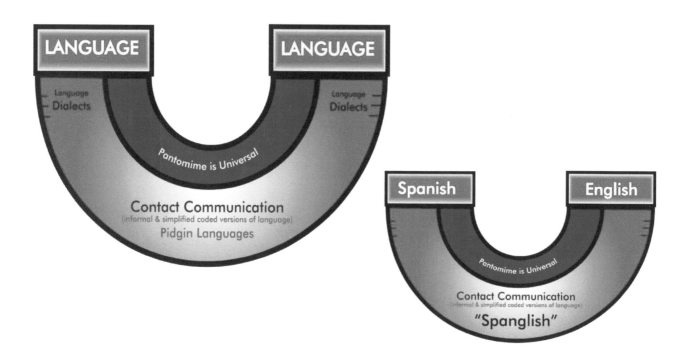

LANGUAGE   LANGUAGE

Language
Dialects

Language
Dialects

Pantomime is Universal

Contact Communication
(informal & simplified coded versions of language)

Pidgin Languages

Spanish   English

Pantomime is Universal

Contact Communication
(informal & simplified coded versions of language)

"Spanglish"

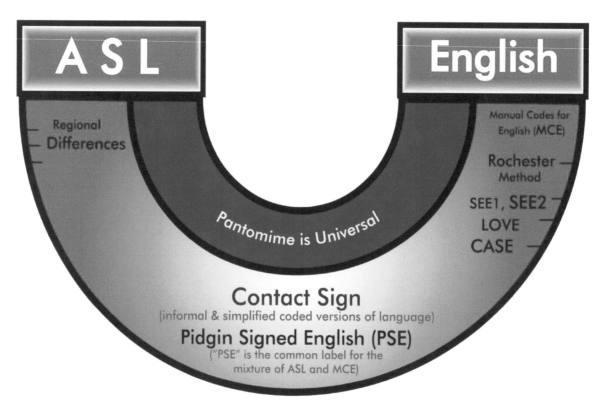

A S L   **English**

Regional
Differences

Manual Codes for
English (MCE)

Rochester
Method

SEE1, SEE2
LOVE
CASE

Pantomime is Universal

Contact Sign
(informal & simplified coded versions of language)

Pidgin Signed English (PSE)
("PSE" is the common label for the
mixture of ASL and MCE)

Deaf Community Membership

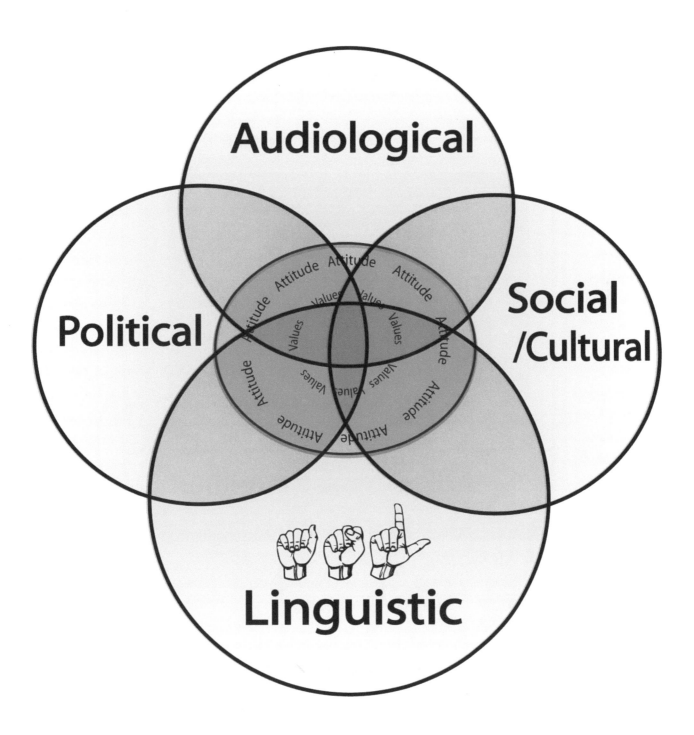

THE 4 AVENUES TO DEAF COMMUNITY MEMBERSHIP

(Adapted from Source: Figure 2.31: "Avenues of Membership in the Deaf Community". p.56
Charlotte Baker-Shenk, D. C. (1980, 1991). American Sign Language: A Teacher's Resource
Text on Grammar and Culture. Washington DC: Gallaudet University Press.)

ASL Syntax Simplified & Explained

[if & when applicable] **Time**   *Time* signs and general signs that establish tense

[Noun or Subject] **"☺" Topic**   The subject, or main point of emphasis of the sentence. Often the noun.

[Verb &/or Adj &/or Object] 👍👎 **Comment**   "Comment" on the *Topic* that was just established.
What the *Topic* is doing (verb) or a description (adjective) of the *Topic* .

[if & when applicable] **Question?**   Question signs may also be first before *Topic* if there is no *Time*, but should be at the end of the sentence too.
First and last or just last in an ASL sentence.

Please note that this is the general "rule of thumb", but exceptions do occur and syntax will vary based on context and inflection.

ASL Syntax Simplified

Time

"☺" Topic [Noun or Subject]

👍👎 **Comment** [Verb &/or Adj &/or Object]

Question?

ASL Syntax Simplification & Explanation by Jacalyn Marosi based on research from WALS, Valli's Linguistics of ASL, The Green Books, and personal observation & experience using ASL in the Deaf community.

Works Cited

Charlotte Baker-Shenk, D. C. (1980, 1991). *American Sign Langauge: A Teacher's Resource Text on Grammar and Culture.* Washington DC: Gallaudet University Press.

Charlotte Baker-Shenk, D. C. (1980, 1991). *American Sign Language Green Books, A Student's Text Units 1-9.* Gallaudet University Press.

Fonts. (n.d.). Futura MD BT, Arial, Arial Bold, Gallaudet, SuttonUS, SuttonGB, Langage des Signes, Signs Language tfb, HandSign, Handsom, Handstand, joeHand2, Wingdings1, Wingdings2, Wingdings3. Retrieved from www.dafont.com; www.fontspace.com; www.signwriting.org/catalog/sw214.html

Leipzig: Max Planck Institute for Evolutionary Anthropology. (2013). *World Atlas of Language Structures.* (M. S. Dryer, M. Haspelmath, Editors, & Creative Commons) Retrieved 8 2013, from WALS: http://wals.info/

Dawnette Reis-Rodriguez. (2013, June 1). HOLMES. (J. W. Marosi, Interviewer) Gooding, Idaho.

Valerie Sutton, Adam Frost. (2010). *ISWA 2010 International SignWriting Alphabet HTML Reference: Writing symbols.* Retrieved from SignBank: http://www.signbank.org/iswa/

Valerie Sutton, Adam Frost. (2013). *SignWriting Hand Symbols Manual.* La Jolla, CA: The SignWriting Press. Retrieved from http://www.signwriting.org/shop/SignWriting_Hand_Symbols_Manual_ISWA2010.html

Valerie Sutton, C. b. (n.d.). *SignWriting.* Retrieved 2014, from SignWriting in the USA: http://www.signwriting.org/usa/

Clayton Valli, C. L. (2011). *Linguistics of American Sign Language: An Introduction* (5th ed.). Washington DC: Gallaudet University Press.

Kayla Wearne. (Fall 2010). *Handshape Game.* North Idaho College, Coeur d Alene, ID.

Cheri Wren. (n.d.). *ASL Handshape Chart.* Retrieved from SignWriting: http://www.signwriting.org/archive/docs5/sw0497-ASLHandshapeChart.pdf

Cheri Wren. (n.d.). *ASL Symbol Sheet.* Retrieved from SignWriting: http://www.signwriting.org/archive/docs5/sw0498-ASLSymbolCheetSheet.pdf

Thank you Students of North Idaho College for offering constructive feedback throughout the years to make this book what has become.

I wish I could cite you all as helpful contributors!

Jacs

Teacher Grade Sheet

Semester/Quarter 1

_____ points for **Quantity:** number of vocab words/signs/glosses   **Vocab Quantity:** _____

_____ points for **Accuracy:** accuracy of Transcription/Description/SignWriting or drawing of vocab

_____ points for **Relevance:** learned this semester (new vs old), and/or relevant to class

_____ **Total Points** out of _____ points possible = _____ %

Semester/Quarter 2

_____ points for **Quantity:** number of vocab words/signs/glosses   **Vocab Quantity:** _____

_____ points for **Accuracy:** accuracy of Transcription/Description/SignWriting or drawing of vocab

_____ points for **Relevance:** learned this semester (new vs old), and/or relevant to class

_____ **Total Points** out of _____ points possible = _____ %

Semester/Quarter 3

_____ points for **Quantity:** number of vocab words/signs/glosses   **Vocab Quantity:** _____

_____ points for **Accuracy:** accuracy of Transcription/Description/SignWriting or drawing of vocab

_____ points for **Relevance:** learned this semester (new vs old), and/or relevant to class

_____ **Total Points** out of _____ points possible = _____ %

Semester/Quarter 4

_____ points for **Quantity:** number of vocab words/signs/glosses   **Vocab Quantity:** _____

_____ points for **Accuracy:** accuracy of Transcription/Description/SignWriting or drawing of vocab

_____ points for **Relevance:** learned this semester (new vs old), and/or relevant to class

_____ **Total Points** out of _____ points possible = _____ %

CPSIA information can be obtained
at www.ICGtesting.com
Printed in the USA
LVHW020436290819
629359LV00003B/16/P